THE ROLE OF THE MYTHIC WEST IN SOME REPRESENTATIVE EXAMPLES OF CLASSIC AND MODERN AMERICAN LITERATURE

The Shaping Force of the American Frontier

J. Bakker

Studies in American Literature
Volume 13

The Edwin Mellen Press
Lewiston/Queenston/Lampeter

Library of Congress Cataloging-in-Publication Data

This book has been registered with the Library of Congress.

This is volume 13 in the continuing series
Studies in American Literature
Volume 13   ISBN 0-7734-9713-7
SAL Series ISBN 0-88946-166-X

A CIP catalog record for this book
is available from the British Library.

The Edwin Mellen Press
Box 450
Lewiston, New York
USA 14092

The Edwin Mellen Press
Box 67
Queenston, Ontario
CANADA L0S 1L0

The Edwin Mellen Press, Ltd.
Lampeter, Dyfed, Wales
UNITED KINGDOM SA48 7DY

Printed in the United States of America

FOR MIA

.

Contents

Acknowledgements

Thanks are due to the publishers of the *Dutch Quarterly Review of Anglo-American Letters (DQR), Neophilologus,* and the Free University Press (Amsterdam) for permission to reprint material.

The chapters on Cooper, Melville, and on the Literary Western were first published as articles in *DQR*; those on Hawthorne and E.L. Doctorow, in *Neophilologus*, while Part Two, chapter 2 (the Popular Western), first appeared as a contribution to *The American West as Seen by Europeans and Americans* (Amsterdam, 1989), edited by Rob Kroes.

I owe special thanks to Ger Janssens of the University of Nijmegen, and John Cawelti of the University of Kentucky, who read parts of the manuscript, and whose critical judgement in literary matters I value.

Introduction

What connects the essays that make up this study is the American West, more accurately the frontier West, even more accurately, the frontier West as myth. Since it is my aim to re-examine its impact on the works discussed in these essays, it may be useful to indicate briefly what I understand the main features of the mythic West to be. In this I follow largely Frederick Jackson Turner, the historian who was the first to provide the theoretical underpinnings on which the study of the West as a scholarly subject was to rest.[1]

Basic to the myth of the frontier West are, Turner thought, the ideas of rebirth and regeneration. Rebirth occurred under the influence of free land; it manifested itself in the shape of a new democratic man, the product of harsh frontier life. Regeneration of both man and society took place whenever civilization came into contact with the wilderness along the frontier; it manifested itself as a process of sloughing off obsolete customs and attitudes, burdensome weaknesses, ancient vices.

Both rebirth and regeneration engendered the myth of frontier democracy, that curious brand of egalitarian individualism that fills to such a large extent the all-embracing myth of the West. But there was still place for one other myth: the myth of the garden, in which nature becomes the source of spiritual values, the source of man's regenerating power.

Put quite simply, rebirth and regeneration are of course nothing else than the two forces that kept the frontier-line moving from east to west, from the Atlantic Ocean to the Pacific Ocean. These forces were progress and success, and both emphasized change and improvement:

---

[1] See Harold P. Simonson, ed. *Frederick Jackson Turner: The Significance of the Frontier in American History*, New York, 1963; rpt 1979.

change, to leave the burdensome past behind; improvement, to win a better, richer future. And if, initially, it was the pioneer who was at the centre of the heroic effort to win the West, facing the dangers of nature and the "savages", at a later stage, it was the self-made man who rose from rags to riches.

But it is as myth that, as critics such as Henry Nash Smith and Edwin Fussell have persuasively argued, the West has exerted its most powerful and lasting influence on American culture and literature.[2] Fussell even goes as far as to believe that the mythic West served as the leading principle for all early American literature, that is, the literature before 1850, but this may be too reductionist,[3] Surely, Cooper's political novels, Hawthorne's *The Marble Faun*, Melville's *Pierre*, Twain's *Innocents Abroad*, to mention only a few, are among the books that can be read without having to invoke the frontier metaphor. But these authors did of course write works in which the frontier serves as the controlling symbol, and in selecting the books discussed in the first part of this study, I have let myself be guided by a simple criterion: if the novel or short story is set on or along the frontier, that is, on or along "the meeting point between savagery and civilization", to use Turner's famous definition, and if events, characters, and interrelationships are influenced by this frontier, then the novel or short story is included for discussion.

In Hawthorne's case this has resulted in the choice of the following stories: "The Canterbury Pilgrims", "Roger Malvin's Burial", "Alice Doane's Appeal", and "The Great Carbuncle", while also *The Scarlet Letter* proved to be sufficiently "Western" to warrant a brief analysis.

---

[2] Henry Nash Smith, *Virgin Land: the American West as Symbol and Myth*, Cambridge, Mass., 1950; rpt 1970; Harvard Paperback 1975. See Book Two.

[3] Edwin Fussell, *Frontier: American Literature and the American West*, Princeton, N.J., 1965, p. 17ff.

Two considerations have guided my choice of *Israel Potter* from Melville's *oeuvre*: firstly, it is generally acknowledged to be his most Western tale; secondly, the novel is underrated and so justifies a revaluation, which, I hope, I have provided.

Thoreau's fascination with the West is not, as I have discovered primarily to be found in his major works, but in one of his shorter pieces, "Walking", also and more aptly called, "The Wild". It has consequently been submitted to a close analysis.

Although Walt Whitman extended the West to include the whole of America, there are parts in his work that are more closely controlled by the Western metaphor than others, and I have concentrated on these. Between 1841 and 1845 Whitman published about two dozen stories, and one of them, "The Half-Breed: A Tale of the Western Frontier", is clearly *pur sang* Western and it is therefore given an exhaustive analysis. Then there is of course *Leaves of Grass*, of which many poems and parts of poems deal with the West or Western elements. They have all been examined so as to arrive at a fairly complete picture of Whitman's relationship with the West.

Any discussion of Mark Twain and the West must begin and end with *Roughing It*, and this is what I have done, examining his complex approach to what he loved and hated at the same time: the West.

There is finally James Fenimore Cooper with whom any work on the impact of the West on American literature must start, and this, too, has been done. As he is the first nineteenth-century American writer of importance, I have compared his seminal Leatherstocking Saga with Thomas Pynchon's *Gravity's Rainbow*, already generally recognized and acknowledged as one of the major works of the twentieth century. What this comparative analysis reveals is that the amazing similarity between these two *chef d'oeuvres* not only extends to thematics and vision, but to the principal characters as well, thus testifying to the continuing impact of the Western element on serious American fiction of the past one and a half centuries.

The second part of this study contains chapters on the modern Western. The first chapter deals with the literary, or adult Western, tracing its development from Owen Wister through Walter van Tilburg Clark and Thomas Berger to E. L. Doctorow, while examining its strengths and weaknesses. The second chapter discusses the popular, or formula Western, concentrating on what links it to the literary Western: violence and the love story. It analyzes the question of why and how these ingredients receive a different treatment in the novels of such typical writers of pulp Westerns as Zane Grey, Eugene Manlove Rhodes, Max Brand, and George G. Gilman. The third chapter is devoted entirely to Larry McMurtry's novels about the Old West, that is to say, to *Lonesome Dove* and *Anything for Billy*. It examines in what sense and to what extent he succeeds in revitalizing the conventions and stereotypes on which the traditional popular Western is based, resulting in what could be called the New Western.

PART ONE

Chapter 1

FROM LEATHERSTOCKING TO ROCKETMAN:
Cooper's Leatherstocking Tales
and Pynchon's *Gravity's Rainbow* Reconsidered

The opening sentence of Thomas Pynchon's *Gravity's Rainbow* (1973),[1] "A screaming comes across the sky", has already achieved some fame as expressing most dramatically the dying cry of Western civilization, "the old theatre", as Pynchon calls it, and which at the end of the novel seems on the point of being destroyed by the Rocket hovering over its tarnished beauty. It could also easily have been the first sentence introducing James Fenimore Cooper's Leatherstocking Tales, and would then no doubt have signified the desperate war-whoop of the Red Indians, heralding the disappearance of their independent existence on the North-American continent.

As Pynchon's novel deals with the one major event of the twentieth century: the final subjugation of Western man to the threat of total control as the result of the emergence of such revolutionary technologies as nuclear physics and rocketry, so Cooper's Tales have as

---

[1] Thomas Pynchon, *Gravity's Rainbow*, London, 1973. All page references are to this edition, indicated in the text by GR followed by page number.

their subject the one major event of nineteenth-century America; the final subjugation of a race, the Red Indians, to white dominance, an event in which technology, regarded by some as a historical force,[2] can also be said to have played a crucial role.

These are not the only correspondences that suggest themselves. In both Cooper's and Pynchon's work the setting is predominantly one of conflict, war. In the Leatherstocking Tales the conflict is between the French and the English, in actuality a continuation of political troubles transferred from Europe to the American colonies, with the Indians in a subsidiary role of nonetheless eagerly sought allies. In *Gravity's Rainbow* the conflict is World War II, or more precisely the end of World War II and its chaotic aftermath, a war once again waged between the major powers of the world, but this time brought to a head on the continent where it started, Europe, with also in a subsidiary role a conquered race, the black Hereros from Africa.

The locale of Cooper's Tales is the region of the Great Lakes, in those early days the frontier, the neutral territory between civilization and the wilderness, a region gradually shifting westwards, in *The Prairie* nearly as far as the Rocky Mountains. In Pynchon's novel the locale has attained global dimensions, encompassing not only the United States and Europe, but also Africa, South America, Japan, Russia and Central Asia.[3] But the main action takes place in the "Zone", that region of war-ravaged Europe where towards the end of the fighting no one is in control yet, where there are no longer distinct patterns, only the

---

[2] Joseph W. Slade, *Thomas Pynchon*, New York, 1974: "Technology is itself a historical force, almost a Zeitgeist, viewed somewhat nostalgically in *Gravity's Rainbow* at a period in time when it lost forever whatever innocence it possessed" (p. 211).

[3] That this global locale is seen as an extension of the American West is suggested more than once in *Gravity's Rainbow*. A village in the Kirghiz steppes is likened to a town in "a wild west movie" (GR 339); Albert Speer looks "remarkably like American cowboy actor Henry Fonda" (GR 448), and Mickey Rooney puts in an appearance at the Potsdam Conference.

potential of new ones, no certainties, and where everybody and everything is adrift, a region, in short, sharing striking characteristics with Cooper's frontier.

More correspondences can still be discerned. In *Gravity's Rainbow* Pynchon reverts again to his favourite plot device, the conspiracy, and in a writer who firmly believes that everything is related to everything else, this need hardly surprise us. But Cooper, too, employs this device, and in a manner no less fantastic.

In dealing with the great social events of their time, Pynchon as well as Cooper have in fact abandoned the realm of realistic fiction and resorted to the fantastic and surrealistic. Cooper's Tales may have a semblance of realism, but as his conception of the frontier, his Indians and the endless series of improbable events that string his Tales together clearly show, it is a kind of realism as distorted as the kind one encounters in Pynchon's work.[4] What it conveys is a world that exists somewhere on the edge of reality and the realm of dreams, symbol, and the archetypal, and the difference between the two writers here is merely that in Pynchon's novels this world has immeasurably expanded, accurately reflecting the development over the past hundred and fifty years of such fields of human interest as philosophy, sociology, psychology, physics, rocketry, literature and the popular arts. In the work of these two writers it is therefore pointless to try and invest action with historical truth, character with personality. The truth of action is determined by the particular medium of the author's minds rather than by historical time and circumstances, and what Cooper said

---

[4] To what extent Cooper's frontier is invented and his division of the Indians into Sioux=Iroquois=bad and Pawnee=Lenape=good arbitrary historically is analyzed by Gordon Brotherston in his article "'The Prairie' and Cooper's Invention of the West" in *James Fenimore Cooper: New Critical Essays*, ed. Robert Clark, London/Totowa, NJ, 1985, pp. 162-86. As he remarks at the end of the article: "In recent decades a whole new initiative in archaeology, ethnography, map-making and the editing of native texts, has begun to provide the rudiments of a history of the Indian in North America, to the extent of terminally upsetting the old frontier shibboleth of the savage, with all its tremendous distortions, suppressions and absences."

of Natty Bumppo, the Leatherstocking figure, also applies to Tyrone Slothrop, one of the main characters of *Gravity's Rainbow*: both are "creations", that is, the vehicles of a writer's deepest thoughts, longings, and anxieties, and here remarkable correspondences force themselves again to the surface.

Cooper's Leatherstocking Tales not only stand at the beginning of the rise of American literature, they also present us with America's first cultural hero, Nathaniel Bumppo, Leatherstocking, Hawkeye, Pathfinder, trapper, or Deerslayer, as he is variously called in the five tales that make up the series. We may meet him in *The Pioneers* (1823) as an ungainly, quarrelsome old man living in a squalid cabin on the outskirts of a settlement, and take our leave of him in *The Deerslayer* (1841) where he has been transformed into a young frontier hero of radiant mythic dimensions, he is and remains the same character: a stoic *philosophe*, of a generous and chivalric disposition, a man, however, who is also a killer, but who during a life time spent on the dangerous frontier has nevertheless managed to preserve his moral integrity, even if not as "hard and intact" as D. H. Lawrence assumed he had.[5]

Pynchon's novel, published a hundred and fifty years later, is not only one of the high points of modern American literature, it also presents us with a character, Tyrone Slothrop, whose life story shows, in a symbolic sense, a remarkable resemblance with that of Cooper's hero. We may meet Tyrone as an intelligence officer in the American army stationed in London, but like a modern Pathfinder he spends most of his time in the Zone, where he too tries to keep his integrity "hard and intact", even though he expresses his moral anxieties by cracking a joke or composing a bawdy song rather than treating us to what makes of Natty Bumppo more often than not such a sententious bore.

[5] D. H. Lawrence, "Cooper's Leatherstocking Tales" in *The Shock of Recognition*, ed. Edmund Wilson, New York, 1943, p. 966. See p. 17.

What motivates Tyrone to flee to the Zone in escape of his pursuers, and the Leatherstocking figure to retreat to the wilderness in flight from the settlements, is also basically the same: fear, the fear of loss of self, of autonomy, or to use Pynchon's favourite term, paranoia. In Natty's case this fear is given its most dramatic expression in *The Pioneers*. Cooper's first Leatherstocking Tale is no doubt about the birth of a settlement, but as such it is also the novel in which we are already made to witness what in Pynchon's novel becomes the overriding concern: the emergence of a bureaucracy, the System, as Pynchon calls it. In *The Pioneers* it is — in its emerging shape — represented by the early settlers; in *Gravity's Rainbow* — in its most advanced form — by The Firm, that is, in concrete terms the world-wide organization of huge corporations and cartels like General Electric, IBM, Siemens, Shell, I.G. Farben, the great multi-nationals, in fact, which can ignore national boundaries, in a geographical as well as in a political sense.[6]

The System's chief aim is, as we learn from both novels, "to do business", to which everything and everyone in the realm of human activities must be subservient. It therefore cannot and will not allow the individual to be in control of his own life.[7] In Templeton, Natty

---

[6] See TLS, January 23, 1987, p. 81: "Doing Without Utopias: An Interview with Václav Havel". In answer to the question "Are you saying that totalitarian régimes such as Czechoslovakia are a possible shape of things to come in the West?" Havel replies: "In my view, Soviet totalitarianism is an extreme manifestation (...) of a deep-seated problem which equally finds expression in advanced Western society. These systems have in common something that the Czech philosopher Václav Bélohradsky calls the 'eschatology of the impersonal', that is, a trend towards impersonal power and rule by megamachines, or collossi that escape human control. I believe the world is losing its human dimension. Self-propelling mega-machines, juggernauts of impersonal power such as *large-scale enterprises* and faceless governments, represent the greatest threat to our present-day world. In the final analysis, totalitarianism is no more than an extreme expression of this threat" (my italics). Later in the review Havel also remarks that "enormous companies like Shell or IBM are — fundamentally speaking — not very different from so called socialist enterprises".

[7] As Richard Godden remarks in his "Pioneer Properties, or 'What's in a Hut?'" in *James Fenimore Cooper: New Critical Essays* (see note 4): "The repression of Natty, of his allies and of all that he has been made to stand for, is essential because

Bumppo, the frontiersman, is constantly watched, spied upon, and hounded by men who, as he himself remarks, are troubled with "longings after other people's business", [8] longings which also include their greed to lay hands on a treasure of silver Natty is suspected to have hidden in his cabin. In *Gravity's Rainbow*, Tyrone is watched, spied upon, and hounded by men of The White Visitation, an Allied agency controlled by The Firm, because he too is suspected of hiding a secret, the secret of being able to predict the whereabouts of the German V-2's, the "treasure" The Firm wants to lay its hands on.

Neither the townspeople of Templeton, nor The White Visitation — purposely set up to increase control over individuals — can ever acquiesce in the individual having secrets. The townspeople because it might deprive them of what they consider their rightful share in material gain; the men of The White Visitation, headed by Dr Pointsman, a fanatic behaviourist, because it deprives them of their belief in cause-and-effect logic, The Firm's chief weapon in exercising control.

To Natty, however, property, money, means nothing, honour and loyalty (the "treasure" he hides in his cabin is old Effingham) everything, an attitude resented by the settlers. To them the right to property and the concomitant right to accumulation is everything, justifying in their eyes the deprivation of others and nature, notions which the Leatherstocking figure deeply detests. But instead of making him exemplary, he comes to be looked upon as dangerous to the peace of society, a view also taken by Pointsman with regard to Tyrone. Tyrone's odd secret not only insults Pointsman's faith in cause-and-effect thinking, the way in which he responds to his "peculiar sensitivity to what is revealed in the sky" (GR 26) is also far too individualistic to

Templeton is palpably the location of an emergent market economy" (p. 126).

[8] James Fenimore Cooper, *The Pioneers*, New York: Holt, Rinehart and Winston, 7th printing, 1966, p. 307.

the latter's liking. Instead of putting it into the service of The White Visitation, Tyrone allows it to make him suspicious of "Them", The Firm, who, as he finds out, want to use him only to further their own ends; who, as he also begins to suspect, have used him all his life. Tyrone rebels and flees to the Zone, not only in order to escape "Their" control but also in order to find the Rocket to which he is related in such a mysterious way. It thus becomes his "Grail" which he must find if he is to know his self. No wonder that the thought of Tyrone "lost in the world of men, after the war", "historically, a monster" if his secret remains unsolved, fills Pointsman with "a deep dread" (GR 144).

If in the area of personal relationships the System's chief aim entails the denial of individual autonomy, in its dealings with the external world it will ultimately result in the annihilation of the organic world, as it is being transformed into a dead world. To understand this it must be realized that in both Pynchon's and Cooper's view the world is "a closed system, cyclical, resonant, eternally returning",[9] a "thing" that should not be tampered with but, on the contrary, left in good repair, an insight ignored by the System. What remains an intuitive understanding in *The Pioneers* — Natty condemning the wasteful ways of the settlers — acquires a scientific underpinning in *Gravity's Rainbow*. Many of the metaphors with which Pynchon seeks to explain the forces that structure the world, the physical as well as the human world, are drawn from the sciences. The metaphor that is relevant here is the one he derives from The Second Law of Thermodynamics which postulates that closed systems — and the earth is a closed system — decline into entropy, that is, into disorder, ending in (heat-)death, if

---

[9] This idea is in fact put forward by the Serpent that appeared in a dream to Kekulé, the famous chemist, and which held its own tail in its mouth, "the dreaming serpent which surrounds the World" (GR 412), a dream which revealed to Kekulé the structure of the benzene molecule. It is a view of the world also held by the Indians, and could therefore have been expressed by Chingachgook, the Mohegan Chief in the Leatherstocking Tales, Natty Bumppo's blood-brother, whose Indian name actually means in English The Big Serpent.

more heat (energy) is drawn from the system than it contains, a process that is irreversible. What the System — The Firm — in pursuing its aim does is "to violate the cycle", leading as the Second Law predicts to a state of entropy, and the rest of the passage from which this and the preceding quotation have been taken is worth quoting in full, since it contains Pynchon's graphic description of the form this state of entropy is to assume in the human world:

> Taking and not giving back, demanding that "productivity" and "earnings" keep on increasing with time, the System removing from the rest of the World these vast quantities of energy to keep its own tiny desperate fraction showing a profit: and not only most of humanity — most of the World, animal, vegetable and mineral, is laid waste in the process. The System may or may not understand that it's only buying time. And that time is an artificial resource to begin with, of no value to anyone or anything but the System, which sooner or later must crash to its death, when its addiction to energy has become more than the rest of the World can supply dragging with it innocent souls all along the chain of life. Living inside the System is like riding across the country in a bus driven by a maniac bent on suicide... (GR 412).

No bus is to be discerned in *The Pioneers* yet, though with the compulsively energetic Richard Jones in mind it is not difficult to imagine who might have been the first "maniac" to drive it across the country, but what *is* discernible are the first signs of the removal "from the rest of the World" of "these vast quantities of energy to keep [the System's] own tiny desperate fraction showing a profit". In the townspeople of Templeton we already recognize the early representatives of the System, initiating on a local scale what on a global scale in Pynchon's novel is continued and completed by The

Firm, the big corporations and cartels which in the world of today control the buying and selling, and consequently "productivity" and "earnings".[10]

As for the "innocent souls" that are being dragged with it, "all along the chain of life": in both Pynchon's and Cooper's work they are not only present but also strikingly alike. In *Gravity's Rainbow* they are the people for whom the System has no use, the people who live amongst "the trivia and the waste" that it produces, the "passed over", the abandoned, the rejected, "the Preterite" as Pynchon, more of a Calvinist than Cooper, calls them. Included in this category are in the first place the black Hereros, corrupted like Cooper's Indians by the white Europeans. These blacks are the survivors of Von Trotha's 1904 massacre in South West Africa, brought to Germany by another important character in *Gravity's Rainbow*, Blicero — Whiteman! — , in Von Trotha's days a young officer, and now the driving force behind the production of the Rocket. It is Blicero who has turned them into Schwarzkommandos, the black Rocket Corps, to serve the Third Reich, in which capacity they have become the first people to derive their identity from the Rocket (to Enzian, their leader Blicero was a Jesus Christ, a "Deliverer"). But Blicero, once a young man "in love with empire, poetry" (GR 660), and still essentially a romantic, has changed into a corrupt Christ, a depraved Nazi, perverted like a Kurtz by the Heart of Darkness. Since love among the whites "had to do with masculine technologies" (GR 324), he has taught the Hereros to be priests of the Rocket, the most advanced product of man's technology, but in actuality "an entire system *won*, away from the feminine darkness held against the entropies of lovable but scatterbrained Mother Nature"

---

[10] Cf. Richard Godden in "Pioneer Properties, or 'What's in a Hut?'": "Cooper provides a pocket history on the development of mercentile capital as profits taken from land speculation are mobilized on behalf of industrial accumulation. Temple planned Templeton as a city, and already wage labour with its attendant class divisions is apparent" (p. 127). See note 7.

(GR 324). In achieving this Blicero has not only alienated them from their own culture which informed them to believe in "Earth's gift for genesis" (GR 316) — their tribal totem is the Erdschwein, "earthpig" — but he has also infected them with his death-wish, his romantic sense of Gotterdämmerung, following the defeat of the Nazis. The Hereros can therefore be said to have been doubly victimized by what Pynchon as distinct from the Preterite and in accordance with Calvinist duality calls the Elect, the powerful, those who are in a position to control and manipulate the others.

But Blicero may still be regarded as an exceptional member of the Elect, a man regrettably destined to change from "prince to fabulous monster" (GR 660), a man yearning to achieve transcendence through a love-death. More representative is that other character who made the invention of the Rocket possible, Laszlo Jamf, like Pointsman a behaviourist, but turned chemist. It is also this man who is responsible for Tyrone's affinity with the Rocket: in the 1920s he conducted an experiment at Harvard for I.G. Farben which was carried out on the infant Tyrone, conditioning him to respond sexually to "a mystery stimulus". This stimulus, actually a chemical component, was later to be used as a vital part in the guiding system of the Rocket. Since Jamf was unable to extinguish entirely Tyrone's response to this chemical, it may furnish a "rational" explanation for the latter's affinity with the Rocket. Now quite apart from the viability of this fantastic experiment, the symbolic significance with regard to Tyrone is clear. He too is in a double sense a victim of the Elect: not only has he been alienated from his human identity by the ruthless application of technology, he continues to be deprived of his freedom by being kept under the Firm's close surveillance, and when he manages to escape from "Their" control in the Zone, by being relentlessly hounded. For suppose he might decide to trade his "secret" to either the Russians, or the Hereros, who like The Firm are also embarked on a frantic search for the German V-2's. This of course could never be allowed.

Tyrone, however, has no interest in "trading" for which he like his ancestors has never shown a great talent, one of the reasons why the Slothrops, although nominally belonging to the Elect, had actually always belonged to the Preterite. Tyrone's main interest is the redemption of his soul, an interest threatened by what The Firm considers the "real business" of the world, which of course *is* "trading", an activity even more rewarding in war than in peace, since war, according to Pynchon, is basically a "celebration of markets" (GR 105). Origin and character, then, destine Tyrone to take up his place among the Preterite, just like the Hereros, but unlike them he does not end up as another priest of technology, nor as a participator in the death-wish of those of the Elect who have experienced defeat. Tyrone's end, as we shall see, is different, resembling that of the Leatherstocking figure, although here too interesting differences begin to emerge.

In Cooper's work the "innocent souls" are also those for whom the System has no use. They are in the first place the Indians, reduced in *The Pioneers* to an inglorious existence of drunken depravity, the indirect result of the system's overriding concern with the profit-motive. True, Cooper makes them choose a fiery death on the mountain which he rather presciently calls The Vision, but the tribute he thus pays them, reiterated in the later Leatherstocking Tales by his revivifying Indian John as the brave warrior Chingachgook, noble Chief of the Delawares, issues from a personal dream rather than from historical reality. The historical reality was that the Indians, like Pynchon's Preterite, were already belonging to the "passed over", the rejected, a category of men, however, which, as we shall see, also includes Natty Bumppo, the Leatherstocking figure. Although one cannot say that in *The Pioneers* Natty submits to the Elect, represented by Judge Temple and his associates, without offering resistance, the fight he puts up to defend and guard his individual autonomy proves futile, what with his misplaced trust in the fairness of man-made law, and his own lack of duplicity with which he could have met his judges on their own ground. Rather than stay after the ignominy of being put in prison and in the stocks, he therefore turns his back on white civilization, and in the rest of the Leatherstocking Tales we only meet him on the frontier, the region where just as in Pynchon's Zone the System cannot wield power yet, and where Natty's particular "gifts" enable him to be in complete control of his own life. But like his obsolete flint rifle to which he stubbornly sticks in preference to the more advanced models that have replaced it, Natty himself, worn out and miserable at the end of *The Prairie*, has become obsolete. His frontier skills of hunter and scout, once the pride of his manhood, are no longer needed and respected, are, in fact, rapidly becoming redundant, as the "sportsmen" hunters begin to slaughter the buffalo by the thousands, firing at them from open trainwindows.

Leatherstocking may die supported on the one side by Middleton, a white man, and on the other by Hard-Heart, an Indian, but the symbolic significance of this scene is illusionary too. The blessing he gives Hard-Heart is to someone who in the most literal sense already belongs to "the passed over", the abandoned, and Middleton, despite the friendship he feels for the young Pawnee, continues to look upon the Indians as "savages", whom he, a firm believer in the white man's "civilizing" mission, cannot but regard as inferior. Natty may stand between them, but he is no mediator, since what he could mediate goes unrecognized: the Indians remain strangers to his Christian "gifts", while the whites find his Indian "gifts" embarrassing, since they stand in the way of "progress".

The Pawnees may honour Leatherstocking as "the just Chief of the Palefaces", but Natty, belonging to the Preterite himself, is in no position to save them from their impending fate. And even if he had been, it is doubtful whether he would have done so. To him, as to

Middleton, the Indians are also basically "savages", "varmint", the only exceptions being the Delawares and the Pawnees, but even among them his heart only goes out to a few individuals, Chingachgook, Uncas, Tamenund, and Hard-Heart. Natty's indifference to the Indians in general is shown nowhere more clearly than in that passage from *The Prairie* in which he tells Bush that he too had fought under General Wayne, "Mad Anthony", the Indian-fighter. The reason why, is revealing:

> (...) I was passing from the States on the sea-shore into these far regions, when I cross'd the trail of his party, and I fell in, on his rear, just as a looker-on; but when they got to blows, the crack of my rifle was heard among the rest, though to my shame it may be said, I never knew the right of the quarrel as well as a man of threescore and ten should know the reason of his acts afore he takes mortal life, which is a gift he never can return![11]

Not only is he ignorant of "the right of the quarrel" with the Indians, the right of the quarrel with the French, or with the English for that matter, escapes him as well. As he remarks in *The Pathfinder* "there is no great difference between an Englishman and a Frenchman, after all",[12] and the reason why he fights on the side of the English, and in the War of Independence on the side of the revolutionists, is to all appearances the same as the one that made him fight the Indians under "Mad Anthony": he happens to be there, and being the man he is, can't resist the call for action.

Natty's allegiance, then, is neither really to the Indians, nor to the whites, which incidentally can also be said of his blood-brother, Chingachgook. As John P. McWilliams puts it, both Hawkeye and The

---

[11] James Fenimore Cooper, *The Prairie*, New York: Airmont Classic 1964, p. 57.

[12] James Fenimore Cooper, *The Pathfinder*, New York: Signet Classic, 1961, p. 393.

Big Serpent "represent no community, lead no men, and defend no
civilization".[13] They are in fact the first and the last of their kinds, and
although Cooper dramatizes through their individual fates the one
major historical event of nineteenth-century America, he has not
attempted to make them representatives of a solution that might have
been an alternative to the one that was being enacted under his very
eyes: the annihilation of one culture by another.

An explanation is not far to seek. Cooper, the man, never really
doubted the prevailing nineteenth-century view that the true meaning of
American history lay in transforming the state of the American
wilderness into a state of civilization. And true civilization was white
civilization, also to Cooper, no matter how severely he criticized the
direction this transformation was taking, no matter how great his
sympathy for the Indians (admittedly *his* Indians rather than *the*
Indians) may have been.

Numbers and superior technology destined the latter to belong
to history's "passed over", and Cooper was keenly aware of what this
meant in terms of individual tragedy, as his Leatherstocking Tales
impressively show. But he never squarely faced the moral problem
inherent in the dispossession of the Indians of their lands and their
culture.[14] The character of Natty Bumppo was created to serve as an

---

[13] John P. McWilliams, "Red Satan: Cooper and the American Indian Epic", in
James Fenimore Cooper: New Critical Essays, p. 156. See note 4.

[14] When Cooper finally set himself the task of actually facing the Indian problem
in *Oak Openings* (1848), the alternative he offers is no alternative at all, but one in
accordance with what remains veiled in the Leatherstocking Tales. In *Oak Openings*
Cooper again presents us with one of his eloquent spokesmen for the Indian
grievances, Onaoh, or Scalping Pete. In contrast with such "a-historical" denunciators
of white injustice as Magua and Tamenund from *The Last of the Mohicans* and
Mahtoree from *The Prairie*, Onaoh seems intended to fulfill a historical role by his
plan to unite the Indian tribes in an uprising against white dominance. He fails,
however, in carrying out his mission, and the cause of his failure is revealing, though
not really surprising if we remember Cooper's basic affirmation of the socio-cultural
values implied in America's westward movement. Watching a Methodist preacher
forgive his Indian murderers before he dies, Onaoh, the savage warrior, is so
impressed that he at once turns into an ardent follower of the Christian faith. He

alternative to the type of backwoodsman that confirmed Cooper's worst suspicions about the course America's Manifest Destiny took, and hardly bears on the Indian problem. But he also must have realized that the Billy Kirbys were inevitable if the nation's westward movement was to succeed. It made his Leatherstocking stand outside history, turning him into a symbol. Which brings us back to Tyrone Slothrop, our modern Leatherstocking. Or is he?

The reason for Tyrone's escape to the zone may be the same as the one that drove Natty to the frontier, but what complicates Tyrone's flight is that he, unlike the Leatherstocking figure, is never sure of his identity. Is he an American Army lieutenant sent on a secret mission to the Zone, about the purpose of which he is kept in the dark but which he nevertheless carries out? Or is he the man who has come to suspect that he is being used as a pawn in The Firm's world-wide game, the purpose of which is "to do business", with friend and foe alike? Tyrone must find out and in order to find out he must find the Rocket, The Firm's latest and costliest commodity in feeding the system's love of death, the secret of Tyrone's conditioning. Under various mythic guises, the latest being a Wagnerian costume which makes him look like Rocketman, he sets out on his quest. It gets him involved in a series of pursuit-captivity-and-escape-adventures as exciting and fantastic as those Cooper regales us with, in which he matches in bravery and resourcefulness Cooper's hero, albeit on a note of hilarious zaniness entirely alien to the latter's writings. But the Rocket keeps eluding him, and so the secret of his identity.

However, what Tyrone does learn on his wanderings North in search of the Rocket is that the total freedom of the Zone appears to be a condition which "not many of us can bear for long" (GR 434).

---

decides to call off his historical mission, thus accepting his nation's fate. He acknowledges the superiority of white civilization and at the end of the novel even blesses the wisdom of the "peace-loving" whites. This "alternative" tells us what Cooper really thought of Indian civilization as compared to white civilization.

Instead of facilitating his search, it causes in the end his undoing. What the Zone lacks is a meaningful pattern, dooming those inside to go on "kicking endlessly among the plastic trivia (...) trying (...) to make sense out of, to find the meanest sliver of truth in so much replication, so much waste" (GR 570). Conditioned to function within the System, primarily on the cause-and-effect principle, Tyrone lacks the means of making sense of his existence in the Zone, the world where there are no meaningful patterns yet, where everything is fluid. He consequently finds himself in a vacuum, and since he lacks a solid sense of self he is soon convinced that both outside and inside the separateness of the self there is nothing, a void. Like Natty, Tyrone cannot live in The Firm's rigidly patterned and deterministic world, but unlike the Leatherstocking figure, whom the nineteenth-century Cooper has furnished with an unshakable sense of self, he cannot live in the as-yet-unstructured world of the Zone either. Chaos starts engulfing him, and instead of being present "at his own assembly", he witnesses his "disassembling".

Tyrone, the Rocketman, also becomes a symbol, a "charismatic" figure like Leatherstocking, but unlike the latter not, as Joseph Slade believes, "without a following, never to be rationalized, never to redirect a death-loving System".[15] Pynchon's view of Tyrone — a character who can neither live inside nor outside the System — may seem to betray an even gloomier determinism than Cooper displays in the creation of Leatherstocking, but this proves to be deceptive. Pynchon is not really a nineteenth-century adherent of the principle of excluded middles, as Cooper was, who could only conceive dualities; civilization and wilderness, red and white (never to mingle), total control and absolute freedom, love and hate, good and evil, redemption and bondage, life and death, an approach largely responsible for his stereotyped

---

[15] Slade, *Thomas Pynchon*, p. 210.

characterization and the rigidity of his novels' ideational content. That Tyrone was sent to the Zone to be present at his assembly, that is, to find and assert his recovered self, but "was being broken down instead, and scattered" (GR 738), is only one story about his end. There are also those who believe that "fragments of Slothrop have grown into consistent personae of their own", and if that is what happened, "there's no telling which of the Zone's present population are offshoots of his original shattering" (GR 742).

Considering the people towards whom the sympathies in *Gravity's Rainbow* are directed, there is little doubt that, if this is the true story of Tyrone's end, these "offshoots" should belong to the Preterite, and not only does this refute Slade's conclusion that Tyrone is outside history, which would put him on a par with the Leatherstocking figure, it also points up another important difference in the symbolic significance of these two characters.

To Pynchon it is only the Preterite who have retained "a few chances for mercy" (GR 610), and the novel furnishes a number of instances to substantiate this view. If through Tyrone, Pynchon seems to demonstrate what may happen if conditioning by the System cannot be extinguished, Roger Mexico, the statistician for The White Visitation, is there to prove that the System's control need not be absolute. Roger, an anti-Pointsman, knows of the latest developments in the sciences, and he too has embraced the belief in the principles of indeterminacy, the theory that recognizes chance and hence the possibility of free will. He even looks forward to the day when scientists will "have the courage to junk cause-and-effect entirely, and strike off at some other angle" (GR 89), thus providing a scientific justification for the call to abolish a view of the world, determinism, which inevitably issues in "a culture of death" (GR 176).

Since the Preterite's stake in the affairs of The Firm is still negligible, it is among them that any organized form of opposition could arise, and when Roger sees that such an opposition, called the Counterforce, is actually taking shape — the Zone being increasingly controlled by the Firm again — he joins it. It is also Roger who still believes in the traditional idea of love as an antidote to "the culture of death", and it is he who does all he can to save Tyrone from Pointsman's evil machinations, causing in fact the undoing of Major Harvey, one of Tyrone's most persistent pursuers, a lunatic version of Cooper's Hiram Doolittle from *The Pioneers*.

Tyrone can count on more loyal friends among the Preterite, one of the novel's few saving graces considering its all-pervasive apocalyptic mood: Geli Tripping, the witch, Bodine, the seaman, Otto and Felix, even Von Göll, the one-time filmmaker turned blackmarketeer, who eventually leads Tyrone to the Rocket base at Peenemünde, "The Holy Center", although by then Tyrone has lost interest in the Rocket. Unable to find it he has already started to "scatter".

There is no denying that Roger Mexico has secret doubts about whether the Counterforce will ever be forged into an organization sufficiently strong to challenge the System, the Preterite being notoriously unconcerned with ideas and therefore hard to unite for consorted action. But when at the end of the novel the Rocket, falling a mile per second, reaches the last delta-t, the book's hope that it remains "an unmeasurable gap" instead of becoming "the infinitesimal fraction of a second" before "this old Theater" will be destroyed, is pinned on the Preterite, not on The Firm. It is a slight hope, but as Pynchon's fascination with probability and indeterminacy theories may tell us, there is no longer a specific scientific reason to reject it out of hand. Chance seems to play its role in the universe — Ludwig's love for his lemming saves it from drowning; Byron, the bulb, escapes destruction — , determinism may not be the be-all and end-all of existence.

One of the numerous ideas underlying *Gravity's Rainbow* is that it was America's pursuit of Manifest Destiny that caused the world to miss "the fork in the road" (GR 556)[16] that could have led it away from "the culture of death". This idea is also strong in Cooper's work, and like Pynchon he was also inclined to put the blame on the Elect, the Haves. But unlike Pynchon he did not expect anything from the Preterite, the People, as he called them, in reversing the individious direction the world had taken.

Cooper believed in the right to property, holding that "most of the ordinances of civilized society, that are concerned with that interest, are founded on reason, and ought to be rigidly maintained".[17] It firmly made him belong to the Elect, although he insisted on making a distinction among them. There was on the one hand the financial élite, the bankers and the emerging industrialists, whom he held responsible for much that had gone wrong in his country; on the other hand there was the landed gentry, a natural aristocracy, upholders of trusted moral values and virtues, of true civilization. In this class Cooper put his faith. But it was a class that as a social and political force was already in the process of being rapidly replaced by the class of financiers and entrepreneurs. And in so far as judge Temple is still a member of the landed gentry he is a nostalgically remembered image of an idealized past; in so far as he too is becoming an entrepreneur, considering his

---

[16] Thinking of Tyrone's ancestor William Slothrop who wrote a tract *On Preterition* in which he argued "holiness" for the Preterite "without whom there'd be no elect", and that if we have to love Jesus, we have to love Judas too, the narrator muses: "Could he have been the fork in the road America never took, the singular point she jumped the wrong way from? Suppose the Slothropite heresy had had time to consolidate and prosper? Might there have been fewer crimes in the name of Jesus, and more mercy in the name of Judas Iscariot? It seems to Tyrone Slothrop that there might be a route back — maybe that anarchist he met in Zürich was right, maybe for a little while all the fences are down, one road as good as another, the whole space of the Zone cleared, depolarized, and somewhere inside the waste of it a single set of coordinates from which to proceed, without elect, without preterite, without even nationality to fuck it up..." (p. 556).

[17] James Fenimore Cooper, *The American Democrat*, New York, 1838; Penguin, 1969, p. 188.

"bias to look far into futurity, in his speculation on the improvements", he reflects the shift that was taking place in the nation from an agrarian to an entrepreneurial stage, a shift Cooper as man deplored but which he as artist registered. Yet, even his disappointment about the direction Jacksonian democracy had taken on his return from Europe in 1833 could not make him change his mind about the People, the Preterite among his compatriots, since, as he thought, their only interest was also money, "without heart, taste or discrimination".[18]

To sum up: what informs the conception of both Natty Bumppo and Tyrone Slothrop is a premise that does not seem to have changed over the past hundred and fifty years, the premise that it is a man's right to exist as a man, as a uniquely defined individual, and to realize his humanity as fully as possible.

The forces that work against exercising this right are also basically the same for both characters. They are primarily technologies, co-opted by The Firm in pursuing its chief aim, which is "to do business", an activity that curtails individual freedom and that may eventually lead to a state of entropy if it is allowed to go unchecked.

The opposition against these forces assumes a similar form for both characters: they rebel, but in trying to escape from the Firm's control, they withdraw from civilization, Natty by retreating to the frontier, Tyrone by disappearing into the Zone, actions that are not inspired by any political or ideological motives. Natty's allegiance is neither to the Indians nor to the whites, while Tyrone is indifferent to the Allied cause in which he serves as an American officer. Their only

---

[18] Heinz Ickstadt: "The more he [Cooper] became entangled in lawsuits and public altercations (...), the more it seemed to him that it was the larger public which was corrupt or easily corruptible — without knowledge of, nor care for, the institutions, without heart, taste or discrimination, its only interest money and the fast success." ("Instructing the American Democrat: Cooper and the Concept of Popular Fiction in Jacksonian America" in *James Fenimore Cooper: New Critical Essays*, p. 23). See note 4.

commitment is to themselves, a strictly personal one: how to preserve individual autonomy.

The only way to achieve this leads to a return to nature, away from the labyrinthine complexity of civilization: Natty, a nineteenth-century creation, in the full understanding and acceptance of his mystic bondage to the wilderness, as exemplified by the last word he utters before he dies, an emphatic "Here!"; Tyrone, a twentieth-century creation, without any understanding, nature representing to him not much else than a source of undirected sexual energy, as exemplified by the image portending his dissolution in the Zone: "a stout rainbow cock driven down out of the cubic clouds into Earth, green, wet vallyed Earth, and his chest fills and he stands crying, not a thing in his head, just natural" (GR 626). It makes both characters stand outside history. In Natty's case because Cooper has made him too much a man of one piece, a man who knows of no compromise between absolute freedom and total control, and therefore unfit to play a social role. In Tyrone's case because Pynchon has made him too little a man of one piece, and therefore equally unfit to break out of what has conditioned him.

Natty's position is particularly ironic. The qualities Cooper has invested in him are precisely those that would enable people to live in harmony with nature, the one way of recognizing true civilization, as Kay S. House put it.[19] That Cooper did not envisage a way of making the Leatherstocking figure play a social role in furthering the creation of such a civilization must, as I have argued, also be ascribed to his own position as a member of the Elect. Through Natty he was able to vent his criticism of the deplorable direction American civilization seemed to be taking, while at the same time he made him the vehicle of his own nostalgia for an idyllic past without social and personal

---

[19] Kay S. House, "James Fenimore Cooper: Cultural Prophet and Literary Pathfinder" in *American Literature to 1900*, ed. Marcus Cunliffe, London: Sphere Books, 1973, p. 123.

restraints. But his allegiance was to the Elect, not to the Preterite, the People, and it is from this stance that Cooper's efforts to distinguish the penniless and illiterate Natty Bumppo from the People derive their significance. He not only provided him with a set of aristocratic qualities (contempt for the merely mercenary, an absolute sense of honour and privacy), but he also took great pains in pointing out that his frontiersman moves on a foot of equality with officers and gentlemen, something that is especially noticeable in *The Pathfinder*, the novel where we meet Natty in the prime of life.

Tyrone's position in *Gravity's Rainbow* is equally ironic, and in much the same way as Natty's. His affinity with the Rocket seems to destine him to play a role in the state that "begins to take form in the stateless German night, a state that spans oceans and surface politics, so sovereign as the International or the Church of Rome, and the Rocket is its soul" (GR 566). People like Tyrone who had been suspicious of the old state, could be expected to be useful in bringing a new state to birth. But Tyrone, though generous and brave, is too occupied with his own private affairs, too uncommitted, too much a product of "the mindless pleasures" fed to him by the mass media, the popular arts, to be able to understand the significance of the Rocket beyond the fact that in some mysterious way he is related to it.

With the invention of the Rocket (revolutionary technology) mankind has arrived for the second time at "the fork in the road" which, if it were missed again, would mean a continuation of "this cycle of infection and death" (GR 724), so characteristic of human history. But this time man might refuse to take the wrong fork. The rocket is not merely doomed to fall down, symbolic of ceaseless destruction, it can also overcome earth's gravity, symbolic of transcendence. What is likely to happen is that the pull of earth's gravity proves the greater force. This apocalyptic view no doubt informs the conception of both Tyrone and Natty. When Tyrone dissolves at the end of *Gravity's*

Rainbow, he hears the explosion of the atombomb dropped on Hiroshima ringing in his uncomprehending ears; when Natty dies at the end of *The Prairie*, he dejectedly hears the shouts of Manifest Destiny ringing in his. But the rigidity of Cooper's approach to both character and vision is lacking in Pynchon's. What Pynchon shows is a healthy suspicion of any rigidity in the conceptualizing process, finding herein no doubt support in the discovery of the principle of indeterminacy. It may explain why he does not look upon the individual and society, the wilderness and civilization as separate and opposite entities, but as fluid and interacting categories, infinitely variable as the spirit takes man. Chance, and therefore choice is possible, enabling him to oppose the Systems which after all are as much the products of human ingenuity as the technologies they so cannily co-opt but which nonetheless remain the greatest threat to his humanity. It is this threat that gave rise to a concern which has not perceptibly changed over the span of one and half centuries, as the work of both Cooper and Pynchon bears witness to.

Chapter 2

NATHANIEL HAWTHORNE:
"The Canterbury Pilgrims"; "Roger Malvin's Burial"; "Alice Doane's Appeal"; "The Great Carbuncle"; *The Scarlet Letter*

There is that memorable passage in Hawthorne's Introduction to *The Scarlet Letter*, "The Custom-House", in which he imagines the scorn his stern, practical, and energetic Puritan forefathers must have felt for him, if they had known what he, their nineteenth-century descendant, would turn out to be: "A writer of story-books!" To them, Hawthorne presumed, it was an occupation rated not much higher than that of a "fiddler".

However, the end of this passage, so full of the typical Hawthornean brand of self-effacing mockery, is significant: "And yet, let them scorn me as they will, strong traits of their nature have intertwined themselves with mine."[1]

What these strong traits included was not only the profoundly moral view of life Hawthorne shared with his Puritan ancestors but also

---

[1] *The Scarlet Letter*, "The Custom-House", The Centenary Edition of the Works of Nathaniel Hawthorne, vol. I: Ohio State University Press, 1974, p. 10.

an unmistakable toughness of mind, and it is no doubt this latter quality which made Edwin Fussell conclude that like Cooper "Hawthorne was at heart a Western writer; and even more persistently than Cooper, he was determined to see himself in a Western light".[2]

Hawthorne, to be sure, was not a Thoreau, the Natty Bumppo who had gone to Harvard, which is not to say though that he was not familiar with Natty's beloved woods and lakes. In 1818, when he was fourteen, an impressionable and formative age, Hawthorne spent a year in the house of an uncle who lived in the town of Raymond near Lake Sebago in the state of Maine and which at that time had still all of the natural beauty pertaining to the American wilderness so brilliantly described by Cooper in his Leatherstocking Tales. If we recall that in 1818 the Missouri region was considered the Far West and Independence an outpost of white civilization, then Maine was the West at that time, and here Hawthorne lived, "like a bird of the air, so perfect was the freedom [he] enjoyed";[3] like a Natty Bumppo almost, hunting, gun in hand, and fishing trout, just as a century later young Hemingway would do in the woods of Northern Michigan.

The impact of the West on Hawthorne's work is discernible in a great many of his stories and even, as we shall see, in his famous novel of adultery, *The Scarlet Letter*. Furthermore, his conception of the West has much in common with Cooper's and Melville's in that he too believed that it was a repository of new potentialities which enabled man to open a more satisfactory "intercourse with the world" than had been possible for him before the Westward movement gained its full momentum.

Yet, Hawthorne's reliance on the West as a shaping force in his

---

[2]   Edwin Fussell, *Frontier: American Literature and the American West*, p. 69, and p. 85.

[3]   As quoted by Henry James in his *Hawthorne* in *The Shock of Recognition*, ed. Edmund Wilson, p. 440.

work is at once more complex than either Cooper's or even Melville's. Nowhere else is this better illustrated than by his short story "The Canterbury Pilgrims", perhaps not his best, but one that can be said to epitomize the various elements that constitute his view of the West.

As can be expected from the kind of author Hawthorne is, all the characters that he gathered round the fountain outside the Shaker village have representative value. The young Shaker couple, Josiah and Miriam, about to leave their village in order to join the Oregon expedition, can easily be seen as representative of all those who opted for a change in their lives, either to flee from oppression and stagnation, as is the case with this young couple, or to improve their material circumstances, as seems to have been the case with the other characters introduced by Hawthorne. The latter, the Canterbury pilgrims proper, no doubt represent the various groups of people who did not make it "out West", and whose woeful life-stories are meant to warn the youngsters against exchanging the security of the Shaker village for the hardships and uncertainties they are going to face among what they designate as "the world's people".[4]

The first story told by the pilgrim who announces himself as a poet, "a thin and stooping figure", may fail to make a deep impression on the young Shaker couple, unfamiliar as they are with this particular species of humankind, but Hawthorne's intention of introducing this "varse-maker" as his first commentator on the Western experience cannot be mistaken. Part of what motivated the Westward movement no doubt resided in the allurement of the unknown, the exotic, the desire for a grander, more exciting existence, all impulses which may be brought together under the appellation "poetic", but the actuality of winning the West required first and foremost a strong arm and a tough mind rather than the poet's "voice of song" and his "delicacy of feeling"

---

[4]   The Centenary Edition, vol. XI, *The Snow Image*, p. 121. All further page references are to this volume.

(p. 124). It explains why, to quote Fussell once again, in the actual West "the very atmosphere of society [was] averse to mental culture, and all refinement [was] so systematically as well as practically decried as to have fallen into absolute discredit".[5]

It is this fall into "discredit" of what the poet holds highest that has disillusioned him. His talents unappreciated, his labour unremunerated, he has turned his back on the West, taking refuge in the Shaker village which, although condemning him to spend the rest of his days among drab utilitarians and spiritual and religious conformists, at least will not let him starve.

However, the poet's urgent appeal to the young couple to stay where they are and to give up their plan to go West — a spiritual desert as well as a place barren of human sympathy — goes unheeded. Young Josiah has no intention of being a poet, nor "Heaven be praised" has his bride, so there is little chance of their going to suffer the disappointments our poet faced. Besides, all they know of what being a poet means is that he makes verse, and helpful Miriam, who fears that the practical Shakers will object to receiving in their midst such an impractical person as a verse-maker, innocently suggests that he might make himself useful by polishing up their "rough" hymns. But the poet hardly heeds her words, ignoring this final insult to his calling. Too self-absorbed he simply turns away in order to compose "A Farewell to his Harp", which later with two or three other pieces he "took the first opportunity to send by one of the Shaker brethren to Concord, where they were published in the New Hampshire Patriot" (p. 126). He, too, finally manages to turn personal failure into artistic success, a phenomenon which, considering Hawthorne's own persistent sense of personal failure, and despite the overt irony with which he so amusingly presents it here, no doubt continued to strike him as a perplexing paradox.

---

[5] Fussell, p. 11.

The second pilgrim who tries to dissuade the young couple from leaving the protective, though depressing security of the Shaker village, represents another class of people that played an important role in winning the West: the merchants, the traders, the financial speculators, whose primary aim was neither to found a new Eden, nor to pursue America's Manifest Destiny, unless it could serve as a convenient pretext for what they were really after, which was quick profits. It was an aim that could result in either sudden riches or in equally sudden ruin, and to all appearances both had happened to this victim of personal greed and impersonal fate, but again Josiah and Miriam, the young Shakers, are not impressed by the merchant's tale of woe. They are content with the proceeds of an honest day's work, which they can earn everywhere, even among "the world's people" and what more should they want? "Nothing more", as the girl piously affirms.

However, the third story they hear is altogether different, commanding their keenest attention. It is told by "a sunburnt countryman of tall frame and bony strength", the sort of man that belongs to their kind, the people who have no desire to be rich overnight but who expect to be rewarded with a decent and comfortable living for the hard work they put in. But even to that expectation, modest as it may be, the West has failed to come up, for as the hardy countryman tells his audience, no matter how long and arduous you worked, it got you nowhere: you grew poorer and poorer until you couldn't bear it any longer, gave up in despair and headed for the Shakers, abandoning personal initiative and freedom for mere sustenance, thus giving the lie to Benjamin Franklin's saying that God helps those who help themselves ("I thought it a matter of course that the Lord would help me, because I was willing to help myself", p. 128).[6]

---

[6]   Cf. what Patricia Nelson Limerick in her *The Legacy of Conquest: The Unbroken Past of the American West*, New York: Norton, 1987, has to say about this aspect of the West: "We are willing to work hard, many of these people thought, and hard work ought to earn us a fair reward. The end of the Western rainbow was

44

But the countryman knows better now. And even this was not the worst. The worst was the effect the back-breaking toil had on what began in love and ended in indifference: the loss of hope, the loss of affection, alienating husband from wife, parents from children.

What both the poet's and the merchant's stories failed to do, the simple and stark tale of the countryman seems to achieve: the young Shakers hesitate. But their hesitation lasts no longer than an instant: "'We will not go back,' said they. 'The world never can be dark to us, for we will always love one another'" (p. 131).

The pyschological truth that speaks from their response is simple and of all times: one never learns from other people's experience, only from one's own, if one learns anything at all. Love to the young is consequently always enduring, always capable of coping with life's darker sides, and always capable of moving the proverbial mountains.

By having the young couple decide to go West, despite the countryman's dire warnings, Hawthorne seems to show himself here in tune with the country's prevailing ideology which held that the Westering impulse was the force *par excellence* of human progress, and that the pioneering settlers, engaged in conquering the wilderness, remained the standard bearers of white civilization.

Yet, as the countryman's story makes sufficiently clear, he was also quite aware of the West as the destroyer of hopes and dreams, when the back-breaking work of transforming the wilderness into civilization taxed human strength and resillience beyond endurance, leaving the settlers, after a life-time of brutal and lonely toil, with nothing more to show for themselves than material and spiritual impoverishment, the forgotten victims of the nation's pursuit of its Manifest Destiny.

What Hawthorne perceived with an equally sharp eye was the

---

supposed to hold at least a modest reward, but for many Westerners the pot with the treasure seemed to have been ransacked sometime before their arrival" (p. 152).

existence of still another West, the West as a mere economic object, relentlessly exploited by the big financiers, traders, restless speculators who by winning or losing fortunes overnight, turned the West into a huge fraud.[7]

Yet, behind and above these realities Hawthorne never lost sight of the over-arching idea of the West as a continuing source of renewal, of new possibilities to break free from stagnation and oppression, from the monotony of a limiting settled existence, as exemplified by the young Shaker couple. It is this idea that, as Tocqueville had already observed and Emerson had affirmed, was "full of poetry (...) the hidden nerve which gives vigor to the frame",[8] a poetry the youngsters enacted, but which the "real" poet in the story failed to express and to convey to his Western audience.

Hawthorne was no doubt serious in his contention, transmitted through this poet, that the actual West was a cultural desert, in which the flowers of artistic achievement rarely bloomed, and if so, went unnoticed, but again this belief does not remain unqualified. Hawthorne's portrayal of the story's poet is not merely ironic but highly critical as well. What this poet clearly fails to do is what he as a poet is supposed to do, and this is, if one agrees with Wallace Stevens, "to help people to live their lives".[9] The poet in Hawthorne's story believes that

---

[7] Cf.: "If we look upon the frontier as a place where the spirit of capitalistic accumulation could flower without restraint, we can perhaps begin to recapture its significance for American history in general", in "Symbol and Idea in Virgin Land" by H. Nash Smith in *Ideology and Classic American Literature*, eds. Sacvan Bercovitch and Myra Jehlen, New York: Cambridge U.P., 1986, p. 32.

[8] Alexis de Tocqueville, *Democracy in America*, transl. Henry Reeve, ed. Henry S. Commager, New York, 1947: "Nothing conceivable is so petty, so insipid, so crowded with paltry interests, in one word so anti-poetic, as the life of a man in the United States. But among the thoughts which it suggests there is always one which is full of poetry, and that is the hidden nerve which gives vigor to the frame" (p. 292). Also cf. R.W. Emerson in *Works* (12 vols [1903-4]. 11: "They [who] complain about the flatness of American life have no perception of its destiny. They are not Americans" (p. 544).

[9] Wallace Stevens, *The Necessary Angle*, New York, 1951, p. 29.

the function of his verse is "to breathe the celestial soul of thought" into it, but if he had breathed into his poetry a fair dose of earthly thought instead, he might have been of more use to the hardy pioneers. He also accuses his audience of "insensibility to the ethereal essence of poetry", but again they might have shown less insensibility if he had confronted them with a less purified form of poetry's essence. In that case the world would probably not have lacked "the ear of taste", and as a consequence not have put him "in a middle state between obscurity and infamy". Also the poet's reaction to this lack of recognition is not exactly conducive to helping people to live their lives: as he vows, he will have nothing more to do with them and deprive them of "a thousand bright creations" which he could have given them , leaving it further to posterity "to cry shame upon the unworthy age that drove one of the fathers of American song to end his days in a Shaker village".[10]

All this, as the poet's activities after the composition of his "Farewell to his Harp" may show, should not be taken too seriously, as we should not take too seriously the poet himself, since, despite his "bitter words", he was, as Hawthorne informs us, "a kind, gentle, harmless, poor fellow enough, whom Nature, tossing her ingredients together without looking at the recipe, had sent into the world with too much of one sort of brain and hardly any of another" (p. 124).

In these comments on the artist one no doubt hears a reverberation of the scorn Hawthorne thought he himself deserved from his Puritan ancestors for being a mere "writer of story-books", but what they chiefly confirm is the idea that there are artists and artists, and that the West had no use for the kind of artist who, while reaching for

---

[10] In an interesting reassessment of his classic *Virgin Land: The American West as Symbol and Myth* (1950), H. Nash Smith admits in "Symbol and Idea in Virgin Land" (see note 7) that he had insufficiently taken into account the worst aspects of the Westward movement, aspects already touched upon in Hawthorne's "The Canterbury Pilgrims", in that the ideas of "civilization", "free land", "frontier individualism" were also used to hide or rationalize such effects as oppression, greed, lack of human concern and disillusionment (pp. 21-36).

the stars, ignored "the hidden nerve" which gave "vigor" to what drove young Shaker couples westward.

If from "The Canterbury Pilgrims" the West emerges as an exhilarating promise, a destroyer of hopes, and a gigantic fraud all at once, in "Roger Malvin's Burial" Hawthorne deals with still another aspect of the West, the side that reveals what was inherently dark and tragic in the irresistible advance of white civilization into the wilderness.

Winning the West also meant encountering the autochthons, the Red Indians, and from the very first contacts between white and red in the early seventeenth century up to the Battle of Little Big Horn in 1876 which heralded the end of organized Indian resistance on the North-American continent, these encounters have shown a wearisome sameness: although in the beginning not without a modicium of good will on both sides, they soon soured as a result of all sorts of misunderstandings, leading to mutual mistrust, broken promises, and finally to outbreaks of hostility, invariably ending in brutal slaughter, burning, and looting.

That these bloody skirmishes were always sought or provoked by the early white settlers seems unlikely, but sometimes they were, as in the case of the well-known "Lovewell's Fight" (1725), in which John Lovewell, a Massachusetts Indian fighter, and a number of his band of scalp bounty hunters were decoyed in Maine by Pequawkets and killed. Hawthorne's story tells of two survivors of this encounter, Roger Malvin, a middle-aged settler, and young Reuben Bourne, his prospective son-in-law.

The curious thing is that in the opening paragraph of the story, in which Hawthorne briefly situates the event in its historical context, he seems to concur with the official version of this fight when he writes that the "bravery displayed by both parties was in accordance with civilized ideas of valor, and chivalry itself might not blush to record the

48

deeds of one or two individuals". It is a somewhat unexpected eulogy of what in fact was an encounter between a party of scalp bounty hunters and a band of Pequawkets that had found them out.

The impression that Hawthorne wrote his introductory paragraph in accordance with "History and Tradition" as conceived by the dominant ideology of his time is further strengthened by the fact that he calls Lovewell "the captain of a scouting party of frontier-men" who led men in "the defence of the frontiers", and that he repeats the view that the fight "broke the strength of a tribe", thus effecting peace "during several ensuing years". [11]

But although Hawthorne may have concurred with prevailing nineteenth-century historical views in presenting us with the traditional version of Lovewell's Fight and its beneficial effect on frontier life, in describing the effect it had on one individual participant he followed his own psychological insight and artistic intuition.

At a first reading "Roger Malvin's Burial" seems to belong to the type of Hawthornean tales that deal with moral failure and the disastrous effect this may have on a person who has to live with the memory of it, while being unable to come to terms with it.

We meet Roger Malvin and Reuben Bourne in the midst of the "howling wilderness". Both are in bad shape, exhausted from their

---

[11] The Centenary Edition, vol. X, p. 337. All further page references are to this volume.

Michael J. Colacurcio in his *The Province of Piety: Moral History in Hawthorne's Early Tales*, Harvard U.P., 1984, believes that Hawthorne's introductory paragraph is ironic (note 17, p. 556), and he may have a point, although it is difficult to detect where and how exactly the irony in this particular case works.

Another explanation of Hawthorne's swallowing Bancroftian historiography hook, line, and sinker is provided by George Dekker, who in his *The American Historical Romance*, Cambridge U.P., 1987, argues that it was Hawthorne's aim in his "patriotic" tales "to have it both ways: to apotheosize the Puritans as founders and liberators while injecting notes, sometimes obvious and sometimes not, that remind us of their acts of destruction and confinement" (p. 148). There is something to be said in favour of either approach. What is clear to me is that by subscribing to the official version of the past — seemingly or not seemingly — , Hawthorne brings out more starkly the fact that the way the individual experiences an event has nothing to do with the significance history accords it.

wounds incurred during the fight with the Pequawkets as well as from their three days' march, which still leaves them half-way between the field of battle and the settlements they are headed for. Roger Malvin is, in fact, mortally wounded, and he knows that they will never make it. He therefore urges his younger companion to move on alone and try to reach the settlements before his strength fails him as well. Reuben, however, refuses to leave the older man. If Malvin dies, he wants to be at his side and bury him, and if this entails his own death as well, so be it. But Malvin will not hear of this, Reuben's responsibilities should be with the living, with Dorcas, Malvin's daughter and the young man's wife to be. Reuben hesitates, but recalling the promise he made Dorcas to defend her father with his life, he grows firm again in his refusal to leave Malvin. The older man then tries another tack, pointing out to Reuben that, if he went, he was bound to encounter a rescue party on his way to the settlement, which would enable him to speed up help that might then still come in time to save Malvin.

This time the fierce desire to live and the prospect of future happiness with Dorcas prove too strong to Reuben. Pretending that the point Malvin makes has convinced him, and suppressing the knowledge that his wounded companion is beyond help, he agrees to go.

What becomes quite clear from Hawthorne's subtle narration is that Reuben, although terrified by the thought of having to die in vain, does not really want to abandon a dying man, yet does so, because his will to live is stronger than his sense of loyalty.

As Malvin predicted, Reuben does encounter a rescue party, but he is in no position to lead them to Malvin. Suffering from complete exhaustion, his mind wandering, he is transported to the settlement, where, nursed by Dorcas, it takes months before he has recovered from his hardships. In reply to Dorcas's questions about her father's fate, Reuben, unable to tell the truth, creates the impression that he stayed with him until he died, after which he buried him. He is acclaimed a hero by the settlers, and everybody rejoices in his marriage to Dorcas which takes place after he has fully recovered, but from that day on Reuben carries with him a secret he cannot reveal to anybody, least of all to those he loves most, Dorcas and his young son Cyrus, soon to be born. It is the secret of his moral cowardice, and just as in the case of Young Goodman Brown and Dimmesdale, it is the concealment rather than the deed itself that poisons his life, a condition aggravated by the knowledge that he had never redeemed his vow to bury Malvin's remains. It transforms Reuben, just as Goodman Brown, into "a sad and downcast, yet irritable man" (p. 350), who gradually deteriorates, losing not only the love and respect of his neighbouring settlers, but also in the end his farm and land which he started to neglect.

He finally decides to leave the settlement and move farther Westwards into the wilderness in order to start a new life. Accompanied by Dorcas and their only son Cyrus, now a comely and promising boy of fifteen and deeply loved by Reuben, he sets out for the tract of land he and Cyrus had cleared and made ready for cultivation the previous autumn.

However, this time Reuben seems unable to follow a straight course to their destination, which is about a week's journey through the virgin forest, but leads his small family farther north instead, into a region "of which savage beasts and savage men were as yet the sole possessors" (p. 253). Some mysterious force compels him to swerve from his course and direct his steps to the rock where eighteen years ago he had left Roger Malvin "unburied in the howling wilderness". It is near this spot that they decide to camp, and it is before this rock that the fatal accident occurs. Setting out in search of game, Reuben and Cyrus leave Dorcas in opposite directions. Reuben, without realizing it, as in a trance, is led in a circle, arriving in the vicinity of the rock where the undergrowth is particularly dense and bushy. Perceiving sudden motion here, and believing it to be game, he fires and a low moan tells him that it was a lucky shot. The moan, however, is not from some animal but from the dying Cyrus, accidentally shot by Reuben, his father. Dorcas, believing that the shot is Cyrus's and wondering why it takes him so long to return with the game, leaves the campsite to meet him halfway, but finds Reuben instead. Something in his rigid posture fills her suddenly with cold, shuddering fear, and when she finally realizes that the object Reuben is staring at in ghastly despair is the dead body of her son, killed on the same spot where eighteen years ago Roger Malvin, her father, perished, she collapses. The effect on Reuben, however, is twofold: on the one hand grief, naturally, on the other, redemption. As Hawthorne concludes his tale: "The vow that the wounded youth had made, the blighted man had come to redeem. His sin was expiated, the curse was gone from him; and, in the hour, when he had shed blood dearer to him than his own, a prayer, the first for years, went up to Heaven from the lips of Reuben Bourne" (p. 360).

There is something disturbingly odd about this end. Although the words that make up this concluding passage all have a New Testament ring — "redeem", "expiate", "sin", "curse", "prayer", "Heaven" — , they derive their real significance from Old Testament if not pagan sources. Reuben, compelled by some deeply primitive urge, sacrifices his son, the most precious treasure he has to offer the gods, in order to feel one again with the universe, from which he had been alienated for eighteen years, following his failure to redeem the vow he once made to a dying man.

Is it exposure to different cultural values that accounts for Reuben's act, based as it is on the belief that only the making of a human blood sacrifice can redeem a man's sense of guilt of having sinned against the order of the universe, a belief also held by Red Indian tribes of North-east America? The impact of the wilderness on the ethical and moral behaviour of the white is not an uncommon theme in Hawthorne's work, and the outcome is as a rule never conceived by him as entirely favourable. For a large number of characters in Hawthorne's fiction it can in fact be described as "demonizing", and the most telling example that immediately comes to mind is of course Hester Prynne's husband, the man who, unknown to her, was "held in bonds among the heathenfolk".[12]

When we meet Chillingworth for the first time in *The Scarlet Letter*, he is described by Hawthorne as "clad in a strange disarray of civilized and savage costume" (p. 60). But the effect of the Indianizing to which Chillingworth had been exposed is not limited to mere appearances. During his Indian captivity he had not only "gained much knowledge of the properties of native herbs and roots" (pp. 119-20), he had even "enlarged his medical attainment by joining in the incantations of the savage priests" (p. 127).

What he must also have imbibed was a good deal of the savage spirit of revenge for which his Indian captors were known, turning him into a preying demon that in the end not only destroys poor Dimmesdale but himself as well. And even the manner in which this is done reminds us of certain popular practices among the Indians. But there is a significant difference. Rather than openly enjoying torture and cruelty in its cruder, physical sense, Chillingworth, an educated white man, derives his joy and satisfaction from practicing it on a more refined psychological level: probing into and dissecting the clergyman's mind, he strikes where it hurts most, working on the man's sense of spiritual failure and moral guilt.

Another telling example of the pernicious influence of the wilderness on white Christians is of course provided by Hawthorne's version of the Hannah Duston tale, the story of the housewife from Haverhill. Together with her nurse Mary Neff, she was taken captive by Abenaki Indians in 1697 during King William's War, but managed to

---

[12] The Centenary Edition, vol. I, p. 61. All further page references are to this volume.

make her escape by tomahawking her captors while they were sleeping, though not before taking their scalps as a bounty, no doubt in retaliation for the murder of her new-born child and why not gain some profit from the harrowing events she had lived through as well?

The source of this popular captivity tale is, as we know, Cotton Mather, who had heard it either from Hannah Duston herself, or from her pastor, and who then recorded it as a tale of heroism performed to the greater glory of God in his *Magnalia Christi Americana* (1702). The story also drew the attention of Thoreau, who included his version in *A Week on the Concord and Merrimack Rivers* (1849).[13]

Hawthorne's version of Hannah Duston's story shows interesting differences with Thoreau's. Contrary to Thoreau, Hawthorne makes no attempt to keep up the pretence of giving an objective account of Hannah's horrifying experiences. He is, in fact, uncommonly outspoken in his sympathies and antipathies, his praise and condemnation, though even here the picture he draws is never entirely black or white.

In the Indians' attack on the settlement, Hawthorne describes them as "raging savages", but oddly enough the inhuman act of the Indian who dashes out Hannah's baby's brains against Thoreau's "apple-tree" is recorded without censure, and the appalling practice of the Indians to kill all the captives who are too weak to keep up with their forced march also goes without comment. What does receive attention is the fact that these Indians — all Roman Catholics — strictly observe their prayers, and as Hawthorne writes, "What can be more touching than to think of these wild Indians, in their loneliness and their wanderings, wherever they went among the dark, mysterious woods, still keeping up domestic worship, with all the regularity of a household at its peaceful fireside" (p. 229). True, Hawthorne continues to call them

---

[13] Both Thoreau's and Hawthorne's version of the Hannah Duston tale are included in *The Indians and Their Captives*, eds. James Levernier and Hennig Cohen, Westport: Greenwood Press, 1977, pp. 156-59, and pp. 224-30 respectively. I have used Levernier's collection, so all page references are to this volume.

"savages", "barbarians", but he does not fail to notice that what "scanty food" they had, was shared with their prisoners, as if they "had all been the children of one wigwam".

Hawthorne shows himself far less empathic when he deals with Hannah Duston. Although he is quite willing to admit that there were grounds for Hannah to justify her feelings of outrage and revenge, considering what the Indians did to her baby and the rest of her family, he condemns in no uncertain terms her act of slaughtering the seven Indian children, calling her "the raging tigress", whom the Indian boy she had saved because she had grown fond of him "did well to flee from". But Hawthorne's moral outrage reaches its greatest pitch when he records Hannah's taking the dead Indians' scalps, and the curses he invokes on what he now qualifies as "the bloody old hag" range from drowning in the river, burial in a swamp, to starvation in the forest. But none of all this happens to her. She safely reaches home, receiving the bounty on the dead Indians, and in her old age, even a pension "as a further price of blood" (p. 230).

Contrasted with "this awful woman" is Thomas Duston, Hannah's husband, "that tenderhearted, yet valiant man", whom Thoreau does not mention at all, but who in Hawthorne's tale is made the centre of the author's warmly-felt sympathy.

Although Goodman Duston in Hawthorne's version abandons his wife and their new-born baby, leaving them to the mercy of the marauding Indians, his seemingly craven conduct is actually the result of a courageous decision. Facing the agonizing choice between saving the lives of either Hannah and the baby or those of his other seven children, he has the balance tipped in favour of the latter, a choice probably clinched, as Hawthorne slyly suggests, by Duston's knowledge of his wife's formidable character: she might hold her own where the children did not stand a chance.

How right Goodman Duston was in his assessment of Hannah's

unflinching toughness is proved by the ten Indians, left dead and scalped in their wigwam, but also Duston himself, the historical Duston, that is, can hardly have been the tender-hearted fellow Hawthorne imagined he was. This becomes apparent when we learn that it was Thomas Duston himself who petitioned the General Court to award his wife a compensation for the bounty on scalps, which, ironically, had just expired when Hannah returned. (The request was granted, and Hannah Duston received 25 English pounds.) What Duston's petition discloses is that he must have felt no qualms in requesting money on behalf of his wife for scalping seven Indian children, from which we may safely infer that he was not particularly disturbed by Hannah's savage deed. In itself this can of course hardly be considered unusual — the early settlers had to be a hardy breed; besides, scalping was officially sanctioned — but it does throw some doubt on the man's tender-heartedness, of which Hawthorne makes so much.

If one recalls that Hawthorne can generally be looked upon as a cautious and even-tempered author, one may wonder what could have caused him to take up the kind of biassed stance as exemplified by this particular story. The explanation is likely to be found in the source of the Hannah Duston tales: Cotton Mather, the seventeenth-century Puritan historian, and no friend of Hawthorne's.

Mather, in accordance with the traditional Puritan typology, compared Hannah Duston to the Old Testament heroine Jael, the woman who slew the Canaanite general while he was asleep (Judges 4:17-22), and he clearly admired Hannah, approving of her bloody retaliation, in which he saw God's providence. It is in all likelyhood this approval and this belief that outraged Hawthorne, who could only see this as "hard-hearted, pedantic" bigotry on the part of the divine, Mather, and who, he thought, "seem[ed] trebly to exult in the destruction of these poor wretches, on account of their Popish superstitions" (p. 229). It explains the harsh tone in which Hawthorne censures Hannah's deed. Through her, he in fact lashes out at the unfeeling self-righteousness, so characteristic of the kind of seventeenth-century Puritanism that even in "the deep, dead slumber" of the Indians before daybreak, the heavy sleep that enabled Hannah to do her cruel handiwork, saw a sign of God's assent to their slaughter.

Like Thoreau's, Hawthorne's greater tolerance of the Indians' savagery seemed to find its origin in his realization that they, the Indians, did not pretend to be better than they were, contrary to the whites who on moral grounds condemned in them what they themselves were equally capable of doing, and, given the right circumstances, never shrank from doing.

The two stories which exemplify this while dramatizing succinctly the issues involved are "Young Goodman Brown" and "Alice Doane's Appeal". The condemnable things in these stories range from what Hawthorne himself in "Alice Doane's Appeal" calls "the many varieties of wickedness", illicit sexual passions, to plain murder, all deeds which the stories' main characters thought they were incapable of ever doing, but which they nevertheless did, apparently because the circumstances were "right".

What made these circumstances right was the fact that they, the early Puritan settlers, lived in close proximity of the wilderness, which, it is true, might bring out what was best in man, spiritually and morally, as exemplified by Cooper's Leatherstocking figure, but which more often than not could also bring out what was most evil in him. It is in this connection not accidental that in Hawthorne's description the wilderness — nature, in a metaphoric sense, the West — is invariably referred to in these two stories as "rude", "dark", "haunted", "heathen", a place "where no church had ever been gathered, nor solitary Christian prayed", where the echoes laugh "like demons", the habitat, too, of the Indian powows, "who, after their fashion, know almost as much deviltry as the best of us".[14]

"Almost" — the distinction Hawthorne makes here is typical again of his lenience towards the savagery of the Indians: their deviltry may be great, but it is never as great as the white man's, probably because what attracts the latter so powerfully to the wilderness is as great as what repels him: the lure of the unknown, the escape from communal control, the complete abandon to supposedly demonic forces. These conflicting pulls constitute an explosive mixture, which, when brought to ignition, may severely affect the sanity of a person's judgement, as in the case of Goodman Brown when he accepts an invitation to attend a witches' sabbath in the deep forest, resulting in his loss of faith; as in the case of Leonard Doane, whom it turns into a murderer.

Although not everything in life depends on prevailing circumstances — character, too, plays its role — , much of what happens in the history of man does depend on them, and the meeting ground of the wilderness and civilization, the frontier, the "West", was one stage in America's history that provided the circumstances which could make a man lose his religion or make him regress to a state of savagery; circumstances such as traumatic encounters with the Indians, total isolation from communal and civilized living, the back-breaking toil that never seemed to result in anything worth showing, or the attraction of the New World's freedom turned into licence or lawlessness, the experience that scarred Goodman Brown.

Despite Brown's relapse to savagery in the forest, however, he does not become a "fiend", perhaps because he might, as Hawthorne intimates, only have dreamt the witch-meeting. But the effect it has on his character and life is as profound as if he had actually gone through the terrifying experience of attending the witches' sabbath.

---

[14] The Centenary Edition, vol. X, p. 81. All further page references are to this volume.

It is life on the frontier, the early "West", that allows and enables Young Goodman Brown to journey into the dark recesses of his humanity, even if he only dreamt it, and it ends by turning him into a lonely, embittered man, distrustful of God and man alike, as he is unable to acknowledge in himself what he condemns in his fellow townspeople, which is the attraction of evil.

The story "Alice Doane's Appeal" also reveals its fuller significance when seen in the historical context of America's Westward movement involving the inevitable clash between two entirely different cultures, the white man's and that of the Red Indian. In this story the clash takes the not uncommon early seventeenth-century form of a night-attack by Indians on one of the settlements, attacks which would end for the whites either in death, or escape, or abduction. In the case of the Doane family all three contingencies seemed to have taken place: the parents meet with death, the children Alice and Leonard manage to escape, while there may have been a third child, Leonard's twin brother, who is abducted, but who was then evidently recaptured, brought up in the Old World, but taken back to the New World again, where he reappears in the lives of Alice and Leonard as Walter Brome, the young man who falls in love with Alice, without knowing that she is his sister. Alice returns his love, but Walter is killed by Leonard before anything unseemly has happened. (Alice's "appeal" to the spectre of Walter Brome invokes a reply that absolves her "from every stain", to the dismay of the prurient ghosts and the devil who flee "as from the sinless presence of an angel".[15]

Life on the early frontier, then, was known to give occasion to these kinds of fatal encounters, but that was not all. The principal reason why Leonard kills Walter Brome is sexual jealousy, and this too results directly from the conditions of early frontier life: loneliness,

---

[15] The Centenary Edition, vol. XI, p. 227. All further page references are to this volume.

isolation, danger of imminent Indian raids forged close ties between brothers and sisters, so close, in fact, that the risk of their acquiring an incestuous nature was far from imaginary. Leonard not only kills a rival, a brother and his father in Walter Brome, he is also the perpetrator of an even more "unutterable crime", incest, a crime that can only be committed "in madness or a dream", and for which he, Leonard, is now moved by "dark impulses to meditate violence against the life of Alice", no doubt from the biblical demand to punish her as well as himself for the fact that he not only loved her "with the strength of sisterly affection" but also with "that impure passion which alone engrosses all the heart", the kind of passion in fact Leonard could never forgive Walter for having for Alice, but which he himself was not allowed to have either.

That Leonard's crimes are not to be looked upon as rare and isolated instances, becomes apparent from Hawthorne's extraordinary evocation of the graveyard scene at the end of the story. None of the dead that emerge from their graves "to revel in the discovery of a complicated crime" — the murder of Walter Brome, a deed "as foul a one as ever was imagined in their dreadful abode" — appears to be innocent, virtuous, without sin. From the very first settlers, "those old illustrious ones, the heroes of tradition and fireside legend", to the most recent arrivals, the murdered Walter Brome; from the victims of the witch-hunting years in the seventeenth century, falsely accused by the priest, former friends, even children, of consorting with the devil, to their victimizers, "a guilty and miserable band; villains who had thus avenged themselves on their enemies, and viler wretches, whose cowardice had destroyed their friends; lunatics, whose ravings had chimed in with the madness of the land" (p. 279), — no one passes the test.

The fiend himself, that is the devil, could have been responsible for this sorry state of affairs, but, as the narrator tells us, it is not the

devil who is to blame, but "his good friend, Cotton Mather", proud
Cotton Mather, "the representative of all the hateful features of his
time; the one blood-thirsty man, in whom were concentrated those vices
of spirit and errors of opinion that sufficed to madden the whole
surrounding multitude" (p. 279).[16]

It is they, the fundamentalists, as we would call them today, who
were basically responsible for the vitiated relations among the white
Puritans, leading to the hangings on Gallows Hill, as well as for those
between the whites and the Indians that invariably resulted in night-
raids and wars.

The interpretation of "Alice Doane's Appeal" is not entirely
determined by its early-frontier context. Freudians, for example, will
have a field day, as the story not only contains a classic dramatization
of the Oedipus complex but a case of incest and fratricide as well.

There is finally "The Great Carbuncle", the story that seems to
come closest to fulfilling what Fussell describes as Hawthorne's
ambition "to betray in fiction the ultimate secrets of the Great West".[17]

It is not difficult to conceive the Great Carbuncle in this story as
the all-inclusive symbol of the Great West, the significance of which
keeps changing, dependent upon the kind of person that falls under its
mysterious spell.[18] There is first the "tall, lean, weather-beaten man",

---

[16] Hawthorne is uncommonly harsh towards Cotton Mather here. In
Grandfather's Chair he shows himself much milder, even if one takes into account the
fact that this work was primarily addressed to a young audience. He does hold Cotton
Mather responsible for the witchcraft excesses, but in *Grandfather's Chair* he believes
that Mather did not act "other than conscientiously". The difference seems to provide
another instance of Hawthorne's great ambivalence towards his Puritan ancestors.

[17] Fussell, p. 85.

[18] Cf. Colacurcio: "Even more sobering, perhaps, is the gradual recognition that,
above or behind all this local theology, conceived in parody and resolved in sentiment,
the tale is actually pressing to evoke the American Master-Theme: somehow the
Carbuncle, bunk or not, represents the Idea of America itself" (*The Province of Piety*,
p. 512). One need not be a Turnerian of course to equate the Idea of America itself
with the American West. Besides, the story, as the narrator tells us, originates from
an Indian legend — which speaks of a mysterious lake, incidentally — , and what in
the popular mind is more strongly associated with the Great West than the Indian?

"clad in the skins of wild animals", the Natty Bumppo-type to whom the West had become "the passionate dream of [his] existence". His restless search for the real West, which earned him the name of "Seeker", has already taken him past middle age into his sixtieth year, without finding though what he has been looking for, but which, when found, he intends to keep for himself, not to share with anybody else. When at last he stands face to face with the giant Gem, he is struck dead, perhaps because the joy of success, the realization of his quest, has killed him, as Matthew suggests, or perhaps because "the very light of the Great Carbuncle was death"[19], but more likely because the Seeker's attitude towards the Great Carbuncle — the Great West — is as selfish as that of the rest of the company of adventurers in search of the Gem. The West belongs to him, and to him only, and in this — understandable — selfishness he does not really distinguish himself from Doctor Cacaphodal, the scientist, to whom the Great Carbuncle — the New Land — serves as a fascinating object of study, the result of which he will lay down in "a folio volume" when he has returned to Europe, "to crown [his] scientific reputation".

Like the woodsman's, the Doctor's interest in the West is entirely self-serving, and this can also be said of the merchant Ichabod Pigsnort, whose sole purpose in getting control of the West (finding the Great Carbuncle) is to keep the state of the world's economy healthy; only then would the prices of all commodities remain stable and high, giving merchants, so he thinks, "a reasonable chance of profit", for they, that is, Pigsnort and his likes, would of course never be fool enough to risk "soul, body, reputation and estate" for an undertaking in which this would not be the case.

What will Pigsnort do once he has found the Great Carbuncle? He will sell it to the highest bidder among the potentates of the earth,

---

[19] The Centenary Edition, vol. IX, p. 154. All further page references are to this volume.

so as to neutralize its great potential of effecting economic changes which might endanger the status quo and the chances of profit, a wise plan, the merchant believes, wiser than any other plan he can think of.

The poet among the prospectors could not disagree more. To him, just as to the scientist, and for that matter to Lord de Vere as well, the haughty nobleman who wants the Great Carbuncle to restore the faded splendour of his ancestral castle, the search is to satisfy personal vanity, that "the splendor of the Great Carbuncle will blaze around [his] name" by enhancing the beauty of his poetry.

Even to the newly-wed couple, the young rustics, Matthew and Hannah, it is the riches embodied in the Great Carbuncle that constitute its greatest attraction to them, but there is a difference. What they look for in the West is warmth and light in which also their fellow men can share, and from which they can derive a firm sense of identity (even in the night the Gem will enable them "to see one another's faces!")

The endearing simplicity that informs the young couple's quest excited "a general smile among the adventurers", with the exception though of "the man with the spectacles", appropriately called the Cynic. Up to now he has successfully punctured the layer of pretentions hiding the real desires that motivate the search for the Great Carbuncle, desires, as he sneers, which are all selfish, vain and foolish.

But the Cynic's own desire, which is to show to the world that the giant gem does not exist, is of course equally selfish, vain and foolish. The cynic, as the saying goes, knows the price of everything and the value of nothing; his "yearnings are downward to the darkness instead of Heavenward", as Hawthorne writes, and he makes short shrift of the Cynic too. Just as the Seeker on beholding the object of his restless search is struck dead, so the Cynic is struck blind because he has come face to face with what he has always denied existed: the presence of "any brightness in the world", and it destroys his *raison* d'âue.

Only young Matthew and Hannah learn the appropriate response to the mysterious call of the Great Carbuncle — the Great West: they reject the desire to take possession of the gem, thus saving themselves from the kind of disasters that are to strike all the other participants in the search. The merchant, captured by the Indians, is held in bondage, ransomed and finally reduced to beggary. The poet's search ends in artistic failure, the "alchymist" forfeits his scientific reputation. Lord de Vere soon rests in "another coffin in the ancestral vault", while the Cynic, wandering through the world "with the desperate idea of catching one feeble ray from the blaze, that was kindling earth and heaven", dies ironically enough in the great fire of London.

The newly-wed couple alone survives the search unscathed, to live a long and peaceful life, but there is of course no gain without loss. In regarding the high promises of the West as dangerous illusions, one reduces the effort of building a new existence there to little more than the slow advancement of a people's standards of living, whether as the result of cultivating the land, or by improving industrial production, both hard and monotonous tasks, lacking all the excitement and glamour usually associated with the winning of the West. As Hawthorne puts it: "(...) from the hour when two mortals had shown themselves so simply wise, as to reject a jewel which would have dimmed all earthly things, its splendor waned" (p. 165).

It is the stern, sober realism as embodied in Matthew and Hannah that carried on and consolidated what had begun in a spirit of wonder and adventure, turning the West into a land of farms, ranches, towns and cities, prosperous though dull, devoid of the magic that the idea of the Great West signified to those few who continued to believe in its mythic potentiality of engendering golden opportunities, unfettered freedom, exciting action and metaphysical yearnings; a land suiting the aspirations of those who could not and would not concede the idea that man is no more than a bundle of sensual appetites craving satisfaction, selfishly and ruthlessly, and regardless of the cost. In the last analysis, the narrator of the story, too, reckons himself among these few, as the concluding lines of "The Great Carbuncle" disclose: "I saw a wondrous light around these summits, and was lured by the faith of poesy, to be the latest pilgrim of the GREAT CARBUNCLE".

Chapter 3

HERMAN MELVILLE:
Israel Potter

Israel Potter: His Fifty Years of Exile (1854) is not only Melville's most underrated novel, it is also his most "Western" novel and consequently, as he himself claimed, his most "American" novel.[1] It belongs to his most political works as well, and it is this quality that, if we look forward, links it with the work of a Thomas Pynchon; it is the Western quality that, if we look backward, connects it with Cooper's work.

The story of Israel Potter is, as we know, based upon a real person whose vicissitudes were recorded by Henry Trumbull in *The Life and Remarkable Adventures of Israel Potter* (1824). Melville follows to some extent Trumbull's account, but his many departures from his source underscore the fact that his version of Israel Potter's life is essentially different from that of Trumbull, whose book clearly belongs to the category of commemorative tales. What Trumbull glorifies in Israel Potter, one of the brave defenders of Bunker Hill, is heroic patriotism. What Melville sees represented in Israel is, as we shall see, of an entirely different order.

---

[1] "His [Ethan Allen's] spirit was essentially Western; and herein is his peculiar Americanism; for the Western spirit is, or will yet be (for no other is, or can be), the true American one", p. 198 in the Standard Edition of *Israel Potter: His Fifty Years of Exile*, Volume XI, London, 1923. All further page references are to this edition.

To what extent the informing principle of Melville's book is the American West becomes apparent when we examine more closely two of Melville's major divergences from his source. In Trumbull's book Israel's birthplace is Cranston, Rhode Island; in Melville's it is the Birkshire Mountains of Massachusetts. The significance of this change reveals itself if we recall that Cranston is situated in the lowlands of Narragansett Basin in Rhode Island, not particularly a place one would associate with the wild West. The region of the Birkshire Mountains, however, — grand, lonely, wild and mountainous — is typically frontier country. The description Melville gives of this region in his first chapter is, in fact, a magnificent evocation of the American wilderness as we may find it in the Far West. It is a place which, as Melville himself put it, "bred that fearless self-reliance and independence which conducted our forefathers to national freedom" (p. 10), that is, the same fearless self-reliance and independence so characteristic of that hardy race of men that was to win the West in the years to come.

The second divergence concerns the account of Israel's woeful existence in London, "the City of Dis". Trumbull devotes no less than half of his book to this episode, describing in detail Israel's many years of hardship and poverty in the English capital. Melville, however, restricts himself to only one brief chapter, in which he quickly summarizes the miserable years Israel spent in that city. Even though it comprised nearly fifty years of Israel's mortal life, it is clear that Melville was not really interested in this period. What did interest him were the causes that led to Israel's foreign exile, and this, I believe, had everything to do with his particular conception of Israel's character.

From Melville's version of Israel Potter's life story the man emerges as a typical representative of the frontiersman: courageous, self-reliant, inventive, skilful as farmer, hunter, trapper, and later as sailor and soldier — all trades Israel takes up at one time or another, excelling in all of them. But he is also a plain man, and although not without some of the proverbial Yankee canniness, basically of a gentle, trusting and loyal disposition, and consequently easily subject to victimization by the unscrupulous. In all of this he resembles to a remarkable degree our prototype of the frontiersman, Natty Bumppo, the hero of Cooper's *The Pioneers*, with whom he also shares, above everything else, a love of freedom, an abhorrence of any form of tyranny. And just as it made Natty flee the settlements, in escape of what he could only see as arbitrary restraints imposed upon his movements by a prying community, so it made Israel fight parental authority first, and colonial oppression later.

His first act of rebellion — against his father, who for some dark reason continued to oppose Irsael's wish to marry the daughter of one of their neighbours — drives him away from the region of his birth, after which he takes up the trade of hunter and trapper, thus becoming a true frontiersman. His second act of rebellion consists in joining the Revolutionary forces in order to oppose another tyrannical father figure, George III of England. *Israel Potter* has been designated as a celebration of American patriotism, and there is no reason to doubt the fervour of Israel's patriotic feelings, but the point to be made is that in his acts of rebellion no other principle is involved than his love of personal freedom. As Melville writes: "It appears that he [Israel] began his wanderings very early; moreover, that ere, on just principles, throwing off the yoke of his king, Israel, on equally excusable grounds, emancipated himself from his sire" (p. 7). In other words, the reasons why Israel became a Revolutionary soldier and why he left home are the same: his abhorrence of external control. No other principle, ideological or political, is involved, and this impression is substantiated as we watch the story of Israel's tribulations unfold.

When, after his part in the heroic defence of Bunker Hill and his subsequent voluntary service on the brigantine *Washington*, Israel arrives in England on the *Tartar* as a prisoner of war, he succeeds in making a daring escape. Roaming the English countryside in search of work and shelter, he is fortunate enough to find a job as a gardener in the employ of a certain Sir John Millet, who takes an unexpected and friendly interest in this Yankee rebel. Although grateful for the kindness this English aristocrat shows him, Israel finds it impossible to address him as Sir John — the appropriate English way. To him it is Mr Millet, and nothing can change his mind. Surprisingly, Sir John, although demurring, does not insist; on the contrary, he even promises Israel not to hand him over to the authorities. Later when Israel "on the good word of Sir John Millet" again, finds employment in the King's Gardens at Kew, he receives the same friendly interest in his person from the king, whom he happens to meet one day. Striking up a conversation with Israel, the king asks him whether he was one of the Yankee rebels who "helped flog" his soldiers at "bloody Bunker Hill" (p. 38). Israel tells him that he was, adding that he didn't particularly like doing it at the time, and the king, impressed by Israel's frank and honest answers, even invites him to join the King's army, holding out to him the prospect of quick promotion, but again Israel respectfully though firmly declines.

In both instances it is not ideology that accounts for Israel's responses, but a sense of personal worth derived from his independent life as a frontiersman, as in the case of Sir John, and of personal integrity dictating him to remain loyal to a cause once embraced, as exemplified by his declining the king's offer. That Melville's Israel is primarily motivated by personal considerations rather than patriotic ones, finds further substantiation in the fact that during all those months that he is employed by the people who offer him protection he makes no attempts to escape. It is not until their protection falls away and he is hunted again as a rumoured Yankee rebel and spy that he starts thinking seriously of how to make his getaway. From this moment on he shares that peculiar sense of paranoia, the feeling of being persecuted by everybody, which also bedevils the lives of characters like Cooper's Natty Bumppo and Pynchon's Tyrone Slothrop. "Who are you?" asks the officer of the ship that Israel in the excitement of the battle boards, only to find himself alone among two hundred enemy sailors:

"A poor persecuted fellow at your service, sir."
"*Who* persecutes you?"
"Everyone sir..." (p. 184).

The answer sums up the upshot of Israel's experiences after he is dismissed from his employment in the King's Gardens. It is not only the English soldiers that are after him, it's also the English sympathizers with the American cause and his own compatriots as well that are after him, the former to throw him in jail, the latter to use him, allegedly for the cause of freedom, in reality for a variety of personal reasons, all threatening him with the loss of freedom. When John Woodcock, Horne Tooke and James Bridges, the English friends who are in league with Benjamin Franklin, take care of Israel, they virtually make him their prisoner while preparing him for his mission to France. This situation does not materially change when Israel reaches Franklin's quarters in Paris, where he is also instantly confined to his room.

Before he arrives at the lodgings of the renowned sage, a curious accident takes place, showing to what degree his vicissitudes in England have fed his growing sense of persecution. When he crosses the Pont Neuf, he is addressed by a boot black who politely though with great insistence offers to polish Israel's shoes. Mistaking the man for a spy, Israel kicks over the box of blacking and takes to his heels, across the bridge, pursued by the incensed Frenchman. Israel's greater agility saves him from being caught, but when later he relates the incident to Franklin, the learned doctor takes him to task for his imprudent rashness which might have delivered him into the hands of the police, and thus have exposed to public scrutiny Franklin's covert activities for the Revolutionary cause.

But this is not the only lesson Franklin teaches Israel in the space Melville devotes to this famous historical figure — three chapters, in fact, which is again an important divergence from Melville's source. In Trumbull's book Israel describes his interview with Franklin in two pages, leaving it to "infinitely abler pens" than his to give the great man his due.[2] Reading the portrait Melville draws of Benjamin Franklin is to become convinced at once that the pen he wields is indeed "infinitely abler" than Trumbull's, but it is of greater interest to see what drove Melville in giving us this brilliant medley of admiring praise and acid condemnation. There is a strong impression that Melville intended to do justice to the Franklin of the official, commemorative records: the exemplary husband and citizen, the printer, philosopher, scientist, author, diplomat and patriot. What is also obvious, however, is that Melville, while admiring the man, did not like him, sentiments which, nearly a century later, also happened to be D. H. Lawrence's, whose main objection to Franklin was, as we recall, that "he [Franklin] tries to take away my wholeness and my dark forest, my freedom. (...) And Benjamin tries to shove me into a barbed-wire paddock and make me grow potatoes and Chicagos".[3] The criticism Melville's Israel voices has a strikingly similar ring, although his attitude towards the "benevolent sage" continues to be reverential.

Franklin not only locks the young hero of Bunker Hill up in his room during his stay in Paris, he also at once starts depriving his guest of whatever could have consoled him a little to his solitary confinement.

---

[2]   Henry Trumbull, *Life and Remarkable Adventures of Israel R. Potter*, New York: Corinth, 1962, p. 51.

[3]   D.H. Lawrence "Studies in Classic American Literature" in *The Shock of Recognition*, ed. Edmund Wilson, p. 924.

Before Israel can even begin to appreciate the thoughtful custom of French hoteliers of placing such luxuries as a bottle of Eau-de-Cologne, a bottle of Otard (brandy), and a bag of sugar in their guests' rooms, Franklin has made the delicacies disappear in his voluminous coatpockets, cheerfully informing his disappointed visitor that Eau-de-Cologne is a "senseless luxury", Otard "poison", and sugar "bad for the teeth". Neither can he allow Israel to enjoy the company of the pretty French chambermaid who, a moment later, trips into his room, all smiles and feminine allurement, since, as Franklin informs him once more hastily, she constitutes another strange custom in Paris, one that young men should be dissuaded from adopting.

Given the circumstances, Franklin's protectiveness seems defensible but at the same time, as becomes quite apparent from Melville's ironic description, America's best-loved Revolutionary hero stands revealed as a rather petty-minded busy-body. Small wonder that Israel sinks into gloom, thinking "every time he comes in he robs me, with an air all the time, too, as if he were making me presents. If he thinks me such a sensible young man, why not let me take care of myself?" (p. 69). Franklin, however, only lets people take care of themselves, when he no longer has any use for them. When Israel, returned to England with Franklin's messages safely hidden in the heels of his boots, fails in his mission because Woodcock dies on the day of his arrival, while his other English friends and accomplices have suddenly absconded or refuse to recognize him any longer, Franklin makes no attempt to find out what happened to Israel, let alone come to his rescue.

There is more in Melville's depiction of Franklin that strikes us as obnoxious, reminding us of certain aspects we have come to associate with Pynchon's Pointsmen, the cause-and-effect fanatics in *Gravity's Rainbow*. For Franklin, too, there is no place in his philosophy for the unknown, the mysterious. In his room, in the Latin Quarter, a large map hangs on one of the walls. It represents the "New World", and contains, as Melville tells us, "vast spaces in the middle, with the word DESERT diffusely printed there, so as to span five-and-twenty degrees of longitude with only two syllables, — which printed word however bore a vigorous pen-mark, in the Doctor's hand, drawn straight through it, as if in summary repeal of it" (p. 49). It is unthinkable to people like Franklin, our eighteenth-century precursor of Pynchon's Pointsmen, that there should remain unknown regions both inside and outside the human mind.

"9 Men in 10 are suicides," Franklin claims in his *Poor Richard's Almanack*,[4] but not, as he thinks, because they belong to the kind of men who understand the world best and therefore like it least, as another of the sage's dicta has it, but more likely because they are unable to reconcile themselves with the fact that so much in life remains "desert", unexplained, or ungraspable. Franklin, in fact, also belonged to this latter category of men, but what no doubt saved him from the suicidal impulse was his aloofness, his lack of real emotional involvement in ordinary life's tribulations, an impression already created by the very first scene in which we are introduced to the "man of wisdom". The weather was warm, as Melville tells us, and Franklin sat in his hot room buzzing with flies. But "the sapient inmate sat still and cool in the midst. Absorbed in some other world of his occupations and thoughts, these insects, like daily cark and care, did not seem to annoy him" (p. 50). "It was a goodly sight to see this serene, cool, and ripe old philosopher," as Melville next informs us with the scarcely concealed irony perceptible whenever he speaks of Franklin. It is a sight, though, which he withholds from Israel. For Israel, Franklin's world is hard to enter, even dangerous: when he walks across the room towards a chair, he finds that the floor is "slippery", so slippery in fact that "his

---

[4] *The Complete Poor Richard Almanacks*, ed. Whitfield J. Bell Jr., Vol. I, Barre, Mass.: Imprint Society, 1970, p. XXI.

unaccustomed feet slid about very strangely, as if walking on ice, so that he came near falling" (p. 51).

When Israel is shown to his room after his first conversation with Franklin, he is in the possession of two books, given to him by the "homely sage", with the urgent request to study them well — besides, "no man should be idle". With the brandy and the sugar gone, and the French chambermaid declared out of bounds, there is not much else left for Israel to while away the time but to comply with this request.

The two books are a Guide to Paris, in English, and *Poor Richard's Almanack*. Reading first the Guide, Israel learns about "the fine things" Paris has to offer, and it makes him even more keenly aware of what Franklin has denied him by imprisoning him in his room. But as the doctor had admonished him, "Business before pleasure". He then picks up *Poor Richard's Almanack*, expecting to find some comfort in it, since, he, Israel, is a "poor fellow" as well, but in this too he is disappointed. The homely wisdom that "there are no gains, without pains", strikes him as rather insulting when addressed to a man like himself, who so far has only experienced the latter, despite all he has done to help the new nation gain its freedom. Disgusted Israel throws down the booklet, wondering what sly intention its author could have had in making him read these two books. Besides, Poor Richard's wisdom is not to his liking; it is also "a sort of sly", and although Israel is willing to admit that his famous host is "one of those old gentlemen who say a vast deal of sense", he suspects that the things they really say "hint a world more". "Depend upon it", Israel concludes his musings on the enigma Franklin poses to him, "he's sly, sly, sly" (p. 70).

What Israel is made to grasp intuitively in the scenes Melville has imagined for him, the reader has already learned from a previous chapter (8), in which Melville, the narrator, has furnished him with a brief, though revealing, picture of Franklin's personality. Likening him to the patriarch Jacob — "A tanned Machiavelli in tents" — , Melville believes that Franklin too was a blending of "the apostolic serpent and dove". He then depicts the doctor, a versatile man, as "a Jack of all trades", even "a master of each", but "mastered by none", that is to say, committed to none, and if this is what Melville meant, then the addition "the type and genius of his land" puts his observations in a peculiar perspective. If Melville saw Franklin as a typical representative of the new nation, it is obvious that he was none too happy about his country's emerging national character.

Franklin's reluctance to take up an exposed position is also subtly indicated in Melville's description of the place where the sage chose to live — midway between the Palais des Beaux Arts and the College of the Sorbonne, a choice not so much dictated by his nature as by his wish to play it safe.[5] But, then, as Melville writes, Franklin was no "poet", rather an "actor", even a "consummate actor", who after "having carefully weighed the world, (...) could act any part in it", the implication being once more that, although Franklin was an actor, playing as easily "a lady's man" as "a man's man, a wise and an old man", he was not so by nature but by choice. And he played it with a mind that "was often grave, but never serious" (p. 61), which may remind us of Hemingway's quip that although seriousness was all right, solemnity was always wrong.[6]

Franklin's multifariousness, as Melville admits at the end of his characterization of the famous man, could only be done justice to by presenting him in contact with different men and different subjects. Presenting him only in contact with plain Israel could not but result in a picture that inevitably showed Franklin "in his less exalted habitudes".

---

[5] Also Paul Jones is not unaware of this. Commenting on Franklin's Revolutionary activities in Paris, he remarks to Israel: "Poor Richard wants to be a little shady in this business" (p. 153).

[6] E. Hemingway, *Death in the Afternoon*, New York: Charles Scribner's Sons, 1932: "(...) a serious writer may be a hawk or a buzzard or even a popinjay, but a solemn writer is always a bloody owl". (p. 192).

However, the underlying irony in Melville's portrayal here is so tangible that the only conclusion one can draw is that for once Franklin, the advocate of honesty and plainness, stands revealed as a man whose "worsted hose", metaphorically speaking, was a more truthful part of his personality than his "honoured hat which once oracularly sat upon his brow" (p. 62).

Oracular, too, is another of Poor Richard's maxims that "God helps them that help themselves". The saying hits Israel in the eye when he reads it, increasing his uncertainty as to what to think of his famous host. The maxim seems to express a cynical truth, but could one accuse that "great and good man" of cynicism? But what if people like Israel Potter couldn't help themselves because they lacked sufficient social status or driving ambition to participate in the games so dexterously played by the powerful? Or what if they did not want to help themselves because if they did, they might hurt others or compromise what they held highest?[7] On whose side was God then?

Israel never consciously poses these questions, although they seem to bother him, but Melville does by introducing the third major character of the novel, Paul Jones. Jones, too, reads Poor Richard's maxim, and he too is impressed by it, but not because it puzzles him. To him it is "a Clincher", a shock of recognition, as it succinctly summarizes his own experience. He is, in fact, so impressed by it that he wants to have a copy of Franklin's booklet, to wear it round his neck "for a charm" (p. 79). Melville's introduction of Captain Paul Jones is another major divergence from his source. In Trumbull's book Israel claims never to have met John Paul Jones; in Melville's nearly one

---

[7]   That Israel belongs to this category of men is substantiated by the following passage. Israel has returned home after an absence of three years, only to find that "his father still remained inflexibly determined against the match, and still inexplicably countermined his wooing", and as Melville continues, "With a dolorous heart he [Israel] mildly yielded to what seemed his fatality; and more intrepid in facing peril for himself, than in endangering others by maintaining his rights (for he was now one-and-twenty), resolved once more to retreat, and quit his blue hills for the bluer billows" (pp. 10-11).

third of the narrative is devoted to this famous Revolutionary naval hero. Melville's principal sources for this section of his book were James Fenimore Cooper's *History of the Navy of the United States of America* (1840) and Robert S. Sands's *Life and Correspondence of John Paul Jones* (1830), but just as he departed from his chief source for Israel's story, so he diverged in significant respects from these two works in his treatment of the Jones episode. One of these changes bears directly on the maxim that shocked Israel, but delighted Jones.

When Jones is finally given the command of a larger vessel, he decides on Israel's instigation to change her name *Duras* into *Bon Homme Richard*. *Duras*, in Israel's view, sounds too much like "durance vile", a term used for imprisonment. The change is made in honour of Poor Richard's saying that "God helps them that help themselves". In Sands's book, however, the new name for the ship is given in compliment to a different maxim of Poor Richard's, namely "If you would have your business done, come yourself; if not, send". Basically the two maxims express the same idea: if you want to get things done, you have to attend to them personally, but the version Melville chooses emphasizes one element in particular: ruthlessness as a condition of the success of extreme individualism, a ruthlessness, moreover, sanctified by divine blessing.

Just as in the case of Franklin, Melville gives us a portrayal of John Paul Jones that aims to do justice to the complexity of this second major figure in America's national pantheon. But although he does not fail to highlight the admirable qualities of the man, his final judgement is wholly condemnatory, a conclusion substantiated by Melville's juxtaposition of Jones to one of the unknown heroes of the Revolutionary war, Israel Potter.

Jones's fierce and unshakable dedication to the Revolutionary cause need not be doubted, but his motives for actively joining as an Englishman America's fight for freedom remain highly questionable.

Personal revenge rather than the call for justice is one. Rejected by his hometown Whitehaven because he was suspected of having flogged a sailor to death, he swore "never again to set foot on her pier, except, like Caesar at Sandwich, as a foreign invader" (p.121). Although Jones has a charismatic personality, enabling him to rouse his men to the impossible — "Captain Paul is the devil for putting men up to tigers", as one of his officers comments (p. 118) — his prime concern is not the welfare of his men, but his unquenchable thirst for honour and glory.

When Franklin in Paris, in reply to Jones's request for a bigger ship, suggests that he might use his own smaller ship as a decoy to capture the English ships, he flies into an unholy rage, rejecting this proposal to act as "a decoy-duck" as utterly degrading. Jones is quite prepared to risk his life for the cause of freedom, but only if it yields "something honourable and glorious" for him. Complaining about the timidity of the American leaders and expressing his impatience with "vacillating Councils", in which "statesmen idle about like the cat's in calms" (p. 74), he exclaims, "My God, why was I not born a Czar!"

Jones is, in fact, more credible as an aspiring Czar, or an Indian chief, to whom he is also frequently likened by Melville, than as an ardent advocate of American democracy. What becomes quite apparent is that he cannot tolerate "degree", not because he is a strong believer in the democratic principle, but because he is unable to acknowledge or accept any authority other than his own. Chasing an English ship close to near the Crag of Ailsa, well over a thousand feet high, Jones suddenly loses his elation when the two ships fall under its shadow, dwarfing both pursuer and pursued to insignificant dots. He orders his men to stop the chase, and hastily turns about. Asked by Israel why he has discontinued the chase, he points to the Crag of Ailsa. To be dwarfed, even by a dead rock, proves unbearable to Jones.

In Paris, where he spends the night in Israel's room, the latter witnesses a curious but equally revealing incident. Too restless to sleep,

Jones silently paces the room. Passing the mirror, he stops, watches himself, then rolls up his sleeve, and "with a queer, wild smile", lifts his arm to the mirror. What Israel, who pretends to be sleeping, sees reflected in the mirror is an arm covered with mysterious tattooings, "a sort of tattooing such as is seen only on thorough-bred savages — deep blue, elaborate, labyrinthine, cabalistic" (p.81). Jones, outwardly dressed in elegant, expensive Parisian clothes, may seem civilized, but inwardly he is still a savage, "a barbarian in broadcloth", and, as Melville elaborates, a sort of prophetical ghost, "glimmering in anticipation upon the advent of those tragic scenes of the French Revolution which levelled the exquisite refinement of Paris with the bloodthirsty ferocity of Borneo; showing that brooches and finger-rings, not less than nose-rings and tattooing, are tokens of the primeval savageness which ever slumbers in humankind, civilised or uncivilised" (pp. 81-82).

What no doubt fascinated Melville in particular about Paul Jones was that Jones, like Franklin, though in a different sense, embodied some of the less admirable traits Melville had come to associate with America's emerging national character. As he said of his native country: "Intrepid, unprincipled, reckless, predatory, with boundless ambition, civilised in externals, but a savage at heart, America is, or may yet be, the Paul Jones of nations" (p. 158). Bearing this in mind, one begins to gain a better understanding of the deeper significance of the fight between the *Bon Homme Richard* and the *Serapis*, celebrated in the annals of the American Navy as one of its most glorious victories.

What receives particular emphasis in Melville's exciting description of this naval engagement is the savagery with which it was fought on both sides. Melville calls it an "unnatural fight", comparing the two ships to "Siamese Twins", obviously because he looked upon it as a fight between people of the same blood. He also calls it a fight over a "disputed frontier", thus connecting it with another fight, equally savage, waged along the American frontier at the time Melville wrote *Israel Potter*. In both cases the fights were distinguished by senseless slaughter and destruction, justifying the questions with which Melville ends his account of Paul Jones's famous battle: "What separates the enlightened man from the savage? Is civilization a thing distinct, or is it an advanced stage of barbarism?" (p. 173).

The questions are clearly rhetorical, for the novel leaves no doubt about the answers they elicit. As long as those in positions of power continue to be self-seeking, merely using those who have put their faith and confidence in them, while remaining indifferent to their individual fates, so long will civilization be an advanced state of barbarism rather than "a thing distinct". Jones, returning from his four-week cruise through the British waters, with the conquered *Drake* in tow, though at a terrible cost of lives recklessly spent, is rewarded by the King of France with a sword and a medal. But, as Melville comments: "Poor Israel, who also had conquered a craft, and all unaided too — what had he?" (p. 150). Just as in the case of Franklin, Israel ceases to exist for Jones the moment he has outlived his usefulness. Jones, too, makes no effort to find out what happened to Israel after his "Yellow-mane", as he affectionately calls him, had mistakenly been transported in mid-ocean from the *Ariel* to the British ship — to face a future of fifty impoverished years as an exile in the British capital. However, not all who were unfortunate enough to be taken to England as Yankee prisoners suffered this fate. This becomes apparent from the story of Ethan Allen, the third figure in the American pantheon of Revolutionary heroes the novel deals with.

With the introduction of Colonel Allen, Melville again deviated from his prime source, Trumbull's account, in which the hero of Fort Ticonderoga is not even mentioned. Why then, one may wonder, did Melville include Allen's story of his imprisonment in England? One explanation, at first sight not implausible, is that Allen's presence serves as a foil to both Franklin and Jones, and Israel as well. In this view Allen represents the true American spirit, essentially Western.[8] He unites the best qualities of both Franklin and Jones without the former's duplicity and the latter's cruelty; qualities which help him to survive the tribulations to which he is subjected in Pendennis Castle.[9]

But, if Allen rather than Franklin or Jones was meant to serve as the true model from which Israel could learn how to be a true American on the one hand, and how to survive without losing his grip on reality on the other, the short duration of his appearance in the novel remains puzzling. He suddenly emerges from nowhere, dominates the stage for one brief chapter, then vanishes again and is heard of no more. Israel himself sees Allen only for a brief moment, and never actually meets him. If the "giant Vermonter" had really been conceived as the novel's moral yardstick, it is not unreasonable to expect that Melville should have accorded him a lengthier and more important part in Israel's life story. There must be another reason for Allen's presence in the novel.

What we may note, when we compare Allen's fate as a prisoner of the British with that of Israel, is that the treatment the Colonel received was far worse than anything Israel suffered during his period of captivity in England. Allen, as Melville tells us, "was treated with inexcusable cruelty and indignity; something as if he had fallen into the hands of the Dyaks" (pp. 198-99). As a prisoner, he was hit over the head by a British commander, kept in irons in the ship's hold on passage to England, and insulted by the ship's officers who looked upon him as "a common mutineer". He did not fare much better in Pendennis Castle. Yet, he was brought back to America, and, as we are informed,

---

[8] John P. McWilliams Jr., *Hawthorne, Melville, and The American Character: A Looking-glass Business*, Cambridge U.P., 1984, p. 188.

[9] William B. Dillingham, *Melville's Later Novels*, Athens & London: The University of Georgia Press, 1986, p. 295.

"in due time, at New York, honourably included in a regular exchange of prisoners" (pp. 200-201). Now the reason for this honourable exchange was no doubt the same as what instigated the initial cruelty to which Allen was submitted: he was a distinguished prisoner of war.

When the first fury about the severe punishment this Yankee officer had administered to the British troups at Ticonderoga had subsided, his position as an important prisoner was acknowledged again, and the harsh and degrading treatment replaced by one more in accordance with his rank. Allen, the man, may have been less than an animal; Colonel Allen, the high-ranking officer, could not be overlooked, and the same question Melville posed in order to point up the difference between Jones and Israel in the way they were treated for war services rendered, can be asked again: "and Israel — what had he?"

This much is certain: what he did *not* have was a position important enough to make him eligible for an exchange of prisoners. What he *did* have — and never entirely lost — was a sense of personal worth, even if no one else bothered to recognize it. To retain it he had only his own resources to rely on, not the examples of Franklin, or Jones, or even Allen. And it is no doubt Israel's "Western" qualities that enabled him to achieve this. After the Allen episode, hearing about the impending threat of being impressed again, he decides to risk his life by deserting from the British merchantman in order to escape to London, hoping to go unnoticed amidst the anonymity of the metropolis. His desertion from the ship is successful, but his safe arrival in London is still a long time in coming. Within fifteen miles of London, Israel is at the end of his tether, physically as well as mentally. Seeing a brickyard, he decides in desperation to seek employment here as a brickmaker, thus joining the "hordes of poorest wretches", the only people prepared by sheer necessity to undertake the kind of work that is "all mud and mire".

What Israel next experiences as one of "the scores and scores of forlorn men engaged in [the] great brickyard" (p. 204), is actually the apotheosis of what he already had a foretaste of in the Shuttle chapter, the chapter in which his involuntary transfer in mid-ocean from the *Ariel* to the British letter of marque occurs, and in which he is also faced with a deliberate denial of his human identity. The chapter describes Israel's attempt to mix in secretly with the ship's crew of some two hundred sailors, because he realizes how dangerous it would be for him if he, a Yankee rebel, was found out. But to be accepted, one ought to belong first, and simply belonging to the human race, even if one has a disposition as friendly and genial as Israel's, is not enough. Neither the company of the main-top men, nor that of the forecastle men are willing to receive him in their midst, or to be concerned with his plight. He is, in fact, forcibly ejected. Also the "holders", the below-deck crew who are lower on the ship's social scale, and even the "waisters,"', "the vilest caste of a ship's company", real "sea-pariahs" (p. 179), refuse Israel admittance to their wretched circle. The acknowledgement of one's human identity only follows social identity, and Israel's implicit insistence on the former taking precedence over the latter is ignored. He is not only considered to be "out of his mind", but as the officer-of-the-deck who interrogates him exclaims, "out of all men's knowledge and memories" (p. 183).

Israel becomes a "ghost", a "phantom", and although he is ultimately permitted to work as a main-top man because it would be foolish not to make use of a first-rate sailor, his weird experience on board of the English letter of marque proves symbolic of his life story in general: he is never acknowledged as an individual in his own right, regardless of birth, background, social position, and nationality, the principle for which he fought at Bunker Hill, but his identity is always a function of his political and social usefulness, and ceases to exist as soon as this can be dispensed with.

This view acquires an even darker colouring in the chapter that describes Israel's brick-making episode. If men and bricks were equally of clay, then, as the philosophical-minded among the brick-makers morosely conclude, "each man was a brick", that is, "a few luckless shovelfuls of clay, moulded in a mould laid out on a sheet to dry, and ere long quickened into his queer caprices by the sun" (p. 206). And just as bricks derive their significance from the wall into which they are built, so "man attains not to the nobility of a brick, unless taken in the aggregate" (p. 207). But even among bricks, dead or alive, there are differences. The kind of "bricks" Israel belongs to are to be found in the first tiers of brick that line the vaults of the kilns. They are scorched, black, twisted, and haggard, hardly to be identified as bricks, but they have their use: they serve to protect the adjacent tiers from overheating, so that these become the "sound, square, and perfect bricks, bringing the highest prices". The topmost layers, too, though inferior to the best, are good enough, but "pale with the languor of too exclusive an exemption from the burden of the blaze" (p. 208).

One can hardly think of a neater symbolic representation of the three social classes among which Israel moves during his adventures abroad: sailors, commodores, and kings. But "bricks" they remain, all of them, moulded in the same mould, and this insight enables Israel to drown his despair about being forced to work for the enemy in an even greater despair as he comes to the conclusion that "Kings as clowns are codgers — who ain't a nobody? (...) All is vanity and clay" (p. 209).

Yet, it is not this pessimistic view of man that sustains Israel in London, after he has finally arrived there in "a tolerable suit of clothes", "several bloodblisters in his palms, and some verdigris coppers in his pocket" (p. 210). What ultimately makes him survive nearly half a century of hardship and poverty in the "City of Dis" are the memories of his native country, America, where for some years he had known what it was to be a free man, a man in control of his own destiny.

What keeps the hope of a dignified existence alive in Israel are precisely his memories of those years, "those well-remembered adventures among New England hills, (...) the scenes of nestling happiness and plenty, in which the lowliest shared" (p. 221). What Melville seems to imply here is that, since all men, like all bricks, are moulded in one mould, it is the circumstances that primarily determine to which particular tier they belong, and that it was in the "Fortunate Isles of the Free" which provided the circumstances most favourable for the greater part of the bricks to become the soundest and the best.

However, as the concluding chapter shows, these circumstances were rapidly and irreversibly deteriorating, already retreating, in fact, to a mythic past. When thanks to the exertions of his only surviving son, whom Israel had never been tired of telling about his happy days in the Promised Land, he is finally able to return to America, it is of course no accident that Melville makes him set foot on sacred soil on the Fourth of July. Israel arrives when the festivities are gathering momentum, but instead of a hero's welcome as one of the veterans of the Revolutionary war, he is hustled by a riotous crowd and nearly run over by a car in the procession, "flying a broidered banner, inscribed with gilt letters: Bunker Hill, 1775. Glory to the Heroes that fought!" (p. 222)

The glory, however, no longer devolves upon the heroes who once fought for liberty and independence, but on those whose rhetoric in celebrating these acquisitions proves most persuasive, and Israel spends the day gazing mutely about him, on the mound in the graveyard which in the Revolutionary days was one of the enemy's strongholds. He notices more changes. Visiting his beloved Birkshires, he has great difficulty in recognizing the scenes of his youth, while no one in the townships remembers him, or has even heard of him. The fields his father used to work are no longer there, and of the old homestead nothing but ruins and the half-burnt hearth has remained.

Israel Potter might as well have never existed. He has, in fact, become what the officer of the letter of marque thought he was, a man "out of all men's knowledge and memories".

Yet, there is the Bunker Hill Monument, testifying to the pious gratitude of later generations who, realizing what they owed the unknown Revolutionary heroes, showed that they had not forgotten them. Melville, in fact, dedicates his biographical account of Israel Potter to this monument, but not to affirm the spirit that conceived it but to expose it. With overt sarcasm he addresses the monument — a symbol too of the birth of American democracy — as "His Highness", implying that the relationship between those who erected it and those to whom it was dedicated was basically what it had always been: the relationship between commodore and sailor, between the self-seekers and the disinterested, between the exploiters and the exploited.

Daniel Webster's famous dedicatory address, delivered when the cornerstone of the Bunker Hill Monument was laid in 1825, is permeated with expressions that exalt "liberty", while Israel Potter had experienced nothing but captivity, even when he was a free man. Webster, also a "commodore", glowingly talked of "glory", "peace", "happiness", holding forth to the veterans of the famous battle about "the reward of [their] patriotic toils",[10] while Israel, forgotten by Franklin and Jones, had been starved in London, and, on his return to America, an old man soon to die, was denied a pension by "certain caprices of law".

Melville ends his dedication by congratulating "His Highness" (already "prematurely gray") on the recurrence of his anniversary, but his concluding wish "that each of its summer's suns may shine as brightly on your brow as each winter snow shall lightly rest on the grave of Israel Potter" is again in keeping with the scathing sarcasm that pervades these first dedicatory pages. It sets the tone of his version

[10]   As quoted by Dillingham in *Melville's Later Novels*, p. 256

of Israel Potter's vicissitudes which like *Moby-Dick* is told in the form of a tale of adventures, but which this time aims at piercing the cardboard reality of America's Revolutionary years. What the novel discloses is how, despite the freedom won, the old pattern of exploiters and exploited rapidly re-established itself, how ambitious commodores remained ambitious commodores, and plain sailors, plain sailors, and how this difference in status determined the extent to which a man could expect recognition of his identity as well as the rewards due to him.

Like Cooper, Melville nostalgically evokes a moment in his country's history in which this pattern seemed to have been broken up, and America provided "the scenes of nestling happiness and plenty, in which the lowliest shared". These scenes made up America's West, whether located in New-England, the Mid-West or the Far West, a region, however, which was already vanishing, not only as a protean idea, in which even Melville himself seemed to have believed for one moment, but also as a geographical entity: on the day Israel dies, the oldest oak in his native hills is blown down, to fade "out of memory", like Israel's name. Melville's fascination with the life story of the real Israel Potter may well have originated in the parallel he could draw between Israel's fate and his own fall into obscurity following the publication of *Moby-Dick*, Melville's own feat of "heroism". Financial reward and full recognition would both have been his, if he had continued to write in the vein of his first popular novels, *Typee* and *Omoo*. But like Israel, Melville belonged to "the disinterested", meaning in his particular case that he could only follow his deepest intellectual and artistic needs in pursuing his vocation as a writer. That it also made him belong to the tier of "bricks" that did not yield the best prices, must have been a harrowing experience which he never expected, though perhaps could have foreseen. On this level Israel Potter's story is also Melville's own story.

Chapter 4

HENRY DAVID THOREAU:
"Walking"

1

All his life Thoreau was to pursue the theme of the West, and practically his whole oeuvre testifies to the persistent nature of this pursuit. The longest sustained discourse on this theme, however, is not to be found in any of his major works — *A Week on the Concord and Merrimack Rivers*, or *Walden*, or *The Maine Woods*, or the twelve volumes of his so-called *Indian Books* — , but in one of his shorter pieces, "Walking", once also and more aptly called "The Wild". What Thoreau actually meant by the West, and why his "needle", though "slow to settle", (...) always settle[d] between west and south-southwest",[1] emerges most clearly from this essay. The West, we are told in "Walking", is "but another name for the Wild", and it is this Wildness that more than anything else constitutes for Thoreau the essence of the West — not Manifest Destiny, nor economic betterment, nor the spirit

---

[1] *Thoreau's Vision: The Major Essays*, edited by Charles R. Anderson, Englewood Cliffs, New Jersey: Prentice-Hall Inc., 1973, "The Wild", p. 139.

of enterprise and adventure with which it is usually associated.[2] No, it is the Wild, a force, attractive in itself, not only, Thoreau claims, in literature but also in life itself, because life "consists with Wildness", and therefore "the most alive is the wildest". In fact "all good things are wild and free", all other things tame and consequently dull. "Even to see the domestic animals reassert their native rights, — any evidence that they have not wholly lost their original wild habits and vigor", as when a "cow breaks out of her pasture early in the spring and boldly swims the river", is something to be thankful for, something to be loved, and therefore, Thoreau concludes, it is "in Wildness" that "the preservation of the World" lies. No matter where one lives in the world, there will always be the city on one side, and the wilderness, the West on the other, and for Thoreau the choice was not difficult: "Let me live where I will, on this side is the city, on that the wilderness and ever I am leaving the city more and more, and withdrawing into the wilderness."

This withdrawal Thoreau accomplished quite literally by living for two years in the woods all by himself, in the famous cabin which he built with his own hands. However, these woods were only a few miles' distance from the homes of his parents and friends. To Thoreau, the wilderness, the West, was never far from the small town of Concord in Massachusetts, and although he travelled somewhat more widely after the Walden episode, Minnesota was as far West as he ever went, with in-between trips to the Maine woods, Cape Cod, and the south-east of Canada. Thoreau may have been a great walker, he was not a great traveller. He, too, seems to have been of the opinion that there is not

---

[2]   *The Correspondence of Henry David Thoreau*, edited by Walter Harding & Carl Bode, N.Y.: New York University Press, 1958; rpt 1974:
"The whole enterprise of this nation which is not an upward, but a westward one, towards Oregon, California, Japan, etc., is totally devoid of interest to me, whether performed on foot or by a Pacific railroad. It is not illustrated by a thought it is not warmed by a sentiment, there is nothing in it which one should lay down his life for, nor even his gloves. (...) No, they may go their way to their manifest destiny which I trust is not mine" (p. 296).

much point in travelling far if you cannot discover the world in your backyard, and the conclusion to be drawn from all this is that to Thoreau the real significance of the West was a condition of the mind rather than one of geography, a notion incidentally already expressed in *A Week*:

> The frontiers are not east or west, north or south, but wherever a man *fronts* a fact, though that fact be his neighbor, there is an unsettled wilderness between him and Canada, between him and the setting sun, or, farther still between him and *it*.[3]

What Thoreau meant by this mysterious "it" is not quite clear. What *is* clear is that this "it" cannot be reached without making a strenuous effort, without putting up a fierce fight, and it is this ability, this "wildness", or, as he later calls it in *Walden*, this "generative energy", [4] which he associated with the West. It is not something merely destructive but rather something creative and expressive of man's true self.

Wildness in the form of the ruthless slaughter that goes on in nature, the eat-and-be-eaten aspect of the wilderness, did not greatly appeal to Thoreau, although he would never deny its considerable pull on people, he himself not excepted. As he admits in *Walden*: once when he saw a woodchuck stealing across his path, he "felt a strange thrill of savage delight", and "was strongly tempted to seize and devour him raw" (*W* 179). Such an experience, as he remarks a few pages further on, makes us "conscious of an animal in us, which awakens in proportion as our higher nature slumbers. It is reptile and sensual, and perhaps cannot be wholly expelled; like the worms which, even in life and

---

[3] *The Writings of Henry D. Thoreau, A Week on the Concord and Merrimack Rivers*, ed. Carle F. Hovde, 1849, Princeton U.P., 1980, p. 304.

[4] Henry D. Thoreau, *Walden or Life in the Woods*, 1854; Doubleday & Comp. Inc., Dolphin Books, rpt. 1960, p. 187. All further page references are to this edition of *Walden*, indicated in the text as *W* followed by the relevant page number.

death, occupy our bodies" (*W* 186).

What this lust for the kill, this aggressive "wildness", reveals is the hunting side of man, constituting the main source of his "generative energy", his creative power, without which a man would cease to be a man, but which at the same time, so Thoreau feels, degrades him. Highly revealing in this connection is an incident he mentions in *The Maine Woods*. Polis, the Indian guide, has shot a moose. When, however, he starts skinning the animal, Thoreau decides to go fishing rather that having to watch the carnage. He dreads the sense of degradation that the killing, cleaning, and eating of animals entail, a dread that in *Walden* extends even to the much more "innocent" sport of fishing:

> I have found repeatedly, of late years, that I cannot fish
> without falling a little in self-respect. (...) There is
> unquestionably this instinct in me which belongs to the
> lower orders of creation; yet with every year I am less a
> fisherman, though without more humanity or even
> wisdom; at present I am no fisherman at all (*W* 182).

However, we should not conclude from these lines that Thoreau's growing revulsion was of a moral nature. "The practical objection to animal food in my case," he observes, "was its uncleanness," an observation which shows us that his objection to fishing, in general to hunting, was aesthetic rather than moral. And this inference is affirmed by what he adds: "And, besides, when I had caught and cooked and eaten my fish, they seemed not to have fed me essentially." The impression that here the author of *Walden* is solely led by considerations of expediency and practicality is then confirmed and strengthened by his final verdict: "It [eating fish, in general animals] was insignificant and unnecessary and cost more than it came to" (*W* 183).

Still, even though Thoreau may have come to reject the hunter, a mode of existence which he considered a passing stage in man's evolution, he continued to believe it necessary to retain the hunter's mode of perception, valuing it more highly than that of the farmer. The latter might represent the next phase in the evolution of man, but in Thoreau's view the farmer was too closely bound to the soil, too great a materialist, to be ever a free soul. His overriding aim in life was to cultivate the earth, all of the earth, and as Thoreau remarks in "Walking", "I would not have every man nor every part of a man cultivated, any more than I would have every acre of earth cultivated: a part will be tillage, but the greater part will be meadow and forest". That is, there should be left plenty of nature, dangerous swamps and wild forests, that "vast, savage, howling mother of ours", so as to offer always a "new country or wildness" to those "who pressed forward incessantly", "who grew fast and made infinite demands on life". Only the continuing presence of this "raw material of life" would keep them sufficiently alerted to their true vocation, which was to perfect man, body and soul. To achieve this the hunter's mode of perception, requiring solitude, chastity and self-restraint, guaranteed better results than the farmer's mode, which was directed at the communal, productivity, and the exploitation of nature's resources, all interests which, as Thoreau believed, were in the way of the individual's growth to complete freedom, for in "Walking" he settles for no less. As we can read in the opening paragraph: "I wish to speak a word for Nature, for absolute freedom and wildness, as contrasted with a freedom and culture merely civil (...) I wish to make an extreme statement." "Walking", in fact, ends in a manner which is as extreme as its beginning. It describes a sunset that bathes the world in such a golden flood as never seen before, a description soon shifting into metaphor, for as golden as this sunset will be man's destiny, when one day "the sun shall shine more brightly than ever he has done, shall perchance shine into our minds and hearts, and light up our whole lives with a great awakening light, as warm and serene and golden as on a bankside in autumn".

It is an astonishing finale, seeming to affirm Fussell's verdict that "Walking" is actually "one long tissue of clichés",[5] clichés such as Thoreau's reiteration of the idea that the only direction to go for ambitious young men was West, and that in general mankind progressed from East to West. But even if Fussell is right, the two most important ideas expressed in "Walking" are still valid, regardless of the fact that it would not be difficult to label them at present as clichés as well. These ideas, then, are on the one hand the belief that civilization, if it is to remain strong and vital, should not lose a certain "wildness", and on the other that the uncultivated, unexplored parts of the wilderness should remain so, and be regarded as "sacred" places, the "strength, the marrow, of Nature", and be treated as such, as the restorers of "the red corpuscles in the blood", as the springs of fertility and regeneration.

In particular the latter idea has acquired an entirely renewed relevance in view of the deplorable state Nature, the wilderness, finds itself in at the moment, that is, in the 1980s. To restore the damage that man has inflicted on the natural environment as a result of reckless exploitation and the concomitant chemical and nuclear pollution would cost about two hundred billon dollars in the United States alone. If one also included the funds necessary to clean up the rest of the Western world, the amount would reach such a staggering height that one might well wonder whether this price was not in ludicrous excess of the increase in material wealth the Western world has gained from this exploitation over the past fifty years. One suspects that there is a sort of natural law that sees to it that gains are always compensated with losses, losses with gains, so that in the final analysis the balance remains even; and this balance is a precarious one between existence and non-existence, a balance only preserved if existence is being

---

[5] Edwin Fussell, *Frontier: American Literature and the American West*, p. 181.

maintained on the level it has always had to the great majority of the people inhabiting this world: one of sober frugality, the one in fact proposed and actually lived by Thoreau.

To Thoreau nature was not merely symbolic of divinity, as it was to Emerson, but to all appearances divine in itself, the actuality of God, and as such visible and audible. As he writes in *The Maine Woods*, deploring the wanton destruction of game and timber: "Every creature is better alive than dead, men and moose and pine trees (...) It is the living spirit of the tree, not its spirit of turpentine, with which I sympathize, and which heals my cuts. It is immortal as I am, and perchance will go to as high a heaven, there to tower above me still."[6] Or take this extract from *Walden*, a fairly typical example of Thoreau's sensuous mysticism:

> In such a day, in September or October, Walden is a perfect forest mirror, set round with stones as precious to my eye as if fewer or rarer. Nothing so fair, so pure, and at the same time so large, as a lake, perchance, lies on the surface of the earth. Sky water. It needs no fence. Nations come and go without defiling it. It is a mirror which no stone can crack, whose quicksilver will never wear off, whose gilding Nature continually repairs; no storms, no dust, can dim its surface ever fresh; — a mirror in which all impurity presented to it sinks, swept and dusted by the sun's hazy brush, — this the light dust-cloth, — which retains no breath that is breathed on it, but sends its own to float as clouds high above its surface, and be reflected in its bosom still (*W* 161-62).

It is interesting to compare this with Hemingway's well-known Gulf

---

[6] Henry D. Thoreau, *The Illustrated Maine Woods*, edited by Joseph J. Moldenhauer, 1864; Princeton, New Jersey: Princeton U.P., rpt 1974, pp. 121-22. All further page references are to this edition.

Stream image from his *Green Hills of Africa*, which he uses as his metaphor of nature's permanence:

> When, on the sea, you are alone with it and know that this Gulf Stream you are living with, knowing, learning about, and loving, has moved, as it moves, since before man (...) [then] the things you find out about it, and those that have always lived in it, are permanent and of value because that stream will flow as it has flowed, after the Indians, after the Spaniards, after the British, after the Americans, and after all the Cubans and all the systems of governments, the richness, the poverty, the martyrdom, the sacrifice and the venality and the cruelty are all gone as the high-piled scow of garbage (...) spills off its load into the blue water. (...) The stream with no visible flow, takes five loads of this a day when things are going well in La Habana and in ten miles along the coast it is as clear and blue and unimpressed as it was ever before the tug hauled out the scow; and the palm fronds of our victories, the worn light bulbs of our great discoveries and the empty condoms of our great loves float with no significance against one single, lasting thing — the stream.[7]

Hemingway's description is even more direct, more concrete than Thoreau's (Thoreau uses the pond as a mirror, and his later sun-images have a certain abstract quality, while Hemingway uses the thing — the stream — itself), but essentially the two passages express the same theme: Nature as the repository of permanent values because it cannot be defiled by human impurity.

We know better now of course. Nature is no longer capable of

---

[7] Ernest Hemingway, *The Green Hills of Africa*, 1935; Penguin Book, 1966, pp. 126-27.

absorbing all the impurities man inflicts. Rather than being the great healer, it has become a commodity like everything else in the human world, but one that in the not-too-distant future may well turn into the great deathtrap. What it proves is that the divinity of Nature ends as soon as man thinks he can do without it. It is not the Godhead that reigns in Nature, instructing man how to behave, but it is just the other way round. Since our ability to harm is infinite, and Nature finite, it may ultimately turn against us, and what distinguishes our particular anxieties from those of earlier times is the insight that man's trust in Nature as the great healer, either in a physical or a moral sense, has as little basis in fact as Ptolemy's conception of the universe. Our ultimate reality is not a mystical union with Nature but a complete separation from Nature, irreparably cutting us off from those primeval sources which as late as the 1930s were thought to be always there, invulnerable to man's harmful and wasteful ways. Reality is no longer "fabulous", to use Thoreau's term, and in "Walking" he anticipated the danger inherent in this change:

> Here is this vast, savage, howling mother of ours, Nature,
> lying all around, with such beauty, and such affection for
> her children, as the leopard; and yet we are so early
> weaned from her breast to society, to that culture which is
> exclusively an interaction of man on man, — a sort of
> breeding in and in, which produces at most a merely
> English nobility, a civilization destined to have a speedy
> limit.

It may amuse us to learn that the worst Thoreau imagined could happen in the 1850s was the production of an English nobleman. It gets less amusing of course when we realize what this exclusive "interaction of man on man" has come to in our own age: instead of English noblemen, the world has witnessed the emergence of a whole class of "undermen", who in the name of progress and the profit nexus are rapidly divesting Nature of all its "wildness", turning her everywhere into desolate, barren wasteland.

2

Parallel and closely linked to Thoreau's pursuit of the West as one of his major themes runs his absorbing interest in the Indians, whom he thought exemplary of the mode of perception he valued most, that of the hunter. Although Thoreau, as Robert Sayre in his *Thoreau and the American Indians* remarks, "scarcely did a thing for them",[8] they were never far from his mind when he read or wrote, and over the years 1847-1861 this interest of his yielded about 3000 pages of notes on the history and the cultures of the Indians, in particular of the Hurons and Iroquois. These notes were collected in volumes, known as Thoreau's *Indian Books*, twelve in all, but never prepared for publication, the main reason being, as Sayre has suggested, that they were used as a source for Thoreau's other writings.

Early proof of the possible truth of this suggestion is to be found in *A Week on the Concord and Merrimack Rivers* (1849), in which Thoreau works out his notes on Alexander Henry and Hannah Duston into stories. The first, the story of the friendship between the white fur-trader Alexander Henry and the Indian chief, Wawatam, is included in the chapter "Wednesday", the second, the account of Hannah Duston and her escape from Indian captivity, is related in the next chapter, the chapter called "Thursday".

The tale of Alexander Henry and Wawatam forms part of Thoreau's disquisition on friendship, and in it he describes the friendship between these two men as one to be remembered with "satisfaction and security".[9] For what caused this friendship between two

---

[8] Robert F. Sayre, *Thoreau and the American Indians*, Princeton U.P., 1977, p. 25

[9] *A Week on the Concord and Merrimack Rivers*, p. 274. See note 3.

men from such different cultures? Thoreau explains: "Metals unite from fluxility; birds and beasts from motives of convenience; fools from fear and stupidity; and just men at sight." That is to say, friendships of just men are concluded through the senses. What in fact is required is the hunter's mode of perception, a mode that understands the value of "fasting, solitude, and mortification of the body" as an overture to attaining this "satisfaciton and security", mystic in nature. True friendship has nothing to do with the merely kind, good, or fair, but is an experience that like any mystic experience is "essentially heathenish", and "free and irresponsible in its nature", by which Thoreau probably meant again that it is basically something that escapes rationality, transcends cultural accretions, and is something that can only occur to those who still have the required natural, pagan-like "naiveté" that makes them available for this kind of experience. As soon as one loses this naiveté, that is, when one "comes out of heathenism and superstition", and starts treating one's friend "like a Christian", then "Friendship ceases to be Friendship". Thoreau, clearly, did not like Christians.

What Thoreau tries to convey is, so it seems, the idea that the only way to solve the historical conflict between white and red on the North-American continent resides in the existence of this kind of friendship. But as the chances of such a friendship ever being realized grow dimmer and dimmer, what with the disappearance of the hunter's mode of perception and its replacement by a different one, it is a solution that is becoming more and more remote. All Thoreau can discover now *vis à vis* the Indians is "charity", the principle that established "the almshouse", leading to "almshouse and pauper relations", unworthy of free men, and preventing them from protecting one another from embarrassments caused by cultural differences.

Moreover, friendship can only thrive, as Thoreau believed, "on homely ground; not on carpets and cushions, but on the ground and on the rocks they [friends] will sit, obeying the natural and primitive laws", that is, in unspoiled Nature, the West, and among people who are still able to obey "the natural and primitive laws". And these people are to be found among the white hunters and the red Indians, as the story of Henry and Wawatam exemplifies, or rather symbolizes, for in Thoreau's rendering both characters are archetypes rather than historical figures. This appears quite clearly from Thoreau's particular approach, which is neither historical nor psychological, but suggestive of recurring elements that make the phenomenon of this friendship timeless: the joy of shared experiences, the sorrow of unexpected partings, the mutual concern transcending cultural differences, a willingness to suspend moral judgement.

The same kind of approach can be noted in Thoreau's version of the story of Hannah Duston (or Dustan, as Thoreau spells it). The very opening already suggests that the events that are about to be divulged are not unique but have representational value. We are introduced to two women and a boy, paddling down the river in a canoe, on the bottom of which lie the still bleeding scalps of ten aborigines. The events themselves are also related in an impersonal objective manner, as if seen from a great distance, preventing the observer from becoming really involved. Thoreau simply records what happened, without any attempt at explaining why these things happened, or should not have happened: the abduction of Hannah and Mary; the killing of Hannah's baby by the Indians; the tomahawking of the Indian family by Hannah and the boy; their subsequent flight and their odd return to the wigwam of their captors in order to take off the scalps of the dead Indians, as evidence in case someone might doubt the truth of their story, an endlessly puzzling consideration. For why would their story not be believed, and what other story could they have told to account for their return but the fact that they had managed to escape?

It is not until the description of their anxious trip home in the canoe that Thoreau drops for a moment this impersonal mask by trying to fathom the fears that must have racked the minds of these three people on their flight through the hostile territory, an Indian lurking "behind every rock and pine", while a hundred and forty-two years later they, Thoreau and his companions, are leisurely looking for a quiet place to spend the night, along the same river, not far from where those bloody deeds were enacted. To the two women and the boy the "primeval forest" through which they fled must have been "a drear and howling wilderness"; to the Indian, however, it was "a home, adapted to his nature, and cheerful as the smile of the Great Spirit", and it is in drawing attention to this contrast that for the first and only time in this story Thoreau seems to express censure: the whites have nothing to seek in the wilderness, for it is the domain of the Indians, whose natural habitat it is.

Thoreau's retelling of the end of Hannah Duston's story of the bloody revenge then acquires again the impersonal tone of recorded history, with one notable exception: the tree against which the brains of Hannah's baby were dashed out becomes in Thoreau's version an apple-tree, and, as he concludes his account, "there have been many who in later times have lived to say that they had eaten of the fruit of that apple-tree".

What Thoreau means by this concluding remark is not quite clear. Does he mean to say that what the Indians did was also done by later generations of whites, or does he mean to imply that what Hanna and those coming after her did was something that can hardly amaze us, since from the moment that Eve, the mother of mankind, ate of the forbidden fruit, it has become part of the human condition? And that event, according to Thoreau's curious manner of computation, did not occur that long ago, only the period of time equalling the lives of sixty old women, "women, such as live under the hill, say, of a century each". There is something to be said for either explanation, while the two together affirm Thoreau's realistic assessment of human nature, which as he implies, has not changed greatly over the centuries.

If it is Thoreau's *Indian Books* that reflect his scholarly interests in everything Indian — their history, their culture — , it is the actual trips to Maine, recorded in *The Maine Woods* (1864), that taught him about real Indians, Indians of flesh and blood. Thoreau made three trips to Maine, one in 1846, of which we are given an account in "Ktaadn", the first chapter of *The Maine Woods*; a second trip in 1853, described in "Chesuncook", the book's second chapter; and a third one in 1897, recorded in "Allegash and East Branch", the third and final chapter of *The Maine Woods*. The book, incidentally, was not edited by Thoreau himself but appeared posthumously.

For the three trips Thoreau and his companions had hired Indians, ostensibly to serve them as guides, but in reality to provide Thoreau as he remarks in "Chesuncook", with an opportunity to study their ways. However, the two Indians, Louis Neptune and his companion, who were to guide them to Katahdin Mountain, the Ktaadn, as Thoreau himself called it, failed to show up. They had been delayed by a drinking bout at Five Islands, and they had not yet recovered from its effects. It was only towards the end of the trip, after Thoreau and his companions had returned from the Ktaadn that the two Indians turned up, eliciting from a disappointed Thoreau the pained exclamation "We thought Indians had some honour before".

Thoreau's disappointment may have influenced his description of the two men, since it is far from flattering, even if we take into account that he seemed to have regarded the two as representative of those Indians corrupted by the white frontier settlements and towns, central Maine being in Thoreau's time frontier country, the "New England's West". "Met face to face," he observes, "these Indians in their native woods looked like the sinister and slouching fellows whom you meet picking up strings and paper in the streets of a city." "There is," as he continues to develop his extraordinary view, "in fact, a remarkable and unexpected resemblance between the degraded savage and the lowest classes in a great city. The one is no more a child of nature than the other. In the process of degradation, the distinction of races is soon lost" (p. 78). For Thoreau to look upon the two Indians here as degraded may have been inspired partly by pique, partly by prevailing prejudices, but the idea that degraded human beings are all alike, regardless of race or colour, cause or reason, is unlikely to have been shared by many of his contemporaries, convinced as they all were of white superiority.

To be noted also in this first chapter of *The Maine Woods* is another striking view of Thoreau's, one opposed again to the general feeling of the times, but testifying again to some deep-seated mistrust on the part of Thoreau of organized society. "In fact," he argues, and for one moment one believes to hear Cooper's Leatherstocking figure speaking, "the deeper you penetrate into the woods, the more intelligent, and in one sense, less countrified do you find the inhabitants; for always the pioneer has been a traveller, and, to some extent, a man of the world; and, as the distances with which he is familiar are greater, so is his information more general and far reaching than the villager's". "Narrow, uninformed and countrified" minds you'll find in the towns about Boston, he claims, "not in the backwoods of Maine" (pp. 22-23), and one suspects that his intense dislike of city-life must be held responsible for this contrary judgement, which may be true in one or two exceptional cases, but surely not for the majority of backwoodsmen.

Thoreau is far more convincing when he describes his encounter with some of the wildest parts of Maine, as he found them along the slope of the Ktaadn:

And yet we have not seen pure Nature, unless we have
seen her thus vast, and drear, and inhuman, though in the

midst of cities. Nature was here something savage and awful, though beautiful. I looked with awe at the ground I trod on, to see what the Powers had made there, the form and fashion and material of their work. This was that Earth of which we have heard, made out of Chaos and Old Night. Here was no man's garden, but the unhandselled globe. (...) Man was not to be associated with it. It was Matter, vast, terrific, — not his Mother Earth that we have heard of, not for him to tread on, or to be buried in, — no. (...) There was there felt the presence of a force not bound to be kind to man. It was a place for heathenism and superstitious rites, — to be inhabited by men nearer of kin to the rocks and to wild animals than we. (...) Talk of mysteries! — Think of our life in nature, — daily to be shown matter, to come in contact with it, — rocks, trees, wind on our cheeks! the *solid* earth! the *actual* world! the *common sense*! *Contact*! *Contact*! *Who* are we? *where* are we? (pp. 70-71)

It is this passage that heralds a significant change in Thoreau's romantic view of Nature. It is still a source of beauty and mystery to him, but its beauty and mystery are terrifying at the same time, since it lacks the principal human attributes of reason, feeling, and care. How, then, was one to deal with it, in particular, since Thoreau was convinced that whites needed a shot in the arm from Nature, from its "wildness", its timeless and inhuman force. Only this would enable them to rid themselves of the physical and mental flabbiness that life in the towns and cities had brought about, for, as Thoreau believed, man was part and parcel of Nature rather than an element of any social system. But how to establish a renewed and revitalizing relationship with Nature? The Indian, Thoreau thought, might provide the answer; they still seemed to have a different, a more meaningful relationship with Nature than the white man, and so, as he writes in "Chesuncook", the second part of *The Maine Woods*, with regard to Joe Aitteon, their Indian guide who did show up this time, he, Thoreau, "narrowly watched his motions, and listened attentively to his observations" (p. 95).

Although Joe Aitteon is an Indian of unmixed blood — a Penobscot — he has adopted the ways of the white man. He is dressed like a lumberman, in fact is one, and, to Thoreau's astonishment, he can be heard to sing "O Susanna" and other popular songs. Although Joe still knows how to hunt, no longer, as he tells Thoreau, could he subsist on what the woods yield as his ancestors could. The reason, however, does not seem to be lack of skill — as Thoreau notices, he still steals through the bushes in a way in which no white man does, that is, with the least possible noise — but a change in mentality: losing track of a wounded moose, the Indian, as Thoreau thought, gave up too quickly for a good hunter. The implication of Thoreau's observation is clear: exposure to life in the white settlements and towns has had an adverse impact on the Indian's patience and endurance in pursuing game.

On this second trip to the Maine Woods watching Indians and hunters, Thoreau also notes that the use they make of Nature is "coarse and imperfect". The conclusion he draws from this observation with regard to the Indians is somewhat odd. "No wonder," he writes, "that their race is so soon exterminated". What follows, however, appears to be the extension of an idea first expressed in the chapter "Higher Laws" from *Walden* (see section 1, p. 90): "I already and for weeks afterward felt my nature the coarser for this part of my woodland experience [that is, Joe's killing of the moose, and the subsequent skinning, "a tragical business"], and was reminded that our life should be lived as tenderly and daintily as one would pluck a flower" (p. 120). If in "Higher Laws" Thoreau looked upon the hunting of animals as a necessary, though passing, phase in a young man's education, enabling him to realize "the better life in him", in "Chesuncook" he rejects the whole idea of killing, believing that "every creature is better alive than dead, men and moose and pine-trees, and he who understands it aright will rather preserve its life than destroy it" (p. 120). Has Thoreau turned vegetarian, or what? To quote once again a passage already referred to earlier: "It is the living spirit of the tree, not its spirit of turpentine, with which I sympathize, and which heals my cuts. It is as immortal as I am, and perchance will go as high a heaven, there to tower above me still" (p. 122). To Thoreau's great indignation, this last sentence was dropped, for the wrong reason of course, by James Russell Lowell, when he edited the text for publication in the *Atlantic Monthly*. More to the point seems Irving Howe's criticism here, when he writes that although Thoreau "seems to offer answers to the problems of life — how we yearn for them! — we see, disappointed, that his answers are mostly literary".[10] For if one should not kill animals, nor plants, what else is there to kill to satisfy that part of man which, according to Thoreau, should not be cultivated? Probably realizing that he has manoeuvred himself into a quandary, Thoreau concludes "Chesuncook" in the following manner:

> The poet's, commonly, is not a logger's path, but a woodman's. The logger and pioneer have preceded him, like John the Baptist; eaten the wild honey, it may be, but the locusts also; banished decaying wood and the spongy mosses which feed on it, and built hearths and humanized Nature for him. But there are spirits of a yet more liberal culture, to whom no simplicity is barren. There are not only stately pines, but fragile flowers like the orchises, commonly described as too delicate for cultivation, which derive their nutriment from the crudest mass of peat.

---

[10] Irving Howe, *The American Newness: Culture and Politics in the Age of Emerson*, Harvard U.P., Cambridge, Mass., 1986), p. 34.

> These remind us, that, not only for strength, but for beauty, the poet must, from time to time, travel the logger's path and the Indian's trail, to drink at some new and more bracing fountain of the Muses, far in the recesses of the wilderness (pp. 155-56).

Poets, artists, that is, highly refined and civilized men, can only start doing their work after the loggers and woodmen have done theirs, that is, the hard but necessary work of making the world fit for human beings, involving a certain amount of destruction (nature) and killing (animals). The artist himself, Thoreau suggests, is unfit to do this. He has to leave this process of "humanizing" the wilderness to more robust natures, but so as not to lose touch with the harsh reality of life entirely, the poet should occasionally follow the logger's, even the Indian's path, obviously to do what he is constitutionally unable to do, which is, to destroy and kill (a little). In theory, this seems to sound all right; in practice, of course, it does not work, and will only lead to disaster. That it seemed to work for Thoreau himself may be explained as follows: in the region where he lived the "wildness" of nature had already largely disappeared. The Indian had ceased to be a threat, and dangerous wild animals such as panthers had become scarce. Life in the white settlements and towns had become pretty dull and undemanding, and any excursion to the still largely unspoiled Maine woods would acquire the nature of a stirring encounter with primitive nature, even though the risks involved were never much greater than facing a spooked moose, the loss of a canoe in one of the many falls, or the possibility of losing one's way in the wilderness. But even this last risk was minimal on account of the presence of Joe Polis, the skilful Indian, who this time served Thoreau as a guide on what was to be his third and last trip to the Maine Woods.

3

Although Thoreau's description of Joe Polis once again testifies to his sympathy for the Indians and his desire to approach them with an open mind, it becomes quite clear that even for a man like Thoreau it was difficult not to be influenced by the popular clichés and stereotypes that largely determined his and his contemporaries' view of the North-American Indian. "I was surprised to see," he observes, "what a foolish and impertinent style a Maine man, a passenger, used in addressing him [Polis], as if he were a child, which only made his eyes glisten a little." Thoreau is equally surprised, however, when he hears that Polis's successful adjustment to the white man's way of life has made him a man of substance, worth $ 6000, the owner of a spacious house and land, and that he was about to buy more land, and that in acquiring it he preferred to deal with white men to Indians, because "they keep steady, and know how" (p. 174). He is even more surprised when he also hears that his guide is a Protestant, and that when he is at home he goes to church and would not work on Sundays, but that if he had to, he wouldn't take money for it. But, as Thoreau wryly observes later, Polis, "did not forget to reckon in the Sundays", when the trip was over and they had arrived again in Oldtown, Polis's hometown, and in this, too, the Indian proved himself to be an exemplary student of the ways of his white brother.

The Indian continues to surprise Thoreau. He would, as he tells Thoreau, like to live in Boston, or New York, or Philadelphia, but he realizes that he, a hunter by profession, would cut a poor figure there. Polis also believes in education, in going to college, and is proud that his son is at the top of his class, and he simply does not understand Thoreau's dislike of white civilization. To Thoreau, who believes that only close contact with nature can bring about spiritual renewal, and that the life of the solitary pioneer or settler in the woods is far more respectable than that led by "the helpless multitudes in the towns" (p.

244), all this is very confusing. It upsets most of his cherished notions about the Indians, who, as he also finds out, are far more sociable than he thought they were. "Polis," as Thoreau writes, "had evidently more curiosity respecting the few settlers in those woods than we. If nothing was said, he took it for granted that we wanted to go straight to the next log-hut" (p. 234), either to exchange news, or to have a chat with the inmates, the "usual way", as Polis thought. But Thoreau and his companion had not come to the woods for that purpose of course; on the contrary, they had come, as they tell him laughingly, "partly to avoid them".

On the whole the Penobscot Indians seemed to be far more social than the whites. They would never take up solitary residence in the deepest wilderness, as a "Yankee or Canada settler" would. The Penobscots would even choose to live in less favourable surroundings just for the sake of being together (p. 291). Polis himself could also be unexpectedly sociable, "exhibit even the *bonhommie* of a Frenchman" (p. 289). He could also be shamelessly "human all too human", as appears from Thoreau's somewhat disapproving description of Polis after the Indian has fallen ill: "He lay groaning under his canoe on the bank, looking very woe-begone, yet it was only a common case of colic. You would not have thought, if you had seen him lying about thus, that he was the proprietor of so many acres in that neighbourhood, was worth $6000, and had been to Washington." Thoreau suspects Polis of putting it on a bit, that "like the Irish, he made a greater ado about his sickness than a Yankee does, and was more alarmed about himself" (p. 290). Thoreau's reaction may show that his sympathy for the Indians did not blind him, and that by comparing them to the Irish, he, too, was not above some of the prejudices of his time. But there were still enough differences between Polis and the whites for Thoreau to remain fascinated by his Indian guide, and especially the matter of how the latter managed to guide himself in the woods did not cease to puzzle him. Polis himself was unable to explain it: "Great difference between me and white man" (p. 185), was all he could say by way of explanation, and Thoreau concluded that the Indian found his way very much like animals do, by instinct, which of course was not much of an explanation either.

Another trait that Thoreau found admirable in Polis was the Indian's alacrity in learning how to adjust himself to new situations. He cleverly made use of the white man's means of transport, the stage coach, to have himself and his canoe carried to the woods in which he hunted. He also learned quickly how to pitch a tent, a feat which the majority of white men would not have accomplished without, as Thoreau believes, having blundered several times. And the Indian's skill with the canoe, in paddling and taking rapids, was simply unrivalled, a judgement Thoreau could give with some authority, as he was quite skilful with the paddle himself — "the great paddler", as the Indian came to call him.

Apart from being a hunter — the best — and a marvellous tracker, Polis also played a leading role in his community. When the Catholics in Oldtown, thereto instigated by the priest, seemed to succeed in ousting the schoolmaster, a Protestant, Polis rallied the Protestants and persuaded them to make a stand. When the priest told them that he was going to cut down the liberty-pole, Polis gathered about twenty young men, painted them "like old times", and instructed them to rush up to the pole and take hold of it the moment the priest and his followers were to carry out their threat. They were not to fight but to raise a racket, sufficiently big to intimidate them, and the stratagem worked. They saved the pole and their school.

The image of Polis, the Indian, as it emerges from this third part of the *Maine Woods*, thus contains both elements that are in accordance with certain popular clichés about the Indians and elements that flatly contradict these clichés. Much of this remains implicit, due largely to

Thoreau's detached, descriptive style. The one but last paragraph of "Allegash and East Branch" is a marvellous example of this implicitness:

> We stopped for an hour at his house [Polis's], where my companion shaved with his razor, which he pronounced in very good condition. Mrs. P. wore a hat and had a silver brooch on her breast, but she was not introduced to us. The house was roomy and neat. A large new map of Oldtown and the Indian Island hung on the wall and a clock opposite to it. Wishing to know when the cars left Oldtown, Polis's son brought one of the last Bangor papers which I saw was directed to "Joseph Polis" from the office.

Far from being a solitary hunter, Polis is a man who lives in a neat, roomy house, in which we find typical instances of white civilization such as maps and clocks: far from being a superstitious pagan, he is a man possessing a good razor; far from being an innocent noble savage corrupted by white civilization and thus doomed to extinction, Polis has adapted to the new conditions in his land. He reads about them in the white newspaper to which he is a subscriber; he has acted upon them and thus successfully built a new existence, having seen the old, traditional way of life disappear. Polis in short does not quite answer to the popular chlichés about the Indians, but at the same time he confirms Thoreau's belief that the Indians still have what the white man has lost, or perhaps never had: the feeling that, when being in close contact with Nature, one is also in touch with something that transcends the human, something one might, for want of a better word, call sacred. As Thoreau himself puts it: "I love Nature partly because she is not man. There a different kind of right prevails. (...) He [man] is constraint, she is freedom to me. He makes me wish for another world.

She makes me content with this."[11]

The essence of this attraction has been characterized in "Walking" as "wildness" — the dark side of Nature, as the Indians understood; the source and raw material of all civilization and culture, as Thoreau believed. Rediscovery by the whites of this "wildness", which, as I may recall, was in Thoreau's view but another name for the West, might serve as an antidote to man's sense of alienation, which, as Thoreau thought, was nothing else but the growing distance between man and his best, most vital self, a belief logically following from his conviction that man was part and parcel of Nature rather than the product of any social system.

In reflecting on Thoreau's relevance to a present-day audience, one may wonder whether there is still any real ground for holding such a conviction, considering the steadily increasing importance of society in determining the nature of our humanity and the decreasing role Nature plays in this process. But in time one is reminded of a remark made by Witold Gombrowicz, a full hundred years after Thoreau voiced his views: "I (...) wanted to be myself, myself, not an artist or an idea or any of my works — just myself. I wanted to be above art, writing, style, ideas".[12] Even in the year 1989, then, it is still possible to believe with

---

[11] *The Journal of Henry Thoreau*, ed. Bradford Torrey and Francis H. Allen, Boston: Houghton Mifflin, 1906, Vol. 4, 443, 445.

[12] "On Bruno Schulz", by Witold Gombrowicz in *The New York Review of Books*. April 13, 1989, vol. XXXVI, nr. 6, 6-7. In this extract, drawn from the first chapter of his Diary 1961-1966 Gombrowicz comments on Bruno Schulz, the Polish-Jewish writer of imaginative fiction (*The Street of Crocodiles*, 1934). In particular the *Monday* entry is revealing. A few excerpts: "(...) I hail, as I have said, from the landed gentry, and this is a burden almost equally strong and only a bit less tragic than to have behind one those thousands of years of Jewish banishments. (...) A landowner — whether he is a Polish squire or an American farmer makes no difference — will always harbor mistrust of culture, for his remoteness from the great centers of human activity makes him resistant to human confrontations and products. (...) Having one leg in the jolly world of the landed gentry, another in the world of intellect and avant-garde literature, I was between worlds. (...) I had a habit of passing myself off as an artist with my relatives in the country (to irritate them), and with artists I passed myself off as a first-rate landed gentleman (to infuriate them, in turn). I was always irritated by artists who were too fanatic. I can't stand poets who are poets too much and painters too devoted to painting. I generally want man not to devote himself to

Thoreau that there is a more important self than the one that is engendered and shaped by family, society, civilization and culture. It is the self that seeks detachment from whatever the creed, fashion, trend or delusion of the day prescribes. It is the hidden source of our freedom, it is our metaphoric West, the only reality worth finding, worth exploring, whether in close confrontation with Nature, as Thoreau did, or with four hundred years of landed gentry life in Samogitia, as Gombrowicz does — confrontations which have one thing in common: a distrust of citified life as a veneer that hides too much.

In the last sentence that Thoreau spoke before he died on the morning of May 6, 1862, only the two words "moose" and "Indian" could be heard.[13] They stand appropriately for the two overriding passions of his life: Nature, and the people whom he thought still had a vital relationship with her, the Indian. Both constituted the West to Thoreau, the American West, which he never really visited.

---

anything entirely. I want him always to be a little detached from what he does. (...) I (...) wanted to be myself, myself, not an artist or an idea or any of my works — just myself. I wanted to be above art, writing, style, ideas."

[13] Robert D. Richardson, *Henry David Thoreau: A Life of the Mind*, Berkeley: University of California Press, 1986, see p. 389.

Chapter 5

WALT WHITMAN:

"The Half-Breed: A Tale of the Western Frontier";

Leaves of Grass

In 1860 Whitman seriously planned to bring out a special "Western" edition of *Leaves of Grass*[1], believing that such an edition would be more attractive to the Western states. However, he needed not to have worried on that score: the original 1855 edition was already sufficiently "Western" as it was, and an explanation for this is not hard to find. To Whitman America was, metaphorically speaking, the West, regardless of whether you were born and raised in New York, California, Texas, Cuba, or in the North or the South of the United States. As we can read in the third poem of "Starting from Paumanok", the cycle of poems that preceded "Song of Myself" in the 1860 edition, the chants celebrating America are primarily

> Chants of the prairies,
> Chants of the long-running Mississippi, and down to the
> Mexican sea,
> Chants of Ohio, Indiana, Illinois, Iowa, Wisconsin and

---

[1]   Edwin Fussell, *Frontier: American Literature and the American West*, p. 416.

Minnesota,

Chants going forth from the centre from Kansas, and
thence equidistant,

Shooting in pulses of fire ceaseless to vivify all.[2]

Whitman, then, extended the West to include the whole of America,
but what he actually understood by the West is less easy to determine.
In perhaps his most famous, though certainly not his best, Western
poem, "Pioneers! O Pioneers!", the West even becomes the playground
in which the future of all mankind is going to be decided, with the
Westerners themselves as a kind of advance party, the "youthful sinewy
races", who "take up the task eternal, and the burden and the lesson"
(of mankind, one assumes), and in this effort, not only they, the
Westerners, but "all the hands of comrades, clasping, all the Southern,
all the Northern" are to participate. And this "Western movement beat"
contains in fact "all the pulses of the world"; all future action will be
here, in the West, in the New World, just as all future literature will be
produced here:

Minstrels latent on the prairies!

(Shrouded bards of other lands, you may rest, you have
done your work,)

Soon I hear you coming warbling, soon you rise and
tramp amid us,

Pioneers! O Pioneers! (p. 232)

Unlike Cooper and Thoreau, Whitman actually visited the prairies and
plains of the Far West, even though he watched them mostly from a
railroad car. This was on his second trip to the West; the first, from
New York to New Orleans and back via Canada, took place thirty years
earlier, in 1848, the trip which is supposed to have been of such crucial

---

[2] *The Collected Writings of Walt Whitman: Leaves of Grass*, Comprehensive
Reader's Edition, edited by Harold W. Blodgett and Sculley Bradley, New York
University Press, 1965, p. 17. All further page references are to this edition.

importance in turning him from a mediocre journalist into America's national poet. Before this happened, however, Whitman's view of the West did not diverge greatly from the one prevailing in the East, although there are, as we shall see, some intriguing differences. This appears most clearly from "The Half-Breed: A Tale of the Western Frontier", the only genuinely Western tale and second-largest piece of the nearly two dozen works of fiction Whitman published between 1841 and 1845.

As Justin Kaplan rightly remarks in his *Walt Whitman: A life*, these works were in "their ambience of symbol, nightmare, and dramas of the inner soul" as much *à la* Poe as *à la* Hawthorne.[3] But also in terms of thematics they were all highly derivative, as Whitman's treatment of such familiar Western themes as lawlessness and revenge in "The Half-Breed" may show, while the ideas that inform his image of the West also appear to be those generally held by his fellow Easterners of the mid-nineteenth century.

The West in this view was usually a region located near the upper branches of the Mississippi, where once "the savage roamed in pursuit of game", a place always full of "adventures".[4] Whitman's Indians too are dignified, brave, and stoic, and one suspects the influence of Cooper here, but the equally stereotyped idea that an Indian can never entirely be trusted, is not absent either. When a series of thefts are reported in Warren, the village where most of the action takes place, the suspicion at once falls on the Redskin. The real culprit however, appears to be Boddo, the half-breed of the story's title, the misshapen offspring of an Irishman who fled from his country to America, and an Indian girl who fell in love with him after he had

---

[3]   Justin Kaplan, *Walt Whitman: A life*, 1980; Bantam Books, 1982, p. 116.

[4]   *The Collected Writings of Walt Whitman: The Early Poems and the Fiction*, ed. Thomas L. Brasher, New York University Press, 1963, p. 257; p. 269. All further page references, if preceded by F, are to this edition.

arrived in the West. This is of course not uncommon, such an affair, that is, be it that in the work of Cooper, Twain, Harte, or Joaquin Miller one would have looked in vain for a sentence like "we were both with the hot blood of young veins" to describe its consummation.

What is also a little out of the ordinary is that the half-breed should be a hunchback, none too bright, and with an unpleasant, even malignant character. Extraordinary, too, is the fact that no one in the settlement knows of the true nature of the relationship between the half-breed and Father Luke, the monk who, whenever he turns up in the region, which is every few months, lives in a cave near the village to devote himself to the self-appointed task of instructing the hunchback, primarily in the religious matters.

The monk of course is none other than the Irishman, the lover of the Indian maid who died while giving birth to their child, the hunchback Boddo. When the Irishman, returning to Warren after a number of years saw what he had sired, he was so crushed by feelings of guilt and remorse that he decided to spend the rest of his life as a monk.

The presence of both a hunchback and a monk in this tale of the West can no doubt be ascribed to the impact of the Gothic novel on nineteenth-century American writing, but the distaste one feels behind the portrayal of the half-breed seems to spring from different sources. One of these may have been the general revulsion from miscegenation prevalent in nineteenth-century America. Another, of a less public origin, emerges when we juxtapose Whitman's description of the half-breed with that of other young men from Warren. This is how the half-breed is described: "He was deformed in body — his back being mounted with a mighty hunch, and his long neck bent forward, in a peculiar and disagreeable manner (...) Among the most powerful of his bad points was a malignant peevishness, dwelling on every feature of his countenance" (F 258).

Peter Brown, the young blacksmith and like the half-breed one of the story's main characters, is a "stout, well-made man", "strongly-jointed", descriptive terms which denote the difference between him and the half-breed, and which even the most bigoted Puritan that ever walked New England's lanes is unlikely to have found offensive. But then we come across the description of Peter's lips, "beautifully cut", and of his neck which "might have been taken by the most fastidious sculptor as a model of that part of the human form in some fine work of art", details which one does not usually find mentioned, or dwelled upon, nor actually expects in a Western story, but which at once sound less odd the moment one remembers Whitman's preference for members of the male sex.

Also the peculiar manner, that is, peculiar from a narrative point of view, in which the third main character, the Indian Arrow-Tip, is introduced, becomes less odd when conceived in the light of this knowledge. On the day of Peter Brown's wedding, Master Caleb and Quincy "stole away", as we are told, "from revellers in the middle of the afternoon, and took a quiet round-about stroll, bringing up, at last, at the dwelling of Quince's father". There they "took a seat on the door-step in front", a front facing the river, "a pleasant prospect". From here they suddenly see Arrow-Tip, emerging, "one of the finest specimens of the Red People", as he is described, or, as the author obviously with unintended irony adds, "rather had the evidence of having once been so".

Arrow-Tip, as it appears, is seriously ill, and has come to Warren to ask the white man whether he has a medicine that can cure his fever. That the Indian heads for the Thornes' homestead is understandable for a number of reasons. He once saved young Quincy's life, and his presence in the house of the Thornes is necessary for the purpose of plot development: it is Arrow-Tip who catches the half-breed stealing, thus providing the latter with a motive for the revenge,

118

which, later, he takes by disobeying Father Luke's request to tell the people of Warren that Peter Brown is not dead but alive, and that as a consequence the Indian is not a murderer and need not be hanged. But Arrow-Tip can of course be introduced in a variety of ways, ways that would serve the story's dramatic purposes much better than the one Whitman ultimately chose. For one thing, we are now ill prepared for the violent altercation that occurs between Arrow-Tip and Peter Brown during the hunting party. Surely, it is a little hard to believe that the actual reason of the fight between the two men should be the Indian's continuously baiting Brown on account of the latter's poor performance in the hunt. Considering the persistent emphasis on Arrow-Tip's behaviour as throughout dignified and stoic, there is nothing in the story to prepare us for such a sudden change of character. Why then did Whitman choose this way of introducing Arrow-Tip and no other? Something over which he apparently had no control drove him to mention and include the close relationship between Caleb and Quincy , the same thing that also made him dwell on male lips, "beautifully cut".[5]

There are other intriguing divergences from the staple Western. When Peter Brown, who was only stunned by Arrow-Tip's blow and then taken to Father Luke's cave to recuperate, realizes that the half-breed Boddo must have failed in passing on the message that Peter is still alive, he at once, despite his weakness, hastens to the village, fervently praying that he may come in time to prevent the angry townspeople from hanging Arrow-Tip:

---

[5] In connection with the Caleb-Quincy relationship it is interesting to read the following passage from Kaplan's *A life*: "Looking back to this period [the period when Whitman taught school], Whitman told Nelly O'Connor that "the grown-up son of the farmer with whom he was boarding while he was teaching school became very fond of him, and Walt of the boy, and he said the father quite reproved him for making such a pet of the boy. Even in this summary version the phrase "quite reproved" suggest a residue of anguish on Whitman's part. Nelly deleted the episode from her published memoir, but it is at least compatible with a story originating in Southold, where Whitman taught for a while, that he got into trouble there and was forced to leave" (pp. 86-87).

Then, with wild and ghastly visage, and with the phrenzied contortions of a madman in his worst paroxysm, Peter Brown dashed along the path and among them. His blood-shot eyes were fixed upon a hideous object hanging in the air. He rushed up to the scaffold — but his limbs failed him, and he could not ascend the ladder. His head vibrated to and fro, like the pendulum of a clock, and he beckoned and tried to speak, though for several moments they could not hear what he said, or rather tried to say.

"Quick! Quick!" came at last from his throat, in a gasping whisper; "cut the rope, he may not yet be dead!"

It was all too late (F 290).

Peter's violent reaction to the half-breed's wilful failure to stop the hanging seems to be in excess of what such a situation in terms of emotions would normally excite in a man of his station in a frontier setting. His anxiety concerns an Indian, who is not only responsible for his precarious condition, but who also did not lift a finger to check whether the man whom he had mortally wounded was really dead or not. Is the blacksmith's mad frenzy to be explained by Whitman's horror of seeing a splendid male destroyed, or is it Peter's innate humanity that demands him to prevent at all costs an innocent man from being hanged? In either case it signifies a striking divergence from the popular nineteenth-century Western tale, in which concern about the value of human life is as a rule restricted to the palefaces rather than to the redskins. This is not to say though that as a story of the West "The Half-Breed" is original; on the contrary, the author's view of the whites and the Indians is on the whole conventional, if not stereotyped. All the Westerners in the story are called "adventurers" and they all look upon one another as "comrades". Miscegenation is reprehended — it results in half-breeds, malignant hunchbacks, throughout the story. At the end the half-breed is made to flee the settlement, and "whether he perished in the wilds, or even now lives a degraded and grovelling life, in some other town, no one can tell".

The hanging of Arrow-Tip, a "good" Indian because he is friendly to the whites, is basically due to the criminal impatience of the townspeople taking the law into their own hands, and evidently the author does not take exception to this mode of law-enforcement: it's "Western" and therefore to be excused.

What is also mentioned without further or implied comment is that the Deer, Arrow-Tip's younger brother, led, as so many Indian chiefs before him had done, "his tribe still farther into the West, to grounds where they never would be annoyed, in their generation at least, by the presence of the white intruders". Obviously Whitman, too, was not greatly troubled by this continual retreat of the Indians on the North-American continent, and only the use of the term "intruders" seems to betray some hidden moral unease on his part.

It is true of course that Whitman was in his early twenties when he wrote "The Half-Breed", which is clearly the work of a beginning writer. It may explain such weaknesses as the clumsy narrative technique, the shaky plot, the over-didactic and preachy tone, the many stylistic infelicities. But what Paul Zweig calls Whitman's "twoness", that is, the simultaneous presence of both originality (however modest in this story) and conventionality (however distressingly cliché-like here),[6] already appears to be a feature of such an early tale as "The Half-Breed".

It is this "twoness" that continues to characterize Whitman's work, and it is interesting, though of course not surprising, to note that in the most creative period of his life, in the years roughly between 1848 and 1860, originality rather than conventionality prevails in his view of the West.

---

[6] Paul Zweig, *Walt Whitman: The Making of the Poet*, New York, 1984, pp. 115-17; 307-8.

Original in the sense of differing from what was generally thought and felt about the Red Indians by Whitman's contemporaries is for example poem 16 of the "Starting from Paumanok" cycle:

> On my way a moment I pause,
>
> Here for you! and here for America!
>
> Still the present I raise aloft, still the future of the States
> I harbinge glad and sublime,
>
> And for the past I pronounce what the air holds of the
> red aborigines.
>
>
> The red aborigines,
>
> Leaving natural breaths, sounds of rain and winds, calls as
> of birds and animals in the woods, syllabled to
> us for names,
>
> Okonee, Koosa, Ottawa, Monongahela, Sauk, Natchez,
> Chattahoochee, Kaqueta, Oronoco,
>
> Wabash, Miami, Saginaw, Chippewa, Oshkosh, Walla-
> Walla,
>
> Leaving such to the States they melt, they depart,
> charging the water and the land with names.

Custer's Last Stand, signifying the end of the red aborigines' organized resistance to the Whites' taking possession of the whole of the North-American continent, was still about fifteen years ahead, but it was of course clear to everybody — certainly in the Eastern states — that the Indians had long ceased to be a major obstacle in the rapid development of the United States to full statehood. All that reminded the white Americans of the presence of the once feared redskins would soon be mere names, but according to Whitman they were not just names: they were strong reminders to the whites of their origin, of how closely they were tied to the natural world — "natural breaths, sounds of rain and winds, calls as of the birds and animals in the woods". The waters and the land of America were in fact "charged" by these names, meaning that into them the spirit of the red aborigines was infused. They, the waters and the land, would thus never completely belong to the whites.

"Song of Myself", the cycle of poems following "Starting from Paumanok" and forming the bulk of the first edition of *Leaves of Grass*, also contains numerous references to Western matter. There are in fact so many that Edwin Fussell thought that the cycle was to a large extent constructed on the pioneer analogy, Whitman's glorified expansion of the self being analogous to America's glorified advancement West. Since on the whole these poems express mid-nineteenth-century American sentiments, evoked by ideas such as the United States as the New World, enacting its Manifest Destiny, they might be called conventionally commemorative. But, Whitman being Whitman, "Song of Myself" also contains views of the West that are diametrically opposed to these current sentiments, and poem 10 of the cycle no doubt provides a good example of this, while at the same time proving what Whitman always took great pains to deny: the surprising extent to which his life and art were inextricably intertwined. Not the raw reality of strictly personally or publicly experienced events was the actual source of his creativity, but this intricate intertwinement of reality and fiction.

The poem relates a number of experiences, some of which are imagined, like the hunting party in "the wilds and mountains" in the first stanza; some are witnessed like the "Yankee clipper", cleaving the waves "under her sky-sails" in the second stanza; others are heard about as the fugitive slave episode in the last stanza suggests. The clam-digging trip in the third stanza may be a boyhood reminiscence, while the description of the trapper marrying a red girl in the fourth stanza is known to derive from a painting called "The Trapper's Bride" by the Baltimore artist Alfred Jacob Miller.

Whitman's depiction of this marriage seems to disclose neither moral approval nor disapproval, but seeing, observing, watching are always highly affirmative activities in Whitman's world, and all the sensual details ("luxuriant beard and curls"; "voluptuous limbs") that intersperse his rendering of this event only emphasize this. We are, it is clear, a long way from the distaste of miscegenation pervading such an early story as "The Half-Breed".

However, in poem 16, "I am of old and young, of the foolish as much as the wise", Whitman presents again his most complacently conservative side, entirely satisfied, so it appears, with the way things are:

(The moth and the fish-eggs are in their place,
The bright suns I see and the dark suns I cannot see are
    in their place,
The palpable is in its place and the impalpable is in its
    place.)

Also poem 34, which records the massacre of Captain Fannin and his company of Texans after their surrender to the Mexicans in 1836, becomes a tale of conventional heroics: all the four hundred and twelve young Texas Rangers that were slaughtered "were the glory of the race of rangers,/ Matchless with horse, rifle, song, supper, courtship", while furthermore in the possession of the right Whitmanesque qualities, "Large, turbulent, generous, handsome, proud, and affectionate,/ Bearded, sunburnt, drest in the free costume of hunters,/ not a single one over thirty years of age".

What nonetheless distinguishes this poem, is the stark, matter-of-fact manner in which the gory details of the actual massacre are singled out, strongly reminding us here, oddly enough, of Hemingway:

A few fell at once, shot in the temple or heart, (...)
The maim'd and mangled dug in the dirt, (...)
These were despatch'd with bayonets or batter'd with the

blunts of muskets, (...)

In poem 35, which describes the sea battle between *Bonhomme Richard*, under the command of John Paul Jones, and the British Ship *Serapis*, fought off Flamborough Head in 1779, Whitman, incidentally, keeps up this matter-of-fact-like registering:

> We had receiv'd some eighteen pound shots under the
> water,
> On our lower-gun-deck two large pieces had burst at the
> first fire,
> killing all around and blowing up overhead.

Or, to give another example:

> Only three guns are in use,
> One is directed by the captain himself against the enemy's
> main mast,
> Two well serv'd with grave and canister, silence his musketry and
> clear his decks.

However, just as in poem 34, Whitman's implied judgement of the event is that of the nineteenth-century American patriot, denouncing the enemy as murderers, rejoicing in the defeat of the English ship, while commemorating this as an heroic feat:

> Serene stands the little captain.
> He is not hurried, his voice is neither high nor low,
> His eyes give more light to us than our battle-lanterns,

lines, though, that end as laconic as an early Hemingway story:

> Toward twelve there in the beams of the moon they
> surrender to us.[7]

---

[7] It is interesting to compare Whitman's treatment of this battle with Melville's in *Israel Potter* (see pp. 78-79). Whitman commemorates the battle as an heroic feat in America's naval history, the official view, whereas Melville focusses on the savagery with which the battle was fought on both sides, making him wonder whether civilization is perhaps "an advanced stage of barbarism".

In poem 36, Whitman's "twoness" reveals itself again. In this poem we are confronted with what the conventional picture of patriotic heroism conceals:

> Near by the corpse of the child that serv'd in the cabin,
> The dead face of an old salt with long white hair and
>   carefully curl'd whiskers.
> For the wounded men there is,
> The hiss of the surgeon's knife, the gnawing teeth of his
>   saw,
> Wheeze, cluck, swash of falling blood, short wild scream,
>   and long, dull, tapering groan,
> These so, these irretrievable.

What these shocking lines tell us in graphic detail is not only what the men irretrievably lose, but also under what desperately crude circumstances they lose it.

Although one may not be certain what Whitman actually understood by the West, "Facing West from California's Shores", a poem from the *Children of Adam* cycle, takes away some of this uncertainty, while confirming once more that in Whitman's work the West is primarily a metaphoric idea rather than a geographical or sociological one:

> Facing west from California's shores,
> Inquiring. tireless, seeking what is yet unfound,
> I, a child, very old, over waves, towards the house of
>   maternity, the land of migrations, look afar,
> Look off the shores of my Western sea, the circle almost
>   circled;
> For starting westward from Hindustan, from the vales of
>   Kashmere,
> From Asia, from the north, from the God, the sage, and
>   the hero,

> From the south, from the flowery peninsulas and the spice
> islands
> Long having wander'd since, round the earth having
> wander'd,
> Now I face home again, very pleas'd and joyous,
> (But where is what I started for so long ago?
> And why is it yet unfound?)

What drives people west is as old as the earth, while the urge behind the drive remains always young (lines 3-5). But on the round earth the west is at the same time east, provided one keeps moving west, until one arrives at the spot from where one started (lines 10-11), a joyous event, but also one that makes you wonder whether the long journey was worth the hardships and dangers, if the end is not at all different from the beginning.

However, this note of profound pessimism about the nature and the purpose of the American experience has disappeared again in such a later poem like "The Prairie-Grass Dividing" from the *Calamus* group:

> The prairie-grass dividing, its special odor breathing,
> I demand of it the spiritual corresponding,
> Demand the most copious and close companionship of
> men,
> Demand the blades to rise of words, acts, being,
> Those of the open atmosphere, coarse, sunlit, fresh,
> nutritious,
> Those that go their own gait, erect, stepping with freedom
> and command, leading not following,
> Those with a never-quell'd audacity, those with sweet and
> lusty flesh clear of taint,
> Those that look carelessly in the faces of Presidents and
> governors, as to say *Who are you?*
> Those of earth-born passion, simple, never constrain'd,

    never obedient,
   Those of inland America.

In this poem the West re-emerges as the land where the American
Adam, the new democratic man, can manifest himself most generously
and most audaciously; a man of an open, uncorrupted, and unclouded
mind, of simple and easy manners, acknowledging no other authority
than his own individual conscience. This is the kind of man that
prospers in the West, the kind of man the West produces. "Always the
West," as Whitman reiterates in "Our Old Feuillage", "with strong native
persons, the increasing density/there, the habitans, friendly, threatening,
ironical, scorning invaders" (p. 171: ll.11-12), no doubt as strong,
friendly, threatening, ironical, and scorning invaders, as he liked to see
himself.

   That these men continue to answer to what Whitman believed
were the typical qualities of the Westerner, is once again emphasized in
another poem from the *Calamus* group, "A Promise to California":

   A Promise to California,
   Or inland to the great pastoral Plains, and on to Puget
     sound and Oregon;
   Sojourning east a while longer, soon I travel toward you
     to remain, to teach robust American love,
   For I know very well that I and robust love belong among
     you, inland, and along the Western sea;
   For these States tend inland and toward the Western sea,
     and I will also.

Whitman himself, as we know, never visited California, but it belonged,
as he thought, to the West and so, in a spiritual sense, he belonged to
it. What it still lacked, however, was "robust love", which, he believed,
he could teach the Californians through his work. Fact is that today
California's attitude towards "robust love" is among the nation's most
tolerant, while this most western state prides itself on the largest

community of homosexuals in the land. Whether this is to be attributed to Whitman's teaching, is of course highly doubtful. A golden sun, and a superb coastline, favouring an easy life style, together with a lively multiracial population, seems a more likely explanation, but the manner in which Whitman's promise to California has been fulfilled constitutes once again one of history's mad ironies.

In contrast with a poem like "On my way a moment I pause" from the "Starting from Paumanok" cycle (see p. 121), Whitman's dealing with the Indians in "Our Old Feuillage" is again depressingly conventional, singularly inane in its meaningless generality:

> In arriere the peace-talk with the Iroquois the aborigines,
> > the calumet, the pipe of good-will, arbitration,
> > and indorsement,
> The sachem blowing the smoke first toward the sun and
> > then toward the earth
> The drama of the scalp-dance enacted with painted faces
> > and gutteral exclamations,
> The setting out of the war-party, the long and stealthy
> > march,
> The single file, the swinging hatches, the surprise and
> > slaughter of enemies; (p. 174: ll. 47-52)

All the well-known clichés about Indians are trotted out, and then left to look after themselves.

Poem 6 of The Sleepers cycle seems to express warm sympathy for the American aborigines, but the curious thing is that Whitman lets his mother be the spokeswoman for this. Once when she was still a girl living with her parents "on the old Homestead", they were visited, as she told him, by "a red squaw", who made a great impression on her on account of "the freshness of her tall-borne face and full and/pliant limbs", a squaw of "such wonderful beauty and purity" that

> O my mother was loth to have her go away,

All the week she thought of her, she watch'd for her many
    a month,
She remember'd her many a winter and many a summer,
But the red squaw never came nor was heard of there
    again. (p. 430)

What is strange is that the homage paid to the American Indians is done by some one in the past, not in the present. And why is it only "remembrance and fondness" that can be given, why not something that could restore the Indian's purpose in life? ("She had no work to give her, but she gave her remembrance/ and fondness"). Or is our reading of the poem wrong, and should we suspect irony, and exposure of hypocrisy? But the poem's tone towards the Red Indian is not ironic, or satirical, but rather a facile, uncommitted sort of sentimental nostalgia.

In "Song of the Broad-Axe" we are treated to a similar evocation of Western life:

The settlements of the Arkansas, Colorado, Ottawa,
    Willamette,
The beauty of all adventurous and daring persons,
The beauty of wood-boys and wood-men with their clear
    untrimm'd faces,
The beauty of independence, departure, actions that rely
    on themselves,

The American contempt for statutes and ceremonies, the
    boundless impatience of restraint,
The loose drift of character, the inkling through random
    types, the solidification;
The butcher in the slaughterhouse, the hands aboard
    schooners and sloops, the raftsman, the
    pioneer,
Lumbermen in their winter camp, daybreak in the woods,

> stripes of snow on the limbs of trees, the
> occasional snapping,
> The glad clear sound of one's own voice, the merry song,
> the natural life of the woods, the strong day's
> work,
> The blazing fire at night, the sweet taste of supper, the
> talk, the bed of hemlock-boughs and the bear-
> skin; (pp. 185-86: ll.34-44)

One may gladly go along with "the beauty of all adventurous and daring persons", and with "the beauty of independence, departure" as well; one may be allured once more by "the American contempt for statutes and ceremonies, the bound-/less impatience of restraint", but refuse to hear again how glad and merry the pioneers and lumbermen are, and how natural they comport themselves.

It is this kind of perverse insistence on the stereotype of merry cheeriness with which the "conquering, holding, daring, venturing" of the Westward movement was supposed to have been achieved that also galls one's reading of "Pioneers! O Pioneers!":

> O you youths, Western youths,
> So impatient, full of action, full of manly pride and
> friendship,
> Plain I see you Western youths, see you tramping with the
> foremost,
> Pioneers! O pioneers! (p. 229)

Still, in complete and dramatic contrast to this poem, written in 1865, is "A Hand-Mirror", which appeared in the 1860 edition of *Leaves of Grass*, testifying to an entirely different mood, as becomes apparent from especially the last lines:

> Words babble, hearing and touch callous,
> No brain, no heart left, no magnetism of sex;
> Such from one look in this looking-glass ere you go

hence,

Such a result so soon — and from such a beginning! (p.
269)

And one may ask oneself whether in "A Hand-Mirror" it was the imminent threat of the Civil War which was perhaps responsible for the despair contained in the last sentence of this poem, and whether in the case of "Pioneers" a tremendous sense of relief that the nation had survived the war might not account for the insistent tone of jubilant optimism so distinctive of that poem. Or is it again an instance of Whitman's "twoness", which refuses to acquire the consistency usually associated with the concept of "oneness", even though his references to the West after 1865 are becoming more and more conventional in that the traditional view of the winning of the West as an heroic event, fulfilling the nation's Manifest Destiny begins to prevail? A typical example is a late poem like "The Prairie States" from 1881, in which Whitman calls these western states "a newer garden of creation (...),

The crown and teeming paradise, so far, of time's
accumulations,

To justify the past." (p. 402)

There may, however, also be an entirely different explanation for the ecstatic element in Whitman's celebratory tone when dealing with the West, and to show what I mean we should take a close look at another later poem about the West, called "From Far Dakota's Cañons", written in 1876 in celebration of Custer's death. Whitman treats this death as a triumph ("I bring no dirge for it or thee, I bring a glad triumphal sonnet"), because:

The fall of Custer and all his officers and men.

Continues yet the old, old legend of our race,
The loftiest of life upheld by death,
The ancient banner perfectly maintain'd,

but he also welcomes it ("O lesson opportune, O how I welcome thee!")
since it revives his own lapsing spirit:

> As sitting in dark days
> Lone, sulky, through the time's thick murk looking in vain
> for light, for hope,
> From unsuspected parts a fierce and momentary proof,
> (The sun there at the centre though conceal'd,
> Electric life forever at the centre,)
> Breaks forth a lightning flash. (p. 483)

What this poem, celebrating the West and all it stands for, seems to tell
us is that "the splendid fever" of deeds like Custer's, however foolhardy
they may look, were the "lightning flash[es]", illuminating "the time's
thick murk". It is this "murk" which occasionally, though in later life
with increasing regularity, bore down Whitman. What in this poem
sounds like facile, buoyantly commemorative ardour for the American
experiment, in particular the Westward movement, is perhaps just that,
but to Whitman it was evidently also something else: a desperate effort
on his part to impose a fixed pattern upon what was happening with
such neck-breaking speed on the Northern continent of America in the
second half of the nineteenth century. This pattern was engendered by
Whitman's deepest wishes rather than the reality of the moment. It was
in fact sheer invention. Just as the man and poet Whitman presented to
the world was sheer invention. But in this he participated in what was
going on around him: the invention of a nation. The extraordinary thing
was of course that by acting on these inventions both Whitman and the
nation started to a large extent to become what they invented: in
Whitman's case it was the generic "I" of his poems, a personage of a
bold, open, generous, physically big, goodnaturedly wicked, yet
reflectively gentle disposition, a person that stood in such marked
contrast to the lonely, withdrawn, severely private man Whitman
actually was, the celebrant of health and success who came from a

family beset by a history of illness and failure. As for America itself: it accepted the adventurous, daring expansive, noisy, and irreverent Jacksonian populism as something that was proclaimed to go with the Westward movement, a style of life that was in such striking contrast to the cautious, restraining, frugal, hierarchical Puritanism of the East coast, which had determined to such a large extent American life in the seventeenth and eighteenth century.

It is probably here that we should look for the origin of the "twoness", so characteristic not only of Whitman's work but of America in general: the juxtaposition of innovative progressivism with staid conservatism. It clarifies why we do not see any development in Whitman's view of the American West, but only a confusing alternation of original and stereotyped ideas in his approach to America's westward movement. It tells us why Whitman and no one else is America's national poet.

Chapter 6

MARK TWAIN:
Roughing It Reconsidered

Trying to decide which information was true about the "Mountain Meadows Massacre", a black page in the history of the Mormons, the narrator of *Roughing It* concludes that "all our 'information' had three sides to it", the three sides being that of the Gentiles, that of the Mormons, and that of the Indians.[1] In the same manner one can say that all the "information" that comes to us in *Roughing It* has three sides to it as well: that of the narrator as tenderfoot, of the narrator as old-timer, and of Mark Twain as the author of the novel.

The information we receive through the tenderfoot tells us of the West as romance, a place full of such exciting things as buffaloes, Indians, prairie dogs and antelopes; a place where one would have all sorts of adventures with desperadoes and Indians, in which one might get killed, or hanged, or scalped, and be a hero and have "ever such a fine time"; a place where one could also visit gold and silvermines and become very rich, after which one would return home and talk about these marvels, calmly, "as if it was nothing of any consequence" (pp. 49-50).

---

[1] Mark Twain, *Roughing It*, 1872; Penguin Book, 1981, p. 157. All further page references are to this edition.

136

What the narrator as old-timer tells us does not really contradict this information supplied by his younger self, but it does put the information in a different perspective, revealing what seems like a more truthful and realistic picture of the West; a picture, however, which is once again altered by the old-timer as writer, that is, by Mark Twain, who, to quote Everett Emerson, never forgot his maxim not to spoil a good story for the truth.[2] So when the tenderfoot joins a party on a buffalo hunt, he may initially feel that he participates in a "noble chase", an exciting adventure, only to learn that if one does not know how to handle a wounded buffalo, the adventure will end in "disaster and disgrace". Unable to control his frightened horse, Bemis, a travel-companion, helplessly undergoes the ultimate humiliation of being chased by a buffalo instead of the buffalo being chased by him. Thrown by his horse, Bemis has to find safety in a lone tree, but even here he is not safe for long. The buffalo, as he later tells his astounded audience, started climbing the tree after him, and if he had not lassoed the beast and, after discharging his Allen gun in its face, succeeded in leaving it hanging twenty feet from the ground, he would not have survived the buffalo's displeasure.

Now this is of course an extraordinary tale, even though the narrator as old-timer reminds his younger self that there are even bigger liers than Bemis. So one should not be too impressed by this story from the West. It is, however, the narrator as Mark Twain, the writer, who is ultimately responsible for the shape of the story by transferring his own story-telling skills to Bemis. In this way Twain not only pokes fun at a whole literary genre, the hunting story, but also delineates a survival strategy for all those who suffer one humiliating experience after the other in that new and strange land, the Far West, a

[2] Everett Emerson, *The Authentic Mark Twain: A Literary Biography of Samuel L. Clemens*, Philadelphia: University of Pennsylvania Press, 1984, p. 67.

strategy as simple as it is ingenious: turn the experience into a joke, and neither the victim nor the reader will feel miserable or shocked any longer.[3]

When in Chapter 32, the narrator and his companions Balloe and Ollendorf get lost in a snowstorm, another romantic adventure in the West, they conclude that the only way to save themselves is to build a campfire and they think they know how to do it from the books they have read. But they fail to make fire with a pistol, or by rubbing two sticks together, as the Indians and hunters do in these books, and when also the horses take off, which they "would never do", but "stay by their masters for protection and companionship in a distressful time like [theirs]", they disgustedly resign themselves to the inevitable: their "last night with the living". And in proper romantic fashion they decide to reform: Ollendorf by pledging never to drink whiskey again; Mr. Balloe, never to play cards again, and the narrator, never to smoke pipe again. When, however, the next day they discover that they are still alive and that they have spent the night fifteen steps away from a stage station, they soon start taking up their old sinful ways again, at first shamefacedly trying to hide it from each other but in the end acknowledging their weaknesses, their lack of principle. Even on this serious matter, then, the romantic tales have proved fraudulent again: reform, as they have learned, is no easier to accomplish than lighting a fire by firing a pistol, or by rubbing two sticks together.

The matrix on which the stories are structured has become clear by now: the tenderfoot eagerly participates in a Western adventure; the old-timer divests it of all romance by disclosing the underlying prosaic

---

[3] See Kenneth S. Lynn, *Mark Twain & Southwestern Humor*, 1960; rpt Greenwood, 1972, pp. 27-28, as well as the following passage: "As both William Dean Howells and H.H. Boyesen testified, women in post-Civil War America came to compose an enormous bloc of the reading population to whom book publishers and magazines of national circulation appealed. How was it possible to talk about eyeball-gougers to *this* audience? and if it was not possible to do so, how could one be honest about the West?" (pp. 164-65).

reality, while the writer, Mark Twain, turns it into burlesque — in the snowstorm episode, by making the starting point of the travellers, Honey Lake Smith's, the same as the place where they spend their miserable night, the stage station. Twain thus inserted, as Franklin Rogers has shown, "a wild, snow-filled day and night of wandering between two places which in actuality were the same".[4]

Although most of the episodes and stories that bear on Samuel Clemens's stay in the West follow this model, Mark Twain, the writer, never employs the structure with any rigidity, thus obviating the risk of becoming monotonous or predictable. A typical example is provided by the narrator's encounter with one of the badmen of the West, the desperado Slade, again a thrilling adventure. Meeting this "ogre, who, in fights and brawls and various ways, *had taken the lives of twenty-six human beings*" (Twain's italics), makes the narrator "the proudest stripling that ever traveled to see strange lands and wonderful people" (p. 110). Here was romance, indeed; romance, however, that is not sustained by anything the "friendly" and "gentle-spoken" man said to the narrator, as he notes when he actually has a talk with the man, and from which he can only conclude that there was nothing remarkable about Slade, unless it was his concern about the comforts of the passengers of the Overland company, of which he was a division-agent. Yet Slade was not simply "a high and efficient servant of the Overland", but "an outlaw among outlaws, and yet their relentless scourge"; a man, who was "at once the most bloody, the most dangerous and the most valuable citizen that inhabited the savage fastnesses of the mountains" (p. 103). How to reconcile this "pleasant person" with the cold-blooded killer of twenty-six human beings, among whom were women and children? How to account for the man's splendid courage in battle, and his desperate pleading for his life when he was finally standing under

---

[4] See Franklin R. Rogers, *Mark Twain's Burlesque Patterns*, Dallas, 1960, pp. 74-75.

the gallows? Even Mark Twain, the writer, is at a loss, and forgetting to burlesque the career of "this bloody, desperate, kindly-mannered, urbane gentleman, who never hesitated to warn his most ruffianly enemies that he would kill them next" (p. 119), he rather lamely concludes that it was "a conundrum worth investigating".

It is the constant interaction of these three voices — the tenderfoot's, the old-timer's, and that of Mark Twain, the author — that gives the novel what at first sight it seems to lack so badly: a sense of unity, that is to say, up to the Sandwich Islands portion. From then on, as most critics have recognized,[5] Clemens, the newspaperman writing for *The Virginian Daily Territorial Enterprise*, takes over, no longer concerned with the rites of initiation that turn the narrator's younger self, an inexperienced naïf, into the latter's older self, an experienced and slightly cynical old-timer.

But even then it is not simply reporting that the voice of the newspaperman does. Mark Twain also takes a firm hand in this, actually creating the kind of West which, ironically, drew Sam Clemens to the Far West in the first place. The reason? Everyday-life in a Western town, in this particular case, Virginia City, simply lacked the kind of events exciting enough to justify a newspaper story.[6] If a reporter still wanted stories, he had better invent them himself, and this is exactly what Mark Twain learned how to do. One or two emigrant wagons passing through the town was hardly interesting. No reporter could ever make a story out of this. Telling his readers, however, that these wagons had passed through hostile Indian country would make a

---

[5] See Henry Nash Smith, *Mark Twain, the Development of a Writer*, The Beknap Press of Harvard U.P., Cambridge, Mass., 1962, p. 35ff. Also, Rogers, *Mark Twain's Burlesque Patterns*, pp. 62-63.

[6] Cf.: "The simple truth is that the American West was neither more nor less interesting than any other place, except in mythology or in the swollen eyes of Westerners, until by interpretation the great American writers — all of whom happened to be Eastern — made it seem so." (Edwin Fussell, *Frontier: American Literature and the American West*, p. 13).

story already considerably more interesting. But reporting that the wagons had been attacked by Indians and that women and children had been wounded or killed, this was truly exciting, this was news, this was "stirring news" (Chapter 42).

What Twain did was of course common practice among quite a few Western newspapermen, and not only among the newspapermen, as becomes apparent from the story of "The Indian Mailrobbery and Massacre of 1856". It throws a peculiar light on the origin of the West's colourful history. There was supposed to have been one survivor of this massacre, but as Twain discovered, this must have been a mistake, "for at different times afterwards on the Pacific Coast I was personally acquainted with a hundred and thirty-three or four people who were wounded during that massacre, and barely escaped with their lives. There was no doubt of the truth of it — I had it from their own lips" (p. 97).

It is therefore a little surprising that Mark Twain should have taken the truth of the news reports in Chapter 49 for granted. It is the chapter that contains extracts from contemporary newspapers, from the *Enterprise* in fact, Clemens's own newspaper, extracts that are meant to show the reader the extraordinary amount of violence the Western mining towns had to put up with. But, as Twain could have known from his own practice as a reporter, and as Jay Gurian has discovered more recently, the "rip-roaring helltowns" that emerge from these extracts were not at all typical of the West. They were, in fact, largely the creation of the editorial policy of certain newspapers, such as, among others, the *Territorial Enterprise* itself, notorious for the commercialized, sensational nature of its reporting as compared to that of, for example, a newspaper like *The Sweetwater Mines*, the pages of which present us with an entirely different picture of a Western mining town, one more in line with the reality of the average hard-working mining community, ran by, as Gurian puts it, "sober, solid middle-class citizens, no more crooked or sinful than your neighbours".[7]

What this uncritical attitude of Twain's towards these reports suggests is the measure of his preoccupation with Western violence, with Western crudity in general. Twain's method of dealing with it, of neutralizing, as it were, its threatening, ugly aspect, is to take refuge again in burlesque, as in Chapter 2, where he pokes fun at his and his companions' weaponry, describing his own weapon, a Smith & Wesson's seven-shooter, as a contraption "which carried a ball like a homeopathic pill, and it took the whole seven to make a dose for an adult", and that of his companion, George Bemis, an "Allen" revolver, as "a cheerful weapon", of which "sometimes all its six barrels would go off at once, and then there was no safe place in all the region, round about, but behind it" (p. 53). Or take Chapter 21, where Mark Twain witnesses for the first time a Western gunfight in Carson City, Nevada, a city in which the Secretary of Nevada Territory and his private secretary, Sam Clemens, were introduced to several citizens, among whom a certain Mr. Harris who was on horseback. Before he had time to get off his horse, however, he excused himself, explaining that he saw a man — a man he was not even acquainted with — who had falsely accused him of robbing a stage coach, an impertinence that could not be suffered with impunity. Riding over to the man, he at once started emptying his six-shooter on him, an act that was immediately reciprocated by the shot-at man. Harris did not survive this shoot-out, although he managed to get home, politely nodding to the Clemenses as he rode by. Twain's laconic description of this display of violence once more turns the

---

[7] Jay Gurian, *Western American Writing: Tradition and Promise*, Deland, Florida, 1975, pp. 31-46. As Gurian notes: "In fact, by examining the real records and newspapers of other Western mining communities, like Sweetwater's, not prey to commercialization in either century, future Western scholars will probably find that neither Virginia City nor *The Territorial Enterprise* was 'archetype' — only apogee. It is time to stop romanticizing our West. The actual history of Western mining settlement in general, has yet to be written. Court and commissioners' records lie untouched in archives while writers dig through earlier glamographs for 'facts'."

incident into burlesque, but from his graphic account of Harris's bleeding wounds one feels Sam Clemens's revulsion lurking.

Another instance of his unspoken abhorrence of this kind of needless and senseless violence is provided by the Honey Lake Smith's episode (Chapter 31) in which the reign of terror by the bully Arkansas is described. Flooding of the Carson River forces the narrator and his fellow companions to be cooped up for eight days in Honey Lake Smith's, a sort of inn on a spot of high ground near the riverbank. "Dirt and vermin", together with cramped quarters, make life uncomfortable during their stay, but what causes the narrator peculiar "discomfort" are a little Swede who is forever singing one monotonous song and a huge ruffian, called Arkansas. The latter, armed with two revolvers and a bowie knife sticking out of his boot, is a man feared by everybody for his aggressively offensive behaviour. The humorous point of the story is of course that it is the landlord's wife who, armed with a pair of scissors, puts a stop to the man's insufferable bullying. Fearlessly, with flashing eyes, she backs him into the middle of the bar-room, where she gives him for all to witness such a terrific tongue-lashing that he is reduced to a state of cowed submission for the rest of his wretched stay.

What is remarkable is that the narrator like the rest of the men is careful not to cause the ruffian any annoyance, putting up with his nasty aggressiveness, and allowing the landlord to be harassed, insulted, and shot at without lifting a finger in his defence. Could it be that Sam Clemens was not a particularly brave man, and that his knack for turning everything into burlesque served as a convenient screen to hide this? One is of course reminded of certain events in his life which might be put forward to substantiate this impression. There is first the mysterious accident that prevented Clemens, an elected lieutenant of the Marion Rangers, from active participation when the Civil War broke out. Not long after he had enlisted, the barn in which he and some of his men were sleeping caught fire. In his attempt at getting out, Clemens fell from the hayloft and sprained his ankle. He had to be put to bed, and when he was up again, he had lost all appetite for going to the war. So when his brother Orion was given the post of Territorial Secretary of Nevada, Twain grabbed the chance to accompany his brother out West as unpaid secretary to the Secretary without a moment's hesitation.

Twain, of course, had every right to refuse to fight in a war in which he could not really believe, but as a proud Southerner who claimed to be descended on his mother's side from the Earls of Durham, his decision not to fight must have made him feel like a deserter, and exposed him to the charge of being a skulker.

A similar situation arose after he had ridiculed the Sanitary fund (the Civil War equivalent of the Red Cross) by suggesting that the funds raised were meant to aid a Miscegenation society somewhere in the East. The joke misfired and he received challenges to duel from four men. But rather than risking his life in a fight over a matter which he could not take seriously, Twain decided to leave Virginia City for California. And again, by what seemed like running away instead of facing the trouble he had caused, he acted against the code of honour of the South, which, as we can read in *Pudd'nhead Wilson*, requires a gentleman to accept a duel when challenged by another gentleman, regardless of all other considerations but those that bear on the idea of honour, for "Honour stood first".[8]

Was it the influence of the democratic, irreverently vulgar West on Clemens's views that made him change his mind about the value of the Southern code of honour? Or had he already begun taking it with a grain of salt before he lighted out for the Territory? Or was it an ingrained aversion to all forms of violence and crudity that made him

---

[8] Mark Twain, *Pudd'nhead Wilson*, 1894; Penguin Book, 1969, rpts 1973, 1975, p. 139.

accept the risk of being accused of cowardly behaviour, ignore the humiliation contained in what looked like so many fainthearted flights on his part? There is, I believe, no reason to assume that Samuel Clemens was less brave or more craven than the next man. What it does reveal is the complexity, if not the profound ambivalence, of his attitude towards the West. Let me clarify this.

That Clemens, in particular the author Mark Twain, greatly liked some things about the West, is beyond doubt. There is first and foremost the sense of freedom which he experienced when he had left behind "the States" and entered the West, perhaps best expressed in the following passage: "There was a freshness and breeziness, too, and an exhilarating sense of emancipation from all sorts of cares and responsibilities, that almost made us feel that the years we had spent in the close, hot city, toiling and slaving, had been wasted and thrown away" (p.54). The tone sounds genuine, even though the second part of the sentence must have sprung from Mark Twain's imagination rather than from the truth of Sam Clemens's biography: up to 1861 he could hardly have seen much toil and slavery in a close, hot city. But the contrast between life in the Far West and life elsewhere in "the States" properly emphasizes the liberating impact the West had on young Sam Clemens's mind.

This evocation of feeling vibrantly alive and happily one with the universe re-occurs a number of times, as in Chapter 5, where he exclaims: "Even at this day it thrills me through and through to think of the life, the gladness and the wild sense of freedom that used to make the blood dance in my veins on those fine overland mornings!" (p. 75); or as in Chapter 17, where he recalls that "it was comfort in those succeeding days to sit up and contemplate the majestic panorama of mountains and valleys spread out below us and eat ham and hard boiled eggs while our spiritual natures revelled alternately in rainbows, thunderstorms, and peerless sunsets. Nothing helps scenery like ham and eggs. Ham and eggs and after these a pipe — an old, rank, delicious pipe — ham and eggs and scenery, a 'down grade', a flying coach, a fragrant pipe and a contented heart — these make happiness. It is what all the ages have struggled for" (p. 161). Even "city-life" in the West was different from everywhere else in the world. Of his stay in Virginia City, Twain writes that it afforded him "the most vigorous enjoyment of life [he] ever experienced" (p. 104).

But on the whole Clemens's vicissitudes in the West constituted one long succession of humiliations and disappointments, however humorously retold by Twain, the writer. It is therefore not unlikely that even his enjoyable experiences in the West acquired their life-enhancing quality largely because of the distance between 1871 when *Roughing It* was finished, and 1861 when the visit to the West took place. As Twain remarks in Chapter 54: "All scenery in California requires *distance* to give it its highest charm" (p. 404). Without this distance one will be struck by its "ruggedness", its poverty of "tintings", its monotonous "sameness", and its lack of variety, all characteristics which in Twain's experience not only applied to the Californian scenery but to the condition of Western life in general.

Even as a classless, freedom-loving region, the West turns out to be a disillusionment. Clemens, arriving in the West, is eager to become a Westerner, to be like these irreverent, egalitarian and independent roughnecks, only to learn that he as an "Easterner" is as much discriminated against as the Westerner is in the East: "and all the time that he is thinking what a sad fate it is to be exiled to that far country, that lonely land, the citizens around him are looking down on him with a blighting compassion, because he is an 'emigrant' instead of that proudest and blessedest creature that exists on earth, a 'FORTY-NINER' " (p. 60).

The particular form social hierarchy had taken in the West is also something that Clemens finds hard to swallow, even though as

Twain, the writer, he finds it easy to ridicule, as when, for example, he describes the abject flattery and obsequious fawning exhibited by the "hairy and half-civilized" station-keepers and hostlers — the lowest in the hierarchy of overland stage-coaching — when they receive the stage-driver, the highest in the hierarchy, "a hero — a great and shining dignitary, the world's favorite son, the envy of the people, the observed of nations" (p. 67). So assured is he of his exalted position that he can afford to show his contempt for the rest of the world, including his passengers, for whom he "had but little less contempt (...) than he had for his hostlers". Also near the top of the scale was the conductor of the coach, but although he was treated by the hostlers and station-keepers "with the best of what was their idea of civility", the driver was "the only being they bowed down to and worshipped" (p. 68).

But then, of course, a driver was usually worth his money, and even though one might find his conduct insufferable, one could at least be thankful for his skill, which had to be considerable. And this was more than could be said of that other well-known Western character, equally highly placed on the social ladder, the man who stood behind a bar, wore a cluster-diamond pin, and sold whiskey, "the cheapest and easiest way to become an influential man and to be looked up by the community at large", as Twain comments in Chapter 48 (p. 346). Yes, to a saloon-keeper was to be looked up to, and "to be a saloon-keeper and kill a man was to be illustrious" (p. 347), for only if you had killed a man, could one be of any consequence, and only if you had killed many men, kept, so to say, your own "private graveyard", could one be a man of great consequence. Since Clemens was unable to kill a man, "nor ever felt a desire to do so" (p. 303), his chances of becoming a real Westerner were slim; those of ever attaining social eminence, non-existent.

Twain may still be able to poke fun at Clemens's sociological observations, but when he has to explain how the jury system works in the Far West, the waves of his moral indignation rise so rapidly that they soon threaten to completely drown the humorist. This jury system, he sternly remarks, "puts a ban upon intelligence and honesty, and a premium upon ignorance, stupidity and perjury" (p. 349). It creates the circumstances in which it becomes almost impossible to punish the guilty and protect the innocent from being cheated, and Samuel Clemens, the tenderfoot, is cheated most of the times. As when, for example, he buys a horse, since every genuine Westerner rides a horse. But Clemens soon discovers that, as "an elderly-looking comforter" puts it, he has been "taken in". The horse happens to be "a genuine Mexican plug", which means that it is only fit for bucking, not for riding, and Twain, the writer, can do little else than turn the outcome of his younger self's gullibility into some priceless farce again.

To be a genuine Westerner also means to become wealthy, and together with his companion — a certain Johnny K — , Clemens decides to get rich by running "a timber ranch" on the shores of Lake Tahoe. The enterprise ends in complete failure, the main reason being that neither young Clemens nor Johnny K — are actually prepared to put in some really hard work; besides, they lack the basic skills to give it a promising start. They prefer devoting their time to admiring the beautiful environment, to smoking, sleeping, rowing, reading, playing cards, and eating the provisions they get from a brigade camp, until, owing to some stupidity no outdoorsman would ever make, their pine forest and practically everything they own goes up in flames. Neither young Clemens, nor Johnny K — , seem to be well-equipped to make it "out West".

It is also this episode that sheds a peculiar light on Twain's attitude towards nature, which is more that of a twentieth-century vacationer in search of physical recreation than that of a romantic worshipper of nature in search of spiritual renewal. "Three months of camplife on lake Tahoe," Twain claims, "would restore an Egyptian mummy to his prestine vigor and give him an appetite like an alligator." Not "the oldest and driest mummies, of course, but the fresher ones" (p. 188).

Deserts, in particular alkali deserts, also lack any significance, practical or spiritual, except for one undeniable thing and that is that after having traversed one in daylight for ten hours they become "a thirsty, sweltering, longing, hateful reality" (p. 164). Of course, young Clemens did not primarily go West in search of spirituality, but what he was totally unprepared for was the complete lack of it, once he had entered the region. On the great plains a woman passenger joins the travellers for about fifty miles, and as she does not say anything and only seems intent on killing mosquitoes, in which she is quite expert, Clemens's curiosity about the woman's Sphynx-like behaviour is aroused. He strikes up a conversation with her, the mosquitoes seeming as good an excuse as any, but soon wished he had never opened his mouth, for after he had, "the Sphynx was a Sphynx no more": "The fountain of her great deep were broken up, and she rained the nine parts of speech forty days and forty nights, metaphorically speaking, and buried us under a desolating deluge of trivial gossip that left not a crag or pinnacle of rejoinder projecting above the tossing waste of dislocated grammar and decomposed pronunciation!" (p. 56). She never stopped till the moment she left the stage coach, having shown herself "a pretty sociable heifer" indeed.

Despite its reputation of having the most colourful history of the United States, the Far West's fund of great stories proves extremely limited, as Clemens learns to his dismay, a state of mind skilfully exploited again by Twain. The fund consists, in fact, of only one story, the story of how Horace Greeley fared when he had to travel from Carson City to Placerville, and incautiously urged the driver, Hank Monk, to ride as fast as he could. Naturally Monk obliged, starting off at such an awful pace that Greeley soon wished he had never uttered a word: when the coach reached Placerville he was more dead than alive. It is the story to which Clemens is regaled whenever a newcomer boards their stage coach, drivers, conductors, chance passengers, Chinamen, vagrant Indians. It is this anecdote that Twain heard 481 or 482 times in a period of six years during which he crossed and recrossed the Sierras between Nevada and California thirteen times, and it had turned his "once stalwart and magnificent manhood" into a "melancholy wreck" (p. 174).

It is not the only time in *Roughing It* that Mr. Greeley causes havoc in an "innocent" 's life. There is also the story in Chapter 70 of the retired preacher Erickson who had once exchanged letters with Horace Greeley, in which he had asked his advice about a curious matter brought to his attention by an anxious mother from Kansas. Her son, as she had told Erickson, was wasting away because he could not realize his one overriding ambition in life, which was to make of a turnip a climbing vine. Perhaps Greeley knew a solution. After all, it was he who had urged young men to go West and accomplish the impossible. In reply to Erickson's request for advice, Greeley had sent a short note, in such an illegible hand, however, that each attempt to make sense of its contents resulted in a different reading, all equally puzzling, except for the unmistakable sexual innuendos which, to the minister's indignation, seemed to become increasingly scurrilous as his readings progressed. At his wits' end he finally wrote Greeley another letter, asking him, though not before pointing out first that there was nothing improper in his relationship with the Kansas mother, whether he would clarify his cryptic note. This the famous man did, and from this rewrite the preacher learned that the Kansas woman's son should stop his experiments at once, since it was impossible to make vines out of turnips.

Even in this version, though, there remains enough for the minister to be puzzled by. For if turnips cannot be made into vines, how, then, is it possible that potatoes can be, and what does it mean that "turnips remain passive", and how is it that "diet, bathing, etc., etc., followed uniformly, will wean him [the son] from his folly"? And what does "so fear not" at the end of the note really mean? What is it that Erickson should not fear? The loss of his sanity perhaps? But he lost it, as the planters told Twain. What the story exemplifies is that rather than serving communication, language is employed to serve entirely different purposes, purposes lacking the rationality of which language is thought to be the chief shaping force. What apart from the piece of sensible advice to the Kansas mother, Greeley's note also contains is something madly irrational, something profoundly anarchic felt to be working behind his advocacy of exploring the West. Of course, the son should stop trying to change turnips into vines, but not because it is madness, but because there are plenty of other madnesses to pursue, promising more immediate results. Buying and selling stock, for example, from real or imaginary claims, located in one's neighbour's backyard, or even in cellars in the very heart of Virginia City. Without having to work the mines, everybody grows rich, until the fraud is exposed and everybody is poor again.

Still, it was in mining that the high promises of the West could occasionally be fulfilled, as it nearly did for Clemens himself, when he and his partner Higbie struck "a blind lead" worth millions of dollars. But becoming rich without having to work for it proves again to be something impossible to achieve for people like Clemens. Owing to a number of odd coincidences he, Higbie and a third partner fail to comply with the mining laws, and they thus lose their claim on the blind lead. The third partner, the foreman Allen, however, refuses to be daunted by some technicality of the law. With a revolver in his hand he insists on his name being added to the new list of claimants, threatening to "thin out" the members of the new ownership if they refused to comply. Allen, fearing litigation, then quickly sold his share for ninety thousand dollars in gold.

Allen is described by Twain as "a manly, splendid, determined fellow, and known to be as good as his word" (p. 298). Clemens, too, might not have lost everything if he, like Allen, had been able to exercise — Western-style — a little more force and a little more determination and daring. This story of Samuel Clemens and his friend Higbie being millionaires for ten days may be true or may not be true, but even if it is not true, it tells us once again those things about Clemens that Twain's humour and burlesque carefully hide from us: his obsessive abhorrence of violence and his tendency to opt for the easy way out, as also exemplified by his passive behaviour in the Honey Lake Smith's episode, his decision not to fight in the Civil War, his departure from Virginia City to California so as to evade a couple of hot-headed dualists. It is therefore no accident that the novel should end with a description of a hold-up, of which this time the author himself, Mark Twain, is the principal victim. In tune with the book's humorous character the hold-up turns out to be a joke, a practical joke played upon the author by his friends. Twain's description of Clemens's reaction to this hold-up, however, confirms again the book's underlying obsession with violence and the narrator's persistent unwillingness to be involved. To Clemens the situation was "most uncomfortably genuine", and what he feared in particular were the guns levelled at him; not, as he later explains, because he expected the putative highwaymen to actually use them but because they, the guns, might go off accidentally. So when, after he is robbed of all his valuables, he is told to keep his hands up for at least ten minutes, he is most anxious not to take them down too early, even if he is made to look like a fool, and nearly freezes. It is again the dangerous unpredictability of life in the West that seemed to upset Clemens most of all. The writer Mark Twain was no doubt powerfully drawn to the wild, dangerous, and riotously farcical aspects of the Far West, and in his style he absorbed its virile character, its forceful directness, its buoyant exuberance in idiom and syntax that pushes the narrative irrepressibly onwards. But as Clemens, the husband of genteel Olivia Langdon, without whose censorship no word of his appeared in print, he was in favour of an orderly, civilized society of citizens who knew that there was a moral difference between a man upholding the law and a man breaking the law. To him the story of the West must have resembled the story of Jim Blaine and his Grandfather's Ram (Chapter 53), also a story that never got told.

What Jim Blaine's business with his grandfather's ram was is never revealed, although plenty of information is imparted to the listener. But it is information totally incongruous with what he is led to expect, just as the emigrant arriving in the West is overwhelmed with information which also appears to be totally incongruous with his expectations. In Jim Blaine's story we hear about a certain Miss Wagner, whose glass eye always popped out, and who was "considerable on the borrow", of items such as Miss Higgins's wooden leg, "to stump around", or the wig of Miss Jacops, to cover her head with — "bald as a jug" — ; Miss Jacops who was the wife of the coffin-peddler, "a ratty old buzzard", who blamed old Robbins for letting him wait two years before he died, and even then he "bursted off" the coffin lid, just to tell Jacops that he did not like his coffins, after which he really died. Robbins's wayward behaviour brings us then to the Hogadorns, a "mighty fine family" from Wellsville, into which family a missionary married, who, however, was "et" by the savages. But "prov'dence don't fire no blank catridges": every savage that partook of the missionary turned out to be a convert in the end. And there's Uncle Lem's death to prove that accidents do not happen: he was there to break the fall of an Irishman who then survived, which he would not have, if he had fallen on Uncle Lem's dog, because the dog would have seen the Irishman coming and have run away. Naturally, because dogs "can't be depended on to carry out a special providence", not even such a splendid dog as Uncle Lem's, which once belonged to Parson Hagar, whose mother was a Watson, and whose sister married a Wheeler, who "got nipped by the machinery in a carpet factory", after which his widow bought the fourteen yards of carpet "that had his remains wove in". Since the church in which the funeral service was held was "middling small", they had "to let one end of the coffin stick out of the window". Burying was impossible, so they planted one end, and let him stand up. They even nailed a sign on, but what it said would never be revealed, as at this particular moment Jim Blaine, uncompromisingly drunk by now, used to fall asleep, never having uttered a word about the story that had lured Clemens to the man's cabin.

Jim Blaine's narrative consists of signifiers that have floated free from their signifieds, and in this it is emblematic of the story of the Far West, which, in Clemens's experience, also unfolded itself with a total disregard for the logic, rationality, order, and expectations continuous with the facts of life as accepted by ordinary, sensible human beings. It is therefore no accident that the chapter immediately following Jim Blaine's meandering, digressing flow of unrelated reminiscences should be one that is exclusively devoted to extolling the virtues of those "Westerners" that did everything to keep up the social values characteristic of civilized living — the Chinese, of whom there were about a thousand in Virginia. They could all read, write and cypher, were orderly, industrious, sane, peaceable and unaggressive, and wasted nothing. They revered their dead and were "a kindly disposed, well-meaning race", and Twain ends this chapter on the following uncommonly harsh note: claiming that no Californian *gentleman or lady* ever abuses or oppresses a Chinaman, he then adds, "only the scum of the population do it — they and their children; they, and naturally and consistently, the policemen and politicians, likewise, for these are the dust-licking pimps and slaves of the scum, there as well as elsewhere in America" (p. 397).

Although Clemens stayed longer in the West than he thought he would — nearly seven years instead of the three months he originally had planned — , he never returned after he had left, except once when he had to be there on a business trip. What this seems to indicate is that he never really looked upon the West as "home", just as he had never considered the region where he was born and raised, the South, as his home, and the reason must in both cases have been the same. As he once wrote to a Missouri friend in 1876: "I think I comprehend their position there — perfect freedom to vote just as you choose, provided you choose to vote as *other people* think, social ostracism otherwise. (...) Fortunately a good deal of experience of men enabled me to choose my residence wisely. I live in the freest corner of the country."[9] In other words, in New England, in Hartford, where Twain lived most of his writing life. There was freedom in the West, just as there was freedom in the South, but only if you belonged to those in power, and were willing to conform to prevailing ethics, which implied putting up with too many shams, too many pretentious falsities, too much crudity and too much senseless violence. Unlike Thoreau who defined the West as wild, believing that in wildness was the preservation of the world,[10] Twain obviously thought that the world had a greater chance of being preserved in the East, in genteel Hartford, in the New England of Hawthorne and Henry James, whom he would not read though, because they bored him with "their niggling analysis". It is a curious paradox, but one commensurate with the paradox that although Twain's finest work was inspired by the South of his boyhood and its stylistic expression shaped by the West of his young manhood, he could not really live in either region.

---

[9] As quoted by Marcus Cunliffe in *The Literature of the United States*, A Pelican Book, 1954, p. 166.

[10] See chapter 4.

PART TWO

Chapter 7

THE LITERARY WESTERN:

Owen Wister, *The Virginian*

Walter van Tilburg Clark, *The Ox-bow Incident*

Thomas Berger, *Little Big Man*

E. L. Doctorow, *Welcome to Hard Times*

1

Western fiction "comes closer than the fiction of any other region to providing an index to America", C. L. Sonnichsen claims in his entertaining and genial study of popular Westerns, *From Hopalong to Hud* (1978)[1]. Of course, the claim is not original. It was, in fact, already made as long as one and a half centuries ago. But James Fenimore Cooper would probably never have made it in public, let alone expressed it with the quiet confidence that speaks from Sonnichsen's dictum. Yet for Sonnichsen to make it with any confidence at all would have been impossible but for Cooper's very achievement: the first and only authentic American hero is a frontiersman, a Westerner, and he is Cooper's creation.

Cooper not only created the avatar of the American hero, he

---

[1] C. L. Sonnichsen, *From Hopalong to Hud: Thoughts on Western Fiction*, College Station, Tex., 1978, p. 4. All further page references are to this edition.

also furnished the basic formulas from which all Western fiction was to develop and without which the Western ceases to be a Western, whether of the popular paperback or of the serious hardback variety.

These formulas have never basically changed since Cooper introduced them. The stock plot has been and still is the story of lawlessness threatening to upset life in a primitive frontier community. Set against a Western landscape as romantic backdrop it involves plenty of action, gunplay, and a love story (sentimental in the commercial Western). The stock characters, following a sharp division between heroes and villains, have been and still are the staples of the popular Western, just as the moral issues of frontier violence have been and still are distinctive features of the serious hardback.

The idea that the West has been of singular importance in shaping American history and the American identity, an idea taken more or less for granted by writers of Western fiction, received scholarly recognition in 1893. In this year, as we know, Frederick Jackson Turner expounded his famous frontier hypothesis, which, briefly stated, claims that what accounts more than anything else for the uniqueness of American history was the experience of the frontier West, and that what contributed more than anything else to the creation of the American identity are the qualities shaped and developed by precisely this experience, qualities such as competitiveness, strength, practicality, inventiveness, materialism, coarseness, restlessness, democratic sense, and above all, rugged individualism.

Although modern historians are inclined to detect more poetical truth than historical fact in Turner's thesis, its impact on how in general Americans look upon their past and consequently upon themselves has been tremendous. What it confirms again is that it is not so much historical truth as the power of myth which shapes people's minds and actions. Yet, surprisingly, it was not until half a century later before this insight was picked up again and given a fresh application in the search for the real significance of the Western novel as the fictional mirror of the American frontier experience. In 1950 Henry Nash Smith published his *Virgin Land: The American West as Symbol and Myth*,[2] a book destined to become a classic in the field of literary studies devoted to Western writing, and largely responsible for its amazing expansion since then.

Smith's study relies for its conclusions to a great extent on the assumption that popular fiction — the nineteenth-century Beadle or dime novel in his case — can reveal more about the basic attitudes of a particular time than the serious novel. What Smith demonstrated was that the Western as popular art could be studied seriously as social history. It was no longer necessary to regard it as mere entertainment. It was revelatory, about the time in which it was written, about the readers who read it. And so it is not surprising that the 1960s and 1970s — the revolutionary decades in which the most vocal part of America seemed to denounce everything the country was thought to stand for, in the past as well as in the present — witnessed an extraordinary surge in academic studies on Western popular fiction, resulting in at least a dozen works on writers of commercial Westerns.[3]

There is no denying that this explosion of fashionable academic criticism has made the Western all but collapse under the weight of new and exotic interpretations. The Western was discovered as the

---

[2] See note 2, Introduction.

[3] To mention only a few beside Sonnichsen: Edwin Fussell, *Frontier: American Literature and the American West*, Princeton, N.J., 1965; James K. Folsom, *The American Western Novel*, New Haven, Conn., 1966; John G. Cawelti, *The Six-Gun Mystique*, Bowling Green, Ohio, 1971; *Adventure, Mystery, and Romance*, Chicago, 1976; Jay Gurian, *Western American Writing: Tradition and Promise*, Deland, Fla., 1975; Richard W. Etulain, ed. *American Literary West*, Manhattan Kansas, 1980; John R. Milton, *The Novel of the American West*, Lincoln and London, 1980.
Unpublished dissertations have been written by Richard W. Etulain on Ernest Haycox, University of Oregon, 1966, and by Neal E. Lambert on Owen Wister, University of Utah, 1966.

160

American Morality Play,[4] as an existential document in which man confronted the landscape of the human soul,[5] as the underworld of the reader's sexual drives, a ticklish dream, the six-shooter turned phallic symbol.[6] Also the Western hero himself rapidly lost his original state of healthy, outdoor robustness. To some he became Christ in cowboy boots, "wielding the thunderbolts of the Almighty",[7] to others "a commercial extension of the drive for private property",[8] or the eternal son, filled with oedipal guilt, in hatred of the father, a villain, who kept the son-hero from his beloved mother.[9]

Yet this solemn quest for the true significance of the Western has not exclusively resulted in the extravaganzas of zealous scholars more gifted with fertile imaginations than discriminatory powers. For one thing, remarkable parallels have been discovered between the development of the nineteenth-century and twentieth-century Western. Just as Cooper can be called the father of the nineteenth-century American hero as hunter, scout, trapper and mountainman, so Owen Wister sired in *The Virginian* (1902) his twentieth-century successor, the cowboy. But whereas it was the commercial offshoot of Cooper's achievement — the Beadle dime novel — which towards the end of the nineteenth century bogged down the Western in an excess of violence, blood lust and sensational horrors, depriving it of all credibility, it was

---

[4] *Time*, March 20, 1959.

[5] James K. Folsom, *The American Western Novel*, p. 32.

[6] John G. Cawelti, *The Six-Gun Mystique*, pp. 81-85.

[7] C. L. Sonnichsen's description of the gunman-hero as presented by Stuart N. Lake in the latter's idealized biography *Wyatt Earp: Frontier Marshall* (1931); *From Hopalong to Hud*, pp. 23-24.

[8] Jay Gurian, *Western American Writing*, p. 62. All further page references are to this edition (see note 3).

[9] Warren J. Barker, "The Stereotyped Western Story, Its Latent Meaning and Psycho-economic Function", *Psychoanalytic Quarterly*, 1955, as quoted by John R. Milton in *The Novel of the American West*, p. 7.

the Wister derivative with literary pretensions which achieved the same result for the Western of the 1970s. Starting with Larry McMurtry (*Horseman, Pass By* 1960), writers like Robert Kreps (*The Hour of the Gun*, 1967), John Benteen (*Apache Raiders*, 1970), George Gilman (*Edge: The Loner*, 1971) and Forrest Carter (*The Vengeance Trail of Josey Wales*, 1971) seemed determined to turn the frontier West into an equivalent of the Holocaust: they not only managed to deromanticize the frontier folk heroes, but also to surpass everything the East had been able to produce in the field of eye-gouging atrocities and kinky sex.

Like Cooper's work, Wister's *The Virginian* contained the hilltops from which both the popular and the serious Western could take flight. Although Wister regarded himself as a serious writer (he counted among his friends not only Theodore Roosevelt and Henry James but also Franz Liszt), the conception of the romantic West stems in large part from him. The cowboy, as he declared in his Introduction to *The Virginian*, is the last romantic figure upon our soil, and the facts seemed to prove him right. In the decades about which he wrote, the period of 1865-1900, a number of historical events occurred which had one thing in common: they were all of epic dimensions. The completion of the first transcontinental railroad, the enormous expansion of the cattle trade by the mid-1880s, the bloody range wars and the last violent clashes with the Plains Indians revivified the Cooperian vision of the West as the land of legend in which Leatherstocking's role as a latter-day Galahad had been taken over by a new hero, the cowboy.

Wister's romantic treatment of the West was taken up and exploited by such writers of popular Westerns as Zane Grey, Eugene Loveman Rhodes, Max Brand, Clarence E. Mulford and Luke Short, while after World War II writers like Louis L'Amour and Henry Wilson Allen continued to produce this type of "clean" Western, the Western which refused to indulge in the cult of filthy language, sexual horrors

162

and gritty realism so maniacally pursued in the 1970s by Robert Kreps *et al*; the Western, in short, as adventure story, the truth of which is "the truth of action and the possibility of a man rising above himself and acting heroically".[10]

Yet *The Virginian* was meant to be more than merely the prototype of the Zane Grey type of Western. Wister's aims were set higher. Like Cooper he wanted to bring together "nature" and "civilization", which in his case took the form of an attempt to reconcile the physical and moral strength of the West with the socio-cultural sophistication of the East. By creating a man who combined the best elements from both regions, Wister intended him to become the exemplary representative of the future of the country. And so we see that Wister's Virginian not only possesses all the characteristics of the mythic Western hero — he is a superb horseman, a deadly shot, a resourceful and dependable leader of men, fearless and chivalric — but that he is also quite willing to improve his diction and writing, read Shakespeare, Walter Scott and Robert Browning (Jane Austen he does not like), learn about Eastern values, and all this with a view to improve his chances of marrying his Eastern schoolmarm, Molly Wood. On top of this he proves to have sufficient business acumen to become a very wealthy man.

What becomes clear from Wister's conception of his main character is that the vision underlying his work is positive and optimistic. It is basically this vision which continues to inform the work of writers such as Wayne Overholser, Ernest Haycox, Wallace Stegner and Jack Schaefer, who established the tradition of serious Western writing, started by Wister, with what critics have come to define as the "adult" Western. Insisting on historical and psychological accuracy in their depiction of the Old West, these authors retain the time-

---

[10] William O. Turner, in a speech to the Western Writers of America *Roundup* for April, 1968, quoted by Sonnichsen (*From Hopalong to Hud*, p. 39).

honoured story of the struggle for survival in primitive frontier settlements. A representative example is no doubt Jack Schaefer's *Shane* (1960), a novel that presents us with the stock situation of a pioneer family fighting for survival against psychotic gunslingers hired by landgrabbing cattlemen. The heroes and villains are still heroes and villains, but they are no longer simple, simple in the moral sense, as the Virginian and his counterpart Trampas still were. Lawlessness (Nature) and order (Civilization) are no longer taken as polar absolutes but as contradictory impulses inherent in human nature. One may still try to reconcile them but it has ceased to be an easy matter, and so has the accompanying frontier violence, glorified in the old popular Western, but in *Shane* acknowledged for what it is and probably always has been: ugly, even when employed in the name of advancing civilization.

Yet, although the heroics in these "adult" Westerns are considerably toned down, the problems of lawlessness and frontier violence approached more subtly, the prosaics of hardship, loneliness and the back-breaking labour of frontier life accorded their appropriate place, in the last analysis they continue to follow the familiar pattern of the traditional Western story in that the white hats always win, and the black hats always perish. It is this situation which has made some critics of Western fiction wonder whether Western writing can ever produce "great" novels, whether in the West, as Jay Gurian put it, "the great questions" can be asked. Gurian himself believes they can, and that some writers have started to ask them, although he is not very optimistic about the result so far. He also makes an attempt to explain why it took so long before the essential human conflicts of good and evil, vision and blindness, love and lust could be portrayed in Western fiction; why, despite the drama of human triumph and failure which the Western scene seemed to offer so abundantly, so few kinds of significant human experience were recreated by Western art. As one possible explanation he mentions the overwhelming geography of the area which reduces "the mind from metaphysical to merely physical capability",[11] a condition unfavourable to art or poetry, he thinks. One may put a question mark here. If Melville could forge art from the vast oceans, why should the vast spaces of the West have daunted the Western artist? Gurian's second explanation sounds little more convincing. The vernacular roots of Western art were inadequate in conveying an important view of experience, he believes. Besides, it fostered anti-intellectualism, preventing the artist from having "ideas". Again one wonders. Didn't Mark Twain's work have vernacular roots, and did it prevent him from having ideas? Gurian's third explanation seems to make more sense. The myth of the West was mainly the creation of the East, he claims; it was developed to provide the industrial, urbanized East with romantic escapist satisfactions, and the writers of Westerns — originally all Easterners — knew how to oblige their audience. Besides, the material which provided the excitement to be lived vicariously by an Eastern audience was, so to speak, ready to hand: cowboys, U.S. marshalls, sheriffs, Indians, settlers, soldiers, scouts, hunters, ranchers, military campaigns, Indian wars, adventures on the cattle trails, in the mining towns, in the mountains, on the scorched plains, the list can easily be extended. The formula story wrote itself, as it were; moreover, it assured easy success and the fast buck, putting a severe strain on any writer of Westerns to go into the trouble of exerting the will and the imagination to transform his material into something new.

This, no doubt, is true for some, for many, but it is hard to believe that it was true for all the writers of Western fiction. Zane Grey, for example, actually the first writer of the formula Western as derived from Wister's *The Virginian*, became a rich man, but only after success had eluded him for many years, lean years in which he wrote

---

[11] Jay Gurian, *Western American Writing*, Chapter 4, pp. 60-65.

his early works — his best according to his critics. From this period, however, also dates his remark that he never cared in the least for the material side of his success (which started after the publication of his *Riders of the Purple Sage*, 1912), and that money meant nothing to him.[12]

One suspects that the reasons why the great questions were never asked in Westerns must be looked for elsewhere. There is of course nothing original in the notion that the nature of the questions asked by the artist are primarily determined by the time and place in which he lives and writes. Unless he belongs to that rare breed of artists who are far ahead of their contemporaries (Emily Dickinson and Herman Melville come inevitably to mind), it is the prevailing vision of the day that to a large extent informs the artist's work. Up to roughly the outbreak of World War II the prevailing view of the West remained pretty much unchanged. Basically it was Owen Wister's as embodied in his *The Virginian*, which dates from 1902.[13] This vision was not by definition a simple one, nor were the questions it posed to the writers trying to give it form, by definition simple. But the answers happened to be simple, reductive in fact, and a closer look at Wister's novel may reveal why.

In Wister's work the West remains what it had been in the nineteenth century, a place of affirmation, where life pulsed with a stronger beat than in the East, where the individual still counted, where he could live away from the artificialities of a highly organized society, and where the old, trusted American values of enterprise, self-reliance, pride in hard work, freedom and the courage to stand up for what one believed in were still upheld. In *The Virginian* the values represented by

[12] Gary Topping, "The Rise of the Western", *The American Literary West*, ed. Richard W. Etulain, p. 31. Quoted by Topping from an unpublished manuscript in the possession of Zane Grey.

[13] Owen Wister, *The Virginian*, 1902; rpt 1979, Signet Classic. All page references are to this edition.

the Westerner (the Virginian) are constantly tested against those embodied by Molly Wood, the Eastern schoolmarm, and found superior.

The Virginian is no doubt romanticized by Wister, but he is not a saint. He has killed men and has known women whose acquaintance Molly Wood and her Eastern family would have found degrading. But the Virginian is not ashamed of his past; he has always upheld the Code of the West: he has never stolen a steer or a horse, never cheated at cards, never accepted an insult without demanding satisfaction, been proud of doing a good job as a ranchhand, and retained despite the low and rough company he has kept a purity of feeling and sense of personal worth which puts him in a position to believe without a trace of hesitation that there is no need for Molly to feel ashamed of having him as a serious suitor. However, the Eastern schoolmarm herself is not so sure of this. Although she is immensely attracted to his splendid physique and perfect manners, his lowly station in life, his lack of polish in speech and diction, of education in general, prove unsurmountable obstacles in allowing her to feel more than friendship. But the Virginian remains confident. Wister has endowed him with a first-rate intelligence: he not only outshoots his opponents, he also easily outwits them. Besides he is quite willing to remedy his lack of schooling, preferably with Molly's aid. Fearing she will give in to her growing love of the Virginian, she decides to return to the East, but fortunately a badly wounded Virginian requires her care and attention, and nothing can now stop the consummation of the romance. But the real test is still to come. Molly may have reconciled herself to the fact that her hero has killed in the past, she cannot accept his killings in the present (the Virginian is forced to hang two rustlers). Torn by conflicting feelings, Molly fights her lonely battle between her Eastern upbringing which tells her that those who take the law into their own hands are guilty of murder, and her love for her cowpuncher. It takes Judge

Henry, the Virginian's employer, an eloquent chapter to convince her that what the Virginian did was his bounden duty as a law-abiding citizen. To understand why the questions raised in *The Virginian* are complex but the answers simplified, it is necessary to follow the Judge's arguments in some detail.

What the authorial voice, Judge Henry and Molly Wood are agreed upon is that "it is not safe to say of any man, 'He did evil that good might come'". Lynching a man without giving him a fair trial is an evil thing, but the question is whether it is always evil. Molly thinks it is, the Judge thinks it is not, believing that it depends upon the circumstances, and in Wyoming the circumstances are bad. For what has happened? The law, as the Judge explains, has been letting cattle-thieves go on for two years, that is to say, the courts, the juries have become corrupt; they are "not dealing the law". The only way to check theft and murder is for the ordinary citizens to take back what they once gave the courts: justice. So the Virginian, the Judge argues, did not *defy* the law but *assert* it. What the Virginian did was "the fundamental assertion of self-governing men, upon whom our whole social fabric is based" (p. 274).

The argument seems conclusive. At any rate Molly can't think of anything to refute it, but it does not put her thoughts to rest. And one can see why. The condition in which every man is free to be judge and executor at the same time is of course an extremely precarious one. It endangers precisely what any judiciary system is expected to guarantee: protection against arbitrariness. However honourable the motives that force people to take the law into their own hands may seem, what they do is resorting to legal anarchy, and this may prove worse than corrupt legality. Wister ignores this important aspect of the problem he deals with and so deprives Western fiction of a chance to pose one of the "great questions".

In this connection it is fascinating to note that the information that Wyoming is a thoroughly corrupt state reaches the unsuspecting reader not until the end of the novel and in a curiously casual, unemphatic way. One almost feels the reluctance on Wister's part to mention it at all. This becomes less odd of course when it is realized that the idea of a corrupt West is entirely inimical to the traditional view of the West. Hence the off-handed way in which it is introduced; hence Wister's inability to make it the focal point of his treatment of the experience of the West. This, as we shall see, could only be done half a century later when the vision of the West had radically changed. As yet, the only form of moral complexity available to Wister has its origin in the accidental: one of the rustlers the Virginian is to hang happens to be an old friend of his. True, this happenstance gives Wister's hero a rough time, and for a short while he is even unhinged by the haunting idea that the trail that mysteriously appears before him and his companion when they travel home through the mountains, might belong to the ghosts of the two hanged men. But when they discover the dead body of Shorty, the ranchhand who has fallen under the evil spell of Trampas and become his accomplice, the Virginian quickly regains his normal imperturbable self. Once he knows that the trail is anything but a ghost trail and that Trampas has killed the likable Shorty in order to improve his own chances of escape, his strange, oppressive mood of moral disarray evaporates completely, and we hear no more of it.

The final confrontation between the Virginian and Trampas — the classic walkdown of all future Westerns — offered Wister a last opportunity to pose one of the "great questions", but again he refused (was unable) to seize it. The very day before the Virginian's wedding Trampas not only accuses him in public of theft and murder but also challenges him to fight it out or else leave town before sunset. Molly, relieved and overjoyed that her hero is still alive after this first confrontation, expects and demands that they leave town at once in order to avoid another "murder", as she calls it, only to hear from her lover that this will be impossible. Leaving before sunset would not only make him lose his self-respect but the respect of his friends and enemies alike, and as the authorial voice agrees: "It had come to that point where there was no way out, save only the ancient, eternal way between man and man", adding, "It is only the great mediocrity that goes to law in these personal matters" (p. 291). However, Molly, white and shaken, will not see it this way. The Virginian does not have to prove his courage — everybody knows that he is a brave man. In addition, hanging the two rustlers may have been a public duty, but this killing is shedding blood in cold blood, and she won't stand for it, so either he forgets about the "ancient, eternal way" or the wedding is off.

Once more the Virginian goes through the convulsions of moral agony: must he sacrifice his manhood on the altar of love? Must he betray the Code of the West and lose his standing among the men of the West in order to win a bride from the East? With lovely Molly in his arms he has a weak moment, but no one need doubt the outcome. Miserable but unable to do his lady's bidding, he leaves, renouncing marital bliss for harsh, manly duty, and after a short, dreadful while, Molly, left behind in her room, hears the three shots: one fired by Trampas, missing the Virginian, two fired by the Virginian, killing Trampas. When he appears before her door again to announce that he has killed Trampas, Molly, thanking God for that, throws herself into his arms, no longer, so it appears, bothered by her New England conscience.

All trials overcome, there is nothing that stands in the way of a bright future with many children and well-earned riches, and quite in accordance with the affirmative sense of life underlying the traditional vision of the West, that's how it should be and, who knows, has been to many. It is, in fact, this affirmation of life which requires the moral problems facing the Virginian and Molly to be solved in a positive sense, and what is more positive than love, which conquers all, deprivation, class, even principle.

However, for the moral problems that beset Wister's hero and heroine to become Gurian's great questions they should have resulted from the political, social and moral tensions that existed in the historical situation of the West. These tensions, to be sure, are touched upon by Wister, but, as I have pointed out, carefully kept in the background. Wister, an Easterner, came to live in the West for reasons of health (physical as well as mental), and since he found what he had come for, it is scarcely surprising that the West should have found in him a firm advocate. And so the crucial questions of how and why not only the Virginian's best friend but a whole state could turn corrupt, driving out the honest people, is only mentioned and never made the focus of his treatment of the West; and so the complexity of the moral problems Wister has his two main characters face is reduced to the chivalric idea of courage, and solved by the conventional notion of love, the love that conquers all.

2

For any author of Westerns to pose and work out the moral issues introduced by Wister where it really hurts, we have to wait till the publication of Walter van Tilburg Clark's *The Ox-bow Incident* (1940).[14] Clark, in fact, is one of the first writers of "adult" Westerns in whose work the impact of a changed view of the experience of the West is noticeable, and who seem to justify Gurian's belief that the great questions have started to be asked in Western fiction.

Clark begins by invoking all the stereotypes of the West, and then proceeds to treating them as a "serious" artist would treat them: he individualizes his characters by showing how and why each of them acts

---

[14] Walter van Tilburg Clark, *The Ox-bow Incident*, 1940; rpt Vintage Books. All page references are to this edition.

in and reacts to the dramatic situations he presents.

Two cowpunchers, Art Croft and Gil, ride into town after a number of months' hard work on the range, heading straight for the saloon, owned by Canby, a hard-eyed Westerner. Here we meet most of the other familiar Western types: ranchers, foremen, cowpunchers, stagecoach-drivers, the minister, the Judge, the deputy sheriff, the storeowner. We witness the classic pokergame followed by the equally classic fistfight. Even the historical situation in Bridger's Wells is familiar, reminiscent of that in *The Virginian*. Rustlers are active in the area, and owing to the leniency and laxity of the law as upheld by Judge Tyler, a politician rather than a lawman and full of blather and rhetoric, cattle stealing continues with increasing boldness and insolence. So when news reaches Canby's saloon that a ranchhand has been killed on the range, presumably by rustlers, the incensed men at once decide to form a posse, even if the sheriff is not in town to deputize them officially. The problem dealt with in *The Ox-bow Incident* is therefore basically the same as the one introduced in *The Virginian*: if the official upholders of the law prove to be ineffective or corrupt, is one justified to take the law into one's own hands? In *The Virginian*, as we have seen, Wister simplified the matter by conveniently overlooking the injustice implicit in Judge Henry's solution. In *The Ox-bow Incident* Van Tilburg Clark cuts right to the heart of the matter by focussing on the fatal consequences this solution may entail: the three "rustlers" who are captured and hanged by the undeputized posse prove innocent, an innocence which could easily have been established if the men had been less impatient with the Law's delay.

What the hanging exemplifies, as Davies, the storeowner, observes, is "that it's more deadly when the law is disregarded by men pretending to act for justice than when it's simply inefficient, or even than when its elected administrators are crooked" (pp. 64-65). It is more deadly not only for the victims but also for each of the self-appointed executioners, who now face the agonizing task of setting their sense of moral guilt right.

Clark pays great attention to what motivates a group of men to go on with what most of them soon come to look upon as bothersome and distasteful, even unjust. He brings out the crucial role of a strong leader, in this case Tetley, the ex-confederate cavalry officer — cool and aloof and in perfect control of himself and the situation — while at the same time Clark succeeds in suggesting the psychological imponderables that account for each individual's taking part in the consorted action. But it is especially with regard to his handling of the problem of moral guilt that Clark raises his Western to the level of serious art.

If it is a strong-willed man that sets the group on a course leading to the deaths of three innocent men, it is also a strong-willed man that could have stopped them from being hanged. It is again Davies who realizes this. What he also realizes is that *he* should have been that man, but wasn't.

It is actually Davies in whom the book's moral action is centred and this is remarkable since he is neither the narrator, nor the novel's central consciousness, a peculiarity I shall come back to later. Davies, an old man, is one of the few men in Bridger's Wells who from the very beginning is opposed to the idea of the men's taking the law into their own hands. When his attempts to stop them fail, he nevertheless decides to ride with the posse, reasoning that he can only dissuade them from any rash action when present. After a stiff ride the posse catches up with three men, driving a small herd of cattle, and assuming they have found the rustlers they capture the men: Martin, the owner, a young man from Los Angeles, who claims to have bought a ranch in the region, and his two hands, an old feeble-minded cowpoke and a tough-looking Mexican. Tetley, cross-examining the captives, comes up with enough incriminating evidence to convince most of his posse that the three men are the rustlers and the murderers of the killed ranchhand (Martin can't show the bill of sale for the fifty head of cattle he bought, and the Mexican can't give a satisfactory explanation how he came in the possession of the murdered man's gun). Davies, however, is still not convinced. He feels intuitively that Martin is not a rustler, nor a murderer, and after he has read the letter Martin has been allowed to write to his wife and which Davies has promised to deliver for him, he is certain. He once more tries to stop the men from going through with the lynching but fails a second time. In his long talk with Croft after they have returned to Bridger's Wells he wonders though whether he really tried hard enough. Davies' case is one of profound irony: of all the men he seems least to blame for the hangings that took place. He came out of it clean, as Croft assures him. If there were any heroes in this sordid affair, Davies could lay claim to the title. But Davies himself is not so sure whether he deserves this praise. *He* was the only one who knew that the men were innocent, even if the kind of evidence he could furnish would not be valid in court. He also knew that most of the other members of the posse were secretly feeling as he did. He could have stopped the hangings if he had had the courage to stand up against Tetley, if necessary by force. But he hadn't, and he had even been glad that he had had no gun to do it. What he feels with growing alarm is that he, Davies, had actually killed the men, not Tetley. The only excuse he can think of — which, if true, might enable him to live on with a modicum of self-respect — is that to stop Tetley would have meant to shoot him, because Tetley, a murderous beast, devoid of human feelings, would never have yielded, and no one could have expected Davies to do such a drastic thing as killing Tetley. But even this straw, to which Davies clings in desperation, breaks. News reaches him that Tetley, in despair over his son's suicide has also taken his own life. Davies cannot but draw one conclusion: this cold, cruelly hard man, who seemed to enjoy the lynching and the harsh treatment to which he submitted his weakling son during the chase and the subsequent hangings, driving the young man to suicide, must have had human feelings after all, and this realization completes the destruction of Davies' own moral being.

There is no doubt that *The Oxbow-Incident* is a fine novel in which Clark seems to prove that the West can be made to serve as a setting where the "great questions" can be posed and investigated. Yet, on closer examination one asks oneself whether Clark really needed the experience of the West to work out the particular problems of moral guilt he raises in his novel. To put it in a different way, is it really the Western setting that determines his subject matter, forcing him to treat it in this and in no other manner?

There is something odd about this book, something that resides in the novel's point of view. The story is a first-person narrative, told by the cowpuncher Croft, but his part in the novel's action is only marginal. He is always off-centre and in no essential way does he affect the course of events. Whenever he acts the result is always futile. His role in the chase and the subsequent hangings is negligible. When he gets shot it is an accident. He merely seems to function as a soundingboard, first to young Tetley when the latter, embittered by his isolation in an environment he hates, explains the hunt in terms of pack instincts which make the weak band together to keep the best down — which, he thinks, is their way of exerting power, for that's what people want, power —; later to Davies, enabling the storeowner to unburden his soul weighed down by his secret guilt.

Although Croft gives the impression that he is more articulate, more perceptive and intelligent than the rest (he is the one who reads books), he is actually one of the "pack", attuned in his conduct to the leader Tetley rather than to a much more discriminating mind like Davies'. That is to say, unlike a Nick Carraway or an Ishmael he is not the novel's moral yardstick. This, in fact, is Davies, but Davies is an old man and a storeowner, not exactly the prototype of the mythic Western hero. Unlike the legendary cowpuncher Davies is the kind of man one may find in any part of the world, and his situation, the Conradian situation of a man who feels destroyed morally because his nerve fails him at a critical moment, is not exclusively a product of the Old West. In other words, it does not inevitably evolve from the formative experience of the West. It has therefore no representative value for the West as such, although it retains of course its universal value. By choosing Davies as the moral yardstick of the novel Clark deprived himself of the chance to make us see the experience of the West from a fresh perspective. He did not really alter the nature of the stereotyped Western, and one wonders why he did not make his narrator, the cowboy Croft, the central character of his moral and psychological drama. Why did he not endow the central hero of the West with Davies' kind of perception and moral consciousness? Could it be that even in Clark's case the prevailing vision of the West was still too potent for him to furnish the traditional Western hero with the kind of sensibility that rather than partaking of or acquiescing in the lawlessness underlying the Westering impulse might respond with moral self-destruction?

There are losers in Clark's tale, and they are no longer exclusively the black hats this time, but they do not basically alter our perspective on a West which, to repeat Gurian's complaint, does not seem to allow the writer to pose the great questions. Clark, to be sure, does pose them but in a context which is not really the product of anywhere else in the world but the West. By showing himself uncertain about what point of view to adopt, he, too, seems to have denied himself the opportunity of uncovering a significance for the Old West which goes beyond the stereotype he obviously wanted to subvert.

3

Thomas Berger's *Little Big Man* (1964),[15] which like Clark's novel belongs to the few "adult" Westerns of literary merit, does present us with losers who change the stereotyped view of the Old West. In Berger's book the great question of good and evil derives its relevance from precisely the frame of reference he employs: the epic years of 1852-1876, the period which covers the most colourful events in the history of the West when the last empty spaces of the American continent were filled with white settlers and the last free Indians, the Plains Indians, were vanquished. Jack Crabb, the 111-year old narrator of the story, took part in all of them, as teamster, prospector, cardsharp, gunslinger, buffalo hunter, army scout, and he is not only present at the Salomon's Fork battle in 1857, at the Indian massacre on the Washita River in 1868, but is also the only "true" survivor of the Battle of Little Horn, the place of General Custer's famous last stand where for the first time in its history the U.S. Cavalry suffered a crushing defeat. Ironically, it was also the end of organized Indian resistance.

What distinguishes Berger's novel from the familiar Western story is that for once the vantage point from which the West is viewed is not exclusively the white man's. Berger achieves this by making Jack Crabb spend some of his formative years alternately among the whites and the Red Indians, the Cheyenne. Like Natty Bumppo Jack is, in fact, both white and Indian, and although an illiterate, endowed with the kind of intuitive intelligence that makes him a keen observer of men and events. Also like Natty Bumppo he is first and foremost a practical man with a lot of common sense. But unlike Natty he is not the stuff legendary heroes are made of. For one thing he is too short and too skinny, and although he does not lack courage, he prefers to be prudent

---

[15] Thomas Berger, *Little Big Man*, 1960; rpt 1975, Bantam Books.

if not shifty. If it means staying alive, he is even prepared to act the courtjester. Besides he is uncouth, unscrupulous, even ruthless, if necessary, although he manages to retain enough decency to remain human. Jack Crabb, in short, seems to combine the characteristics of all those who remained nameless in the opening of the West, but who must have possessed the resilience and the robustness of nature necessary to survive the hardships and brutality of those early frontier days.

What Berger does with the creation of Jack Crabb as his conception of the Western hero is what he does with all the events and characters that have become legendary in the history of the West: he demythologizes them. Central in this demythologizing process is the correction of the traditional view of the Indians. It is quite clear that Berger is in warm sympathy with their way of life and that he condemns the historical role of the whites in their relations with the Red Indians, yet he is careful not to cause the pendulum to swing too far in the other direction. The Indians in *Little Big Man* are not idealized; they are even made fun of occasionally, though on the whole it is the whites who bear the brunt of Berger's ridicule. They are what many nineteenth-century whites thought they were: crude, smellly, shabby, lousy, ignorant and superstitious. But they are not simply savages. Many of the bloody clashes between red and white resulted from misunderstandings generated by cultural differences rather than Indian savagery. The opening chapter is representative: it describes the encounter of a band of Cheyenne and a wagontrain in which, following a series of this type of tragi-comic misunderstandings, Jack's white parents are killed.

On the whole the picture of Indian life that emerges from Jack's observations compares favourably with that of the whites'. The Indian attitude towards children, strangers and — a test-case — homosexuals, shows greater tolerance and consideration than that of the whites in nineteenth-century white society. The Indians may be guilty of all the Christian sins enumerated by the Reverend Pendrake, but they are free of the sins that can make white civilization such an uncomfortable place to live in: the "envyings" and the hypocrisy, particularly in sexual matters. There are other qualities which explain the great attraction of Indian life to Jack. The Red Indians do not attach much value to material possessions, nor are they interested in power, personal, social or political. If they have an ambition it is to be honoured as a great hunter or warrior. Their chiefs, for instance, lead only by example. When Old Lodge Skins, the chief who adopted Jack as his son because he felt responsible for the deaths of his parents, wants to move his tribe, he just strikes his tepee and leaves, expecting those members of the tribe who agree with his decision to follow him of their own accord. Cheyenne society does not lack community feeling but remains basically anarchic. The individual is given a great deal of leeway. The Cheyenne would never fight under leaders they cannot respect, as Custer's white soldiers did under officers they despised. To kill a man in combat is honourable, but to lead two hundred men to a certain death in a senseless, foolhardy attack as General Custer did, the Cheyenne would consider a crime.

When at the end of the novel Old Lodge Skins makes preparations to die — a scene in which Berger soars to great literary heights — the dying Chief summarizes the fundamental differences between the red man's world view and the white man's. The white men, as he explains to Jack, live in straight lines and squares, not like the Indians who live in circles because only then is there no permanent winning and losing. Only then does life remain continuous. Even when a Cheyenne dies he knows that he shall continue to live in everything that is. But the white man only wants to win, although he hates fighting, which the Indian loves, it being part of life, and the Indian loves life, whereas the white man hates life. That's why he can wantonly destroy the buffalo herds; that's why he will not stop before he has vanquished all the Indians, even if he prefers doing it "by scratching a pen across paper or saying something into the wind", for what he is really after is man's soul.

From this juxtaposition one thing becomes quite clear: what favourably distinguishes the Indian world view from the white man's refers to twentieth-century paradigms rather than nineteenth-century ones. Tolerance to children, strangers and homosexuals is part of the socio-cultural attitudes of the 1960s rather than of the 1860s. Rejection of social restraint, emphasis on anarchic, individual freedom, indifference to power, concern for ecological matters, hatred of faceless bureaucrats are articles of faith more fervently held in the 1960s than at any other moment in the history of America. So it is in terms of twentieth-century paradigms that the disappearance of the Indians becomes an event of great dramatic potential, giving rise to some of Gurian's great questions. The question, for example, whether in this collision between two world views not more was lost than won. Once this question can be asked — and it could only be asked until very recently — the moving death of Old Lodge Skins acquires the tragic dimension Berger no doubt intended it to have: the old Chief dies in the full knowledge that the Cheyenne's way of life is finished, that with the irresistible advance of white civilization there will be no future for the Indians — a prospect that would hardly have bothered white community in the nineteenth century.

Yet, Berger is not merely nostalgic. The Indian way of life may be entirely satisfying to those brought up in it, basically it is static, belonging to a past stage in the white man's own social evolution — the stage of pre-industrialization. Jack Crabb prefers Indian life to that of the white man, but he knows that he cannot stay with the Indians. What he misses are not only the amenities he got used to while living among the whites, but also the excitement of the continual changes characteristic of white civilization. As he remarks, nothing ever happens among the Indians.

If one of the signs of major literature is its ability to give meaning to the great social events of its age, then Berger seems to have written the "great" Western Gurian asked for. Yet the meaning Berger attaches to the disappearance of the Indians as a vital force in the experience of the West — no doubt one of the important social events of the nineteenth century — shows a distinct imbalance, and so the novel is not quite as great as the brilliance of some of its constituent parts suggests — such as the marvellous descriptions of the antelope hunt, the battles of Washita and Little Big Horn, the death scene of Old Lodge Skins.

The main reason for this imbalance lies, I think, in Berger's narrative strategy. The novel's central consciousness is Jack Crabb's, and it serves admirably in giving us a fresh perspective on all the important events and legendary characters of the Old West. His commonsensical, deadpan, Huck Finn-like observations furnish the novel's satirical tone, so eminently suitable to deflate reputations and expose the mad incongruities that seemed to have made up the reality of the West. But like Art Croft, Jack Crabb, the man who was there but whose name "is missing from every index, every roster, every dossier", is a marginal figure: he never in any way influenced the course of events, he never in any way was central in the clash of the two cultures, as Old Lodge Skins was, as, for that matter, General Custer was. Of Old Lodge Skins we have a fine portrait. He is neither the savage of the conventional view of the Indians, nor Cooper's noble red man. He may be a shabby, smelly Indian, even a "buffoon" in the eyes of the whites, but he is also a courageous, wise and philosophical man, not a saint, but a man who lives by what he believes in, who stoically goes his own way, though driven relentlessly back in his own territory by the white man, but who nevertheless retains a loving and touching concern for his adopted white step-son, Jack Crabb. His representative value is entirely convincing. With General Custer it is different. Despite Gurian's belief that Custer is one of the three most fully developed characters (Jack Crabb and Old Lodge Skins being the other two), Custer's portrayal is primarily satirical. He emerges as a complete idiot, mad in his histrionic, self-centred conceit of being better than any other man in the world, a man who discourses on Cooper's mistaken view of the Indians as noble red men — they are savages in every sense of the word — after he himself has just committed the savagery of leading, quite senselessly, two hundred men to the slaughtering-table. Jack seems to feel some admiration for Custer despite the man's odious character. What, for example, distinguished him from the Washington politicians was that he had always been his own man, "never whined, snivelled, nor sucked up to another". But this, as Jack also observes, was the rule among the Indians, so from their point of view hardly a distinction. Yet they did not scalp him; out of respect, Jack thinks. But he is quickly undeceived by Old Lodge Skins: no, not out of respect but because he was getting bald.

As Old Lodge Skins' counterpart Berger's Custer clearly lacks stature to bring out the full historical and human complexity of the experience of the West in as far as it impinges on the fate of the Indians. We see "hardass" Custer through the eyes of Jack Crabb, and are thus presented with a wholesome correction of the man's inflated historical reputation. But while achieving this Berger reduces him to a farcical figure, and so detracts from the tragedy implicit in the collision of two inimical world views. We see, through Jack's eyes, the major events of the Old West and are, while gripped by the brillance of Berger's satire, confronted with lunacy and incongruity rather than complex human motivation. While achieving this Berger, in fact, reduces the whole West to farce. Perhaps it was just that, farce, a big hoax. But if this were true, there is reason to doubt whether Gurian was right after all in believing that the great questions can be asked in the West. They can of course be asked, but not, so it appears, before the perspective on the West has fundamentally changed. Where Berger succeeds in writing major literature is when he approaches his materials from a vision shaped and informed by perceptions and experiences belonging to the twentieth century; where he merely entertains us — but what superior form of entertainment — is when he is exploiting, like the writer of popular Westerns, the myth of the West — not the one engendered by the work of Cooper and Wister, but that of the West as a tall story, the West of Mark Twain's *Roughing It*.

Whether this thesis has general validity for all serious Westerns remains to be seen of course. It does find corroboration though in that other modern Western of unmistakable literary merit, E. L. Doctorow's *Welcome to Hard Times*.

4

When with the publication of *The Book of Daniel* (1971) E. L. Doctorow leaped, to quote *The New York Times*, into the first rank of contemporary writers, he had written two other novels: *Welcome to Hard Times* (1960) and a science fiction novel *Big As Life* (1968). Neither had been received with great acclaim — *Big As Life* deservedly; it was, in fact, a failure, as Doctorow himself acknowledged, but *Welcome to Hard Times* was, as I hope to show, clearly underrated.

Ragtime, published in 1975, propelled Doctorow into the best-seller's list. The book was a great popular success, but some critics were not convinced and condemned the novel as trivial. Doctorow's next work, his play *Drinks Before Dinner*, was first performed in New York in 1978. It was followed by *Loon Lake* in 1980, a novel again, dealing with America's depression years, and more overtly experimental than his previous novels.

What all of Doctorow's novels have in common is a concern with history. Each of them deals with an important period of America's past: *Welcome to Hard Times* is set in the 1870s, when the West was still being won; *The Book of Daniel* is based on the Rosenbergs case and depicts the 1950s and 1960s, the transitional years from repression to radicalism; *Ragtime* evokes the 1900s, when American society went through a period of great transformation; *Loon Lake* concerns itself with the depression years, also a crucial period in the American experience.

Yet it would be a mistake to call Doctorow a historical novelist in the ordinary sense of the word. Although he is fascinated by history's official record, it is not his major concern. Objective historical facts are never as objective as the historians pretend they are. Social, political, religious or philosophical tenets, even psychological imponderables, have the power to alter objective facts, a power usually applied — consciously or unconsciously — to serve less than objective goals.

What Doctorow prefers to do is to look behind official history and bridge the gap between public and private experience, thus shedding new light on "objective" facts while disclosing those that have been suppressed or ignored in the process of history becoming official. Yet it is precisely this predilection that has also laid Doctorow open to the charge of being guilty of manipulating historical fact. *Ragtime*, the novel in which he intermingles historical figures with imaginary characters, has particularly provoked the ire of a number of critics. Russell Davies, for example, thought the book to be little more than "a mass of capricious juxtapositions",[16] while Cushing Strout condemned the novel because he felt that "to make historical characters do whatever suits one's fancy makes for amusing entertainment or for political manipulation", adding that Doctorow by doing this corrupted

---

[16] Russell Davies, "Mingle With the Mighty", TLS, January 23, 1976, p. 77.

"the veracious imagination".[17]

But did he? What gives Doctorow's best novels the ring of veracity is exactly the quality of the imagination he brings to his interpretation of the episodes he has selected from American history. Doctorow's imagination is that of the artist, not the historian's or the sociologist's, which is to say that he is concerned with "life as an experience rather than as a postulate for dramatic development". True, life as a postulate for drama also belongs to the writer's "devices and tricks of trade", but since, to continue Doctorow's own line of thought here, it has been appropriated by the media as well as by the disciplines of social sciences, which by now have turned it into one of "the industrialized forms of storytelling", the artist should — more than ever — place the emphasis on "life as an experience".[18]

In doing this Doctorow not only brings to his material the verifiable facts but also his skill of feeling his way into history. What gives Doctorow's interpretation of recorded history its tone of authenticity is that in drawing on official fact he does not forget his own experience of the world. He thus no doubt "colours" official history, making it occasionally even seem "untrue", but nevertheless "true" in the only sense that counts: as a revelation of human motives and aspirations which throughout history have remained pretty much unchanged. What may have changed is the mode in which they manifest themselves. One can therefore understand what Doctorow means when he writes: "I'm under the illusion that all my inventions are quite true (...) whether it happened or not. Perhaps true because it didn't happen."[19]

---

[17] Cushing Strout, *The Veracious Imagination*, Wesleyan U.P., 1981, p. 193.

[18] E. L. Doctorow, *Drinks Before Dinner*, 1978; rpt Bantam Book, 1980. Introduction p. Xiii.

[19] Paul Levine, "Interview with E. L. Doctorow", *Ideas*, CBC Radio, Spring, 1978.

Doctorow, then, is interested in the psychological or existential truth of the historical event, truths which transcend the limitations imposed upon historical truth by prevailing ideologies. It is this that makes him in his best novels a more rewarding historian than the professional historian who only works from recorded fact.

The intriguing question that arises is of course to what extent Doctorow's own approach to history remains determined by prevailing ideologies, and in what sense this may have affected the value of the psychological and existential truths he has discovered about the historical epochs he deals with in his novels.

To examine this question *Welcome to Hard Times* seems particularly suitable, since it is not only a typical genre work, a Western, but also takes up a number of themes already introduced by the father of the genre, James Fenimore Cooper, who wrote his Leatherstocking Tales at a time when the prevailing ideologies were different from those of the 1950s and 1960s.

Just like Cooper's *The Pioneers* (1823), *Welcome to Hard Times* (1960)[20] deals with the birth of a settlement and the Westerner as standard bearer of civilization. However, from the start there is already a significant difference. If in *The Pioneers* the reader finds himself on the paradisiacal shores of Lake Otsego (Lake Champlain), in *Welcome to Hard Times* he is transposed to the dismal flats of Southern Dakota, a region where, as Blue, the novel's narrator and main character, remarks, there is no excuse for a town except that people naturally come together.

The backbone of the settlement of which Blue becomes the unofficial mayor are merchants, shopowners, barkeeps, carpenters, lawmen, young lovers, and even the outcast Indian living on the town's fringes is not wanting. They represent the same sort of people that

---

[20] E. L. Doctorow, *Welcome to Hard Times*, 1960; rpt Bantam Book, 1976. All page references are to this edition.

populate Cooper's Templeton, but that's where the resemblance between Doctorow's pitiful lot and Cooper's genial and cheerful characters ends. Blue himself may remind the reader of Judge Temple in his energetic determination to make the settlement thrive, but again that's how far the resemblance goes. What makes Judge Temple a standard bearer of civilization is quite unambiguous: he believes in a better, bigger and brighter future — his dream, the American Dream. What makes Blue start *his* career as standard bearer is weariness turned to shame: arriving one day in the flats of Dakota, he sees a man, Fee the carpenter, building with quiet assurance a place "right up off the flat ground". Blue might have come West with some of Judge Temple's expectations, but after he had done everything in the Western book with not much more to show than that he had learned "it was enough to stay alive", he had finally realized, watching Fee, that he had moved along too long and that the time to settle had come, and "Fee's place was as good as any now".

Cooper's novel opens with a description of Christmas time in the new settlement, a description D. H. Lawrence has rightly praised as "marvellously beautiful", containing "the loveliest, most glamorous pictures in all literature".[21] Doctorow opens with a description of wholesale slaughter and destruction, containing what easily qualifies as the goriest, most depressing pictures in all literature. In the span of twenty pages half a dozen people are brutally killed or mauled, while practically the whole of Blue's town is reduced to ashes.

What has caused this small-scale holocaust is the outcome of a conflict which, in fact, is also central in Cooper's *The Pioneers*: the conflict between "nature" and "civilization", between "natural" liberty and "civil" liberty, between the liberty to follow one's own natural inclinations and the liberty to do what is right in accordance with man-

---

[21] D. H. Lawrence, *Studies in Classic American Literature*, 1914; in *The Shock of Recognition*, ed. Edmund Wilson, p. 958.

made law.

In Cooper's novel it takes the form of a quarrel over newly-instituted game-laws, the old hunter, Natty Bumppo, becoming the spokesman of all those who protest against what they consider civilization's arbitrary restrictions upon natural liberty, while Judge Temple acquires representative value as the upholder of civil liberty in his firm belief that only man-made laws save us from savagery.

Cooper's treatment and solution of this conflict is ambiguous, to say the least. Although he is clearly in sympathy with Natty's standpoint, he actually shares the Judge's view, and for a solution he knows no better than sending his hero, the old hunter, farther West, into the wilderness, conveniently out of civilization's reach. Of course, Cooper, a descendant of the enlightenment, a firm believer in reason and human progress, can do little else. It also explains why the violence in the novel is restrained, why it remains so surprisingly "clean".

In Doctorow's story the conflict assumes a pitch of vehemence and a degree of complexity which, as will become apparent, can hardly be understood if only the story's historical context is taken into account. In *Welcome to Hard Times* the idea of "natural" liberty finds embodiment in the Bad Men from Bodie, vicious and psychotic men, who were not "ordinary scoundrels" but "who came with the land", and with whom you could no more cope than "you could with dust or hailstones" (p. 7). So when one day a Man from Bodie rides into Blue's town and starts harassing and abusing the townspeople, brutally killing some, committing unspeakable atrocities on others, the rest of the town, including Blue, watch at a safe distance and in helpless horror their houses go up in flames. Blue's half-hearted attempt to stop the Man from Bodie at gunpoint had miserably failed, and he too, panicking, had joined the general flight, leaving Molly, one of the barkeep's prostitutes, at the mercy of the brute despite his promise to protect her. One cannot fight natural disasters, one can only suffer them. However,

Molly, surviving, though badly mauled and burnt in the fire, has a different view of her fellow citizens' strange passivity which she denounces roundly as craven cowardice, and it is especially Blue who has to bear the full brunt of her fury. He of course knows that she is right, and his decision to take care of Molly and Jimmy, Fee's young boy, orphaned by the Man from Body, is his first step on the road leading, as he hopes, to redemption and rehabilitation. For Blue still believes in second chances, the reason, too, why he stays among the shambles of his abandoned town, and starts rebuilding it amost single-handed.

But life, when it has been poisoned at the roots, offers no second chances. Molly, her mind warped by her terrible experience with the Man from Bodie, continues to live in mortal fear of his return. At the same time she is consumed with hatred and a thirst for revenge to which everything else, love, honour, dignity is made subservient. Blue may do anything to try and redeem his failure, surround her with the love and care only a husband can give, he remains the coward who left her behind in the hands of a crazy killer. Becoming a mother to Jimmy, she wins the boy's affection but this too is done with only one purpose in mind: to instill into the boy contempt for the man who stood by while his father was murdered, and to train him for his future role of avenger.

Nothing, as Blue finally realizes, mattered to her, not he, not Jimmy, just herself and her Man from Bodie, for whom she seemed to be waiting like "a proper, faithful wife". Blue's insight into Molly's condition, however, does not stop him from becoming her "final fool". He would, as he admits, do anything for her, always. So when at the end of the novel the Man from Bodie actually makes his reappearance, Blue, outsmarting the man this time, manages to shoot him. Hoping that the sight of the vanquished fiend might end Molly's sick obsession, he delivers him, still alive, to Molly, but quickly realizes that he has again made a terrible mistake. Molly, turning into a ferocious animal, starts stabbing the wounded man to death. Watching in horror what the woman to whom he had become totally devoted is doing, Jimmy faces the dreadful truth Blue had in vain tried to impress upon him: he, too, had only been used, never really loved by Molly. The effect on the boy is shattering: the blast of his shotgun, poised to protect Molly, kills both her and the Man from Bodie.

When Jimmy is gone, Blue foresees that the land will soon be inflicted by the atrocities of another Man from Bodie: Jimmy, "who used to be Fee's boy". He also realizes, despairingly, that he could have saved the boy. He should have sent him away from the place where he witnessed the murder of his father; instead he had left him to the care of Molly, another failure, for she had nourished him on hatred and contempt, and Jimmy, as Blue had noticed "was a child fitted to the land, using all his senses to live with what it gave him" (p. 89).

So far the novel reads like a psychological thriller, set against the backdrop of early frontier life, exemplifying, so it seems, the unorthodox idea that far from being primarily a healthy and liberating experience, frontier life could be profoundly traumatizing as a result of its unmitigated brutality. But the novel is more. Blue's feat of putting the Man from Bodie out of action is not only a failure from a psychological point of view, but also a failure in an entirely different, perhaps even more serious sense. To understand this we have to take a closer look at what really motivates Blue to shoot the Man from Bodie.

When Blue finally decides to stand up to the Man from Bodie, he has no longer the illusion that by killing him he saves his town from evil. He shoots the man when he has already realized that it is not so much the Man from Bodie that matters as the circumstances that call him into being. The Men from Bodie were not like hailstones against which one is powerless, as he once believed; they were not some nonhuman force. Men from Bodie only appeared when the circumstances were favourable, when they were allowed to appear, when they were even welcomed. They were always among the citizens of Hard Times: in fact, their own Man from Bodie had never left town: "it was waiting only for the proper light to see him where he's been all the time" (p. 198).

Blue's fresh insight into the nature of evil — "natural" liberty turned rampant — is actually gained by a deeper understanding of what he meant when he once told Molly that a "settled" town drives the Men from Bodie away. And Hard Times, he believed, had become a settled town, and therefore immune to Men from Bodie. They don't stand a chance, as he assured Molly when she, imploring him to leave the town while there was still time, had remained unconvinced.

What then are the real reasons for Blue's decision to face the Man from Bodie? They are, strictly speaking, emotional ones, no principle is involved. On the one hand there is his feeling of humiliation because Molly has shamelessly promised the town's dumb-witted sheriff her favours if he will kill the Man from Bodie; on the other, blind anger because he once again watches all hell break loose in his town. Yet Blue knows that what he sees happen holds no surprise. For when the news breaks that the mine is closing (the lodes appear to be exhausted) and that as a consequence no road, no stamping mill will be built, Hard Times ceases to be a "settled" town. With the miners pulling out, it loses its only source of income, and therefore its reason to exist. When the townspeople also start moving out, thus weakening the town's social structure even more, the circumstances are favourable for evil to rear its ugly head again, the times rife for the Man from Bodie to reappear. He has, as Blue understands when, horrified, he watches him start his fiendish work again in Zar's Palace, never been away. For he is always there, among those who feel the illicit thrill of watching his atrocities; among the men who, while filling the streets of

Blue's town for weeks, had waited in vain for the work on the road and the mill to start, had spent their money in Zar's Palace, Isaac Maple's store, the Swede's eating tent, with tempers rising, tempers turning vile when the news of the mine's closure gets around and the general exodus of the townspeople who took all but gave nothing starts. The Man from Bodie — Turner, a man with a name after all — may fire the first shot, but after Blue has done what he later comes to look upon as the "most futile" he ever did, even though at the time it made "most sense", that is, shooting Turner, it is these men, the Man from Bodie multiplied, who begin and complete the general looting, burning and killing.

When the orgy of violence and destruction is over, the streets littered with corpses, the town in ruins and abandoned, the only persons left are Blue, mortally wounded, and the Swede's crazy wife, Helga.

Blue's town may never have thrived but for the presence of the gold in the mountains, but what really underlay the lack of vitality, the inability to thrive or even to continue to exist, is again something far more fundamental. As Blue himself in one of his more perceptive moments admits, the end of the town was already in its beginning. He then understands what Molly meant when at the height of the town's prosperity she scornfully pointed out to him that if his town "stretched four ways as far as the eye could see, it would still be a wilderness" (p. 146). For it lacked something, something, Blue thinks, the whole West lacked: "The color dazzles us but when it's too late we see what a fraud it is, what a pinched-out claim" (p. 186).

The West as a fraud, an idea that also informs to such a large extent the writing in Berger's *Little Big Man*. Doctorow, however, abstains from satire. What distinguishes him from Berger is that he focusses on the plight of the white settler confronted with this insight — the West as fraud — , dramatizing its tragic rather than its comic implications.

Like Jack Crabb, Blue, the novel's central intelligence, is a full-fledged Westerner, a man who has done everything in the Western book. What they share is the endurance, the energy and basic optimism with which they pursue their exploits. Blue manages to survive a severe Dakota winter with practically no food and insuffcient shelter. He then starts rebuilding his town from scratch. Alf Moffet, the stagecoachdriver, describes him as a man who, if he was hanging by his fingers from a cliff, would call it "climbin' a mountain". When at the end of the novel he is dying, he considers setting fire to what is left of the town in order to scatter the buzzards, but then rejects the idea: "Someone will come by sometime who will want to use the wood".

Yet Blue, like Jack Crabb, does not belong to the legendary West, a romanticized world with such mythic heroes as a Virginian, a Lassiter, a Harrison Destry.[22] What both Blue and Jack Crabb lack is their success. Blue, for example, can only look back upon failures, moral failure, social failure, economic failure. This can also be said of Jack Crabb, but there is an important difference. Blue's failures have to do with historical conditions rather than with character. He is, one might say, a displaced person. His humanity, his basic lack of interest in material things, his modern insights into what makes a community live and thrive, might have made him a successful director of a twentieth-century Welfare Agency. To be a success in a nineteenth-century frontier town, however, other qualities were required. Those of Zar, for example, the Russian ex-farmer, who has learned that only people who sell are getting rich: not miners, but salesmen; not cowboys but saloons; not those who look for money but those who supply those who look.

Zar is the first man who happens to pass through Blue's town after it has been burnt down by the Man from Bodie, and he arrives in a wagon full of whiskey and in the company of three hookers, for, as he

---

[22] Lassiter is the hero in Zane Grey's *Riders of the Purple Sage*, 1912; Harrison Destry, in Max Brand's *Destry Rides Again*, 1930. See next chapter.

tells Blue, what men are most willing to pay for are women.

What makes Zar decide to stay in what is left of Hard Times is the expectation of profit, no more and no less, and in this he becomes representative of the majority of the people who start converging on the town once it begins to show signs of prospering. Zar is not without ideals: his ideal is a two-story hotel. But when the influx of new arrivals in the town continues and the sanitary conditions are getting unbearable, he is not interested. To improve the situation Blue has to start digging sumps all by himself. When the men who are waiting to get employed become troublesome, Zar does not share Blue's concern. As long as they are drinking his whiskey, he is content, and when Blue suggests that they should create temporary jobs by pouring money back into the town's shaky economy which in addition would also keep the men off the streets, Zar declares him "mad".

Zar and his kind can only exploit the people, the land — until they are exhausted. What they lack is a sense of a bond with the land. As Hayden Gills from the office of the Governor of the Territory wearily complains to Blue when he visits Hard Times to charter the town: "(...) nothing fixes in this damned country, people blow around at the whiff of the wind" (p. 142). The only person in Blue's town capable of growing something on its barren soil is John Bear, the Indian, an autochthon. He, too, is the only one who can heal instead of merely destroying. With the aid of his medicine extracted from the land he nurses both Molly and Jimmy back to health.

Doctorow's view on the history of the Red Indians is implied but as pointed as Berger's. John Bear, pretending to be deaf and dumb, lives in complete isolation from the white community. Yet, when asked to render his medical services he never refuses, though he makes one exception, for Zar, the man who struck him down from behind when he was treating Molly's burnt back — assaulting her, as Zar of course at once assumed. In the beginning of the story his garden patch is trampled down by the Man from Bodie; at the end his shack is torn down and burnt by the white mob.

What the town lacks to justify its existence is not only a bond with the land but also community feeling, a sense of man's common destiny, of a common human goal. In the first dreadful winter spent in the patched-up remnants of the town when even Blue himself begins to doubt whether they will survive, he decides to organize a Christmas party — a suitable occasion, he thinks, to bring people together. The party fails dismally. This is no fault of Adah's, the wife of a minister before she had to stoop low in life to become Zar's partner in procuration. She plays her melodeon and sings the hymns, creating for a moment the appropriate Christmas spirit, but when the drinks offered by Zar begin to take effect, the atmosphere changes. Zar starts insulting Isaac Maple, whose insistence on being paid in cash he resents: he, Zar, has his whiskey and women to trade. Jessie, Mae and the Chinagirl, the three hookers, are getting fresh and vulgar, turning abusive when Jenks shows himself unwilling to pay for what they have to offer. Mary — a former prostitute herself but now become respectable as Blue's putative wife — manages to offend everyone by setting herself apart, prim and haughty in her refusal to join the drinking and singing. Soon the shouts drown the sounds of Adah's melodeon and when the noisy squabble has subsided the company breaks up. The gathering, as Blue sadly realizes, made no longer sense; there was nothing more to say and each of them was alone again, like strangers, hostile in their isolated separateness.

The destruction of the town, then, results from moral rather than economic failure. What gave it birth is not the impulse to advance civilization — the traditional view of the experience of the West — but raw, selfish greed. The West as a fraud, and Blue, a flawed man himself, although in a different sense than his fellow townspeople, is powerless to fight it. He might have been more successful if he had had the kind of ruthless business enterprise of a Zar and the superhuman courage of the legendary Western hero, but he has neither. Instead of writing out claims for himself, he writes them out for others, thereby earning Molly's contempt; instead of facing the Man from Bodie, he flees, thereby deserving contempt in his own eyes. The qualities he does possess — decency, human concern, disinterestedness — make him a fool in Molly's eyes and a madman in Zar's, while they prove totally inadequate to stop the Man from Bodie. For the first time in the history of the Westerns we meet the Westerner as a tragic figure, a man destroyed by the moral and social tensions that existed in the historical conditions of the West, but which are absent from the official records (history) and the fiction based on these records after they have undergone imaginative adaptation (myth).

Blue, a man with a weakness for documents, deeds, and ledgers himself — the novel is actually written in the form of three ledgers — records the story of the West that got lost or ignored because the prevailing ideologies blocked a vision different from the current one. Doctorow's novel presents this vision, a vision that questions the very basis of the experience of the West, suggesting that it was doomed from the outset because it was undertaken from the wrong set of values. The novel can do so because it refers to an alternative set of paradigms derived from experiences which have palled the optimistic view of the Westering impulse, thrown doubt on its justification, whether called Manifest Destiny or the American Way of Life. These experiences — the atomic bomb, the Korean War, the Vietnam War, the McCarthy hysterics of the 1950s, the racial riots of the early 1960s, the assassinations of prominent American leaders, the student uprisings of the late 1960s — belong to the twentieth century. By focussing on the West from this twentieth-century perspective the novel lights up corners which until recently had remained dark, revealing material which not only effects a shift in our historical sense but also touches upon the inadequacy of the human condition in general. It is this material, containing the elements of human tragedy — the source of significant art — , which enables the writer to pose Gurian's great questions, and as a consequence to start writing "great" Westerns.

Whether Doctorow's novel tells us the one and only true story of the West is doubtful but not so important. As Blue concludes, no document — official or fictional — can really "fix life". This is an illusion. But just as the staunch advocates of the popular Westerns claim that these novels give us the West as it should have been, so Doctorow can claim that he gives us the West as it also must have been, given some basic unalterables of the human condition. Breaking through the confines of the Western as genre, a genre engendered by the nineteenth-century conception of the West as a place of infinite possibilities and heroic achievement, Doctorow has written a powerful novel, moving and gripping, in a style as bare and stark as the flats of Dakota, in a mood as relentless and uncompromising as the winter that brought Blue and what was left of his town's community near the brink of extinction.

Yet, though desperate, it is not a despairing novel. In the final analysis it bears witness to something that eludes rational explanation: the miracle that there are always people like Blue who refuse to give in to Hobbes' dictum that life is brutish, nasty and short, even if the omnipresence of wholesale destructiveness and moral obtuseness seems to prove that it is just that. In this sense *Welcome to Hard Times* remains a Western. However, to *call* it a Western may knock the bottom out of a genre that, if the term is to retain its meaning, can only continue to fictionalize historical material and human emotions which, as I have pointed out in the discussion of *The Virginian* refuse to yield any of the "great questions", the treatment of which may lift literature beyond its entertainment level. The "real" Western cannot concern itself with existential problems by reason of the very nature of the vision that called the genre into being, a vision created and shaped out of the need to justify the West as a place of high hopes and epic achievements. It is thus doomed to remain a subliterary activity, leaving us with the following paradox: as soon as the Western becomes "great" it ceases to be a Western. It becomes a Western with a difference, taking its place among what I would call the New Westerns.

Chapter 8

THE POPULAR WESTERN:
Zane Grey, *Riders of the Purple Sage*
Eugene Manlove Rhodes, *Pasó Por Aquí*
Max Brand, *Destry Rides Again*
George G. Gilman, *The Killing Claim*

In February 1987 the famous anchorman Dan Rather interviewed George Bush on the *CBS Evening News* — life. Bush had granted the interview, expecting that it would focus on his presidential campaign. Dan Rather, however, at once started to interrogate Bush about his behaviour in the Iran-*contra* scandal, provoking, as he doggedly persisted in this line of questioning, an angry response from the Vice-President. Bush not only denounced Rather's tactics as unfair, he also set in a counter attack. Would Rather like it, so he asked the *CBS* anchorman, if his overall performance would also only be judged by one unfortunate incident? Bush of course referred to the day in September 1987 when Rather had walked off the *Evening News* set to protest *CBS*'s decision to allow the US open tennis match to cut into the broadcast, leaving the network blank for more than six minutes.

Bush's indignant rebuttal to Rather's mulish persistence was generally applauded, at least initially, but the point I want to make is not to determine whether one ought to join or reject the applause, but to call attention to the manner in which the incident was reported. This is how *Time* magazine described it:

> It was video High Noon. Bush had shut down the legendary media gunslinger from Black Rock. It was the new George Bush (...)[1]

The description is suggestive, but it is suggestive in more than one sense. It also tells us again the extent to which the popular Western continues to furnish the images and metaphors that appeal so greatly to the American mind. But, then, it is the Western which is the only form of popular art that is genuinely American, and in tracing its origin two dates have a particular significance, 1823 and and 1902.

In 1823 James Fenimore Cooper published *The Pioneers*, the first of his Leatherstocking Tales, the novels that introduced the literary Western in nineteenth-century American literature, while at the same time providing the formulas for the Beadle dime novel, the nineteenth-century version of the popular Western.

In 1902 Owen Wister's *The Virginian* appeared. It introduced the literary Western in twentieth-century American literature, while at the same time furnishing the formulas for its subliterary offshoot, the commercial Western.

One may ask oneself of course whether it is necessary to distinguish between the literary Western on the one hand and the popular, or commercial, or formula Western on the other. John R. Milton, for one, believes it is, defining in his scholarly study *The Novel of the American West* (1980)[2] the former as well-written and intended to

---

[1] *Times*, February 8, 1988, no. 6, pp. 20-21.

[2] John R. Milton, *The Novel of the American West*, Lincoln: University of Nebraska Press, 1980, see Chapter I.

illuminate the human condition by introducing significance of theme, seriousness of intent, and multi-dimensional characterization; the latter, as stereotyped, and intended to provide mass entertainment by shamelessly exploiting the myths of the old West. The former, the literary Western, written by writers such as Vardish Fisher, Walter van Tilburg Clark, Henry Ferguson, A. B. Guthrie and Frank Waters, can withstand the application of standard literary criticism; the latter, the popular Western, cannot, because it is written in accordance with a fixed pattern, the main ingredients of which are: a frontier setting, a colourful cowboy hero, a two-sided morality of good and evil, violence and a love story. The literary popular Western is, commercially speaking, only moderately successful; the popular Western as a rule hugely successful, as the books by writers like Zane Grey, Max Brand, Luke Short, Ernest Haycox, and most recently, Louis l'Amour, selling by the millions, abundantly prove.

However, what defines a book as a popular Western is not, as I hope to make clear, the presence of the afore-mentioned ingredients, as these can also be found in the literary Western, while some of them may even be wanting in the formula Western, but first and foremost the underlying vision. And this vision most clearly emerges when we examine the two ingredients that link the popular Western to the literary Western, that is, violence and the love story, in particular violence, to which for brevity's sake I'll restrict myself in my discussion of a number of representative Westerns.

The prototype of the twentieth-century popular Western is no doubt Zane Grey's *Riders of the Purple Sage*. Published in 1912 it was an immediate success, becoming an all-time best-seller, the model for successive generations of popular Western writers.

The violence in *Riders of the Purple Sage* originates from two easily definable sources: on the one hand the thirst for revenge, on the other, the thirst for power. Lassiter, the novel's main character, is the typical mythic Western hero of larger-than-life dimensions, a man known and feared for his lethal gun. When we meet him for the first time he has been on the trail for eighteen years to find and kill the man who abducted his sister Milly Erne. His long search has finally brought him to Jane Withersteen's ranch in a border settlement in Southern Utah, a Mormon community founded by Jane's father, the man, in fact, who, as becomes apparent later, was responsible for Milly Erne's leaving her husband to join the Mormons. Fortunately Jane's father is dead, while also Milly Erne has died in the meantime, and since Jane, as Lassiter learns, had been her best friend, and since she is attractive and in serious trouble herself with the Mormon leaders who want control over her Amber Spring which supplies the region with precious water, he is easily persuaded to stay and ride for her.

The Mormon leadership wields absolute power over the community, and is quite prepared to resort to violence if all other means to achieve this fail. The violence they perpetrate is therefore also recognizable, "rational", since it serves a well-defined purpose. It can be checked if one has the courage and the ability to oppose it. The evil of which it is a sign can also be accounted for: it is the fanatic, religious conviction of being right, of brooking no divergent opinion.

The violence Lassiter's activities entail has no mystery either. He kills Bishop Dyer and his bodyguards in an open fight because Dyer has committed the outrageous act of kidnapping Jane's adopted little daughter Fay. The men who keep Fay captive are also mercilessly hunted down and killed. At the end of the novel when Tull and his henchmen are about to capture Lassiter and his companions, the pursuers are buried under the avalanche of rocks and stones set in motion by Lassiter. The violence of which Lassiter is the agent not only serves justice but is also meant to decrease violence in the future. As he tells Jane: "It [violence] can't be helped. But it can't last always. An' remember this — some day the border'll be better, cleaned, for the ways of men like Lassiter."[3] So what in Lassiter's case justifies violence — even glorifies it — is the fact that it is thought to ensure the advancement of civilization, one of the conventional ideas underlying the experience of the West. Looking at violence from this angle, it thus becomes a positive force, holding no mystery, even serving a noble cause: to make the world safe for civilization.

This positive, life-affirming attitude is again a distinctive trait of Eugene Manlove Rhodes's *Pasó Por Aquí* (1925),[4] one of the most popular Western of the 1920s, a Western with a surprise though, since it lacks two important staples of the Western: the shoot-out and the love-story — not a fist is raised, not a shot fired, not a kiss given or stolen.

The story's outlaw-hero, Ross McEwen, red-haired and twenty-five years old, is also somewhat unusual. He robs a store *cum* bank with an unloaded shotgun borrowed from the storeowner, pays for the goods he buys, and when his pursuers have come too hot on his trail he slows them down by tossing to the wind for all to see the stolen paper money, repeating his free distribution at appropriate intervals. When after days of relentless pursuit his horse gives out, he saddles a steer, riding it not only to confuse his trackers but also to reach the little ranch which might mean the end of a torturous thirst and a moment of rest. However, the place, owned by a Mexican family, turns out to be a sick room, almost a morgue, since all the members of the family are down with diphtheria, some in the last dangerous, choking stage and about to perish.

Tending his patients day and night McEwen manages to hold death at bay, but realizing that he must find doctor's help if they are to

---

[3] Zane Grey, *Riders of the Purple Sage*, 1912; repr. New York: Pocket Books, 1980, p. 302.

[4] Eugene Manlove Rhodes, *Pasó Por Aquí*, 1925; repr. University of Oklahoma Press, 1973, 3rd print 1982.

pull through, he decides to build a fire on the hilltop so as to draw attention to his plight, even though he knows that his smoke signals will bring his pursuers to the ranch. In this he proves right. Pat Garrett, the sheriff, and his deputy notice the fire signals, and they arrive in time to take over from McEwen who from sheer exhaustion is on the verge of collapse. Garrett sends for a doctor and nurses, and with expert help arriving the chances of the family's recovery are fair, thanks to McEwen's quick, timely and valiant first aid.

For a criminal McEwen shows a surprising sense of sacrificial unselfishness, risking life, capture and imprisonment to save a poor Mexican family. But sheriff Garrett is the right man to appreciate his heroic humaneness. When the two men ride off, we know that for McEwen it is not prison but freedom that awaits him, an act of generosity on the part of the sheriff hard to understand by the Eastern nurses, who indignantly object to anyone being allowed to get away with crime. But, as Rhodes suggests, that is not how the Westerner feels. Basically McEwen is a humane and courageous man, and that's what counts, that's what in the last analysis he ought to be judged by.

The outlaw-hero is of course not an unfamiliar character in American popular art. What he seems to fulfill are two interrelated cultural needs: on the one hand he embodies the average American's ambivalence towards the law and the legal system; on the other, he is the projection of his estrangement from a society that has grown more and more restraining and impersonal. What Rhodes adds to this conception of the outlaw-hero is a touch of humour and a whiff of sentimentality.

In 1930 Max Brand published what became one of the most popular Westerns of the period between the two wars: *Destry Rides Again*.[5] Like Lassiter, Harrison Destry, the novel's main character, is

---

[5] Max Brand, *Destry Rides Again*, 1930; repr. New York: Pocket Books, 1944.

one of those mythic Western heroes, wild, reckless and fearless men, quick on the draw, and admired and dreaded by men of lesser stature. Destry, however, meets his peer in the person of Chet Bent, seemingly a friend, but actually his mortal enemy, bent on Destry's destruction. Like Tull in Grey's novel, Bent seems evil incarnate, but what motivates him holds no secret. Just as in *The Riders of the Purple Sage*, it is revenge as well as the thirst for power. Bent holds a secret grudge against Destry: when they were boys, Destry had bested him and Bent had never forgiven him for this. Besides, the prettiest girl in town has fallen for Destry, not for Bent, and Bent wants this girl, Charlotte Dangerfield, not only because she is Destry's girl but also for an important additional reason: she is the daughter of the richest rancher in the region. Bent wants that ranch, as he wants most of the town. His ambitions are boundless and he has sufficient cunning and ruthlessness to obtain what he wants. Robbing the Express — the beginning of his spectacular rise in the county — , he succeeds in planting incriminating evidence on Destry. Destry is tried, found guilty and sentenced to a ten-year imprisonment. The verdict turned out by the twelve jury members is unanimous, not because the twelve men are convinced of his guilt but because the trial has given them an opportunity to settle old scores without having to fear instant retaliation from the man they have passed sentence on. But Destry promises he will call on them when he is set free, and this is what he does after he has served his term.

As may be noted, all the darker passions — boundless ambition, soul-destroying envy, lethal revenge — , the ingredients to make a story exciting, are there, in pretty elementary form, it is true, but easily recognizable as drives that explain human action. Also the violence that Destry's settling accounts with his enemies entails is again remarkably "clean", holds no mystery. Guns blaze, blood is spilled, but it is all done in the cause of justice. The guilty are punished, innocence is redeemed. One can even speak of poetic justice, when in the final titanic fight between Destry and Bent, the latter — finally facing the consequences of his evil and treacherous activities — drops to his death over a steep cliff.

Yet, it is precisely here that Brand, unexpectedly, seems to rise beyond the formula and the stereotype he so cleverly and skilfully manipulates by intimating how thin and wavering the line between life as just and sane and life as indifferent and absurd really is. In this last fight Destry proves again the better man, but not because he is stronger, cleverer and more courageous, but because he has more luck. This realization has a sobering effect on his person and view of life. If it is only luck that stands between survival or perishing, what certainty is left? Existence becomes frightening, absurd. It is this awareness that makes Destry feel an old man, finished and done for, a man who finds no longer any use in the old, simple manner of setting right what is wrong, of opposing evil with a blazing gun. He decides to put away his Colt, believing that to restore life's sanity new ways must be found.

Destry's farewell to arms resembles that of Frederic Henry, the hero of Hemingway's *Farewell to Arms*, like Brand's a novel of the 1930s. But there is a fundamental difference. Frederic Henry's farewell signifies separation from the community of men. In Brand's book Destry's farewell means the end of the old days and the beginning of a new regime in Wham, Destry's town, a regime founded on communal action rather than on individual reliance and prowess. In thus ending his novel Brand continued to subscribe to the traditional view of life underlying the experience of the West, a view basically optimistic and affirmative, and the opposite of what found expression in the work of the major writers of the 1920s and 1930s such as Ernest Hemingway and William Faulkner. The violence one encounters in the work of these writers does not seem to be engendered by economic, or political, or social, or passional forces only, nor by something that can be explained as accident or incident, but rather by the potentiality of evil as it resides in the most ordinary human beings. This renders the violence that confronts us in their work unpredictable, arbitrary, absurd, creating a sense of profound unease and uncertainty with regard to the human condition, which within itself seems to carry evil simply because it is what it is.

To sum up: what this brief discussion of some representative samples of the pre-World War II popular Western shows is the following: first, there is an imaginative variety to be discerned in the handling of the standard ingredients that constitute the popular Western, a variety that even seems to reflect certain current social or political events. What, for example, is responsible for Zane Grey's solution of Lassiter's problems may be the impending threat of World I: when Lassiter topples Balancing Rock, crushing his pursuers, he, Jane and Fay are shut off from the outside world forever. Surprise Valley becomes their private Eden, a solution that may fulfil a sentimental daydream but hardly bears thinking of as a reality. McEwen's sacrificial heroism and sheriff Garrett's generosity in *Pasó Por Aquí* could well be Rhodes's comment on the self-serving hedonism of the 1920s, so disastrously ending in the Wall Streett Crash of 1929, of which one also seems to hear an echo in *Destry Rides Again* when Brand has the hero of his story survive not because he is braver or more virtuous than his antagonist but because he is luckier.

Secondly, this imaginative handling of the ingredients that make up the popular Western does not affect the nature of the vision underlying these novels. In this vision which is basically the same for all Western fiction up to roughly the outbreak of World War II, the West is what it was thought to be in the nineteenth century: a place of affirmation, where the individual still counts, where the old, trusted American values of enterprise, self-reliance, freedom, and the courage to stand up for what one believes in, are still upheld.

If we next view the kind of popular Western written after World War II, we have to distinguish between two kinds of development. The one is not really a development but a prolongation, a continuation of the sort of traditional, Zane Grey-like Western which authors like Nelson Nye, Ernest Haycox, Wallace Stegner, Luke Short, Will Henry and William O. Turner continued to write. To these writers, all members of *Western Writers of America (W.W.A.)*, the Western remained essentially what it had always been, "an adventure story", the truth of which is, as William O. Turner, one-time president of *W.W.A.*, put it in 1968, "the truth of action and open country and the possibility of a man rising above himself and acting heroically". And, as Turner believed, "because of its roots in American tradition it [the Western] has an essential relationship to the American spirit and hence a potential that has not been fully realized." It surely needed, he thought, "writers who see this relationship and articulate it for the modern reader." [6]

The trouble with Turner and his fellow Western Writers of America is, however, that they see this relationship exclusively in terms of a romantic, violent West, and that what they articulate is, as *Time* in a feature article in 1959 wrote, the Western as the American Morality Play, as "an allegory of human life and death in which the forces of good (in white hats) and the forces of evil (in black hats and five o'clock shadow) fight it out on the huge Western stage. Evil always loses. The viewer or reader goes his way fulfilled and satisfied, convinced that the universe is in good hands." [7]

The other kind of development that took place in the production of the popular Western after the war is more interesting. It is the sort of development that follows the fashionable socio-cultural trends of the day, and it led some professional observers to believe that what the

---

[6] As quoted by C. L. Sonnichsen, in his *From Hopalong to Hud*, p. 39.

[7] *Time*, March 20, 1959, "The American Morality Play".

modern pop Western really reflected were the reader's assumptions and prejudices rather than the writer's conception of his subject matter. And what these assumptions and prejudices revealed was mighty strange, quite upsetting in fact, though not about the writers, who simply catered for what the public wanted, but about the readers. Judging by what they seemed to like in the work of a Robert Kreps (*The Hour of the Gun*, 1967), of Charles Portis (*True Grit*, 1968), of a John Benteen (*Apache Raiders*, 1970), or of George G. Gilman, the creator of Captain Josiah C. Hedges, better known as the redoubtable Edge, these readers of the post-World War II popular Western seemed a pretty sick lot, wallowing in the weirdest of abnormalities that in the areas of sex and violence could be imagined.

The remarkable thing is, however, that despite the kinky sex and the gory descriptions of vicious fights, the snapping of bones, the eye-gouging, the bashing-in of heads *cum* oozing brain-fluids, the underlying vision remains familiar, recognizable, does not basically differ from the one that underlies the bulk of the pre-war popular Westerns.

To substantiate this view let us take a closer look at one of George G. Gilman's Edge-novels. Gilman's stories, recommended by his publisher, Pinnacle Books, Inc., as "The Most Violent Westerns in Print", are undoubtedly representative of the post-World War II pop Western, and since it does not really matter which of the more than forty Edge-stories one selects, we might as well examine one of the most recent, *The Killing Claim*, published in 1982.

The protagonist of the Edge-novels is our traditional Western hero of over six feet tall and lean build, with high cheek bones, hawkline nose, thin lips, firm jaw and the familiar ice-blue eyes. Edge's past, too, belongs to the tradition of Western writing: as a former captain in the Civil War he is a man "prepared by countless brushes with death to be ready to face and defeat any new menace that might be waiting to attain him."[8] It is this readiness that makes him particularly successful in avenging the murder of his kid brother and the burning of the small farmstead on which he was born and raised. Enough suffering and cruelty have been visited upon the hero to account for the ruthlessness with which he carries out the revenge. Moreover, tracking down the five murderers and killing them has made Edge step outside the law. He has also become a wanted man, and this completes the romantic picture of the good "bad" hero: a man set against the entire world, a man who can no longer afford to indulge in feeling or emotion, but who must always be on guard and remain detached if he is to survive. A man too who learns to accept this way of life, an invariably violent way of life, who even learns to like it, and who therefore becomes an even more dangerous man to quarrel with.

Gilman, however, introduces two changes, evidently meant to dull the glamour that radiates from the traditional Western hero. He makes Edge a bounty hunter, a profession generally looked down upon by law-abiding and law-breaking citizens alike, and he dilutes the purity of the Western hero's white Anglo-Saxon descent by presenting him as the offspring of a Mexican father and a Swedish mother, calling him throughout the novel "the half-breed". Edge himself, however, does not brook any slighting remarks about his mixed descent, and when the young stage guard John Cox is careless enough to ignore this, Edge forcibly makes him mend his ways by holding a razor blade to his throat, teaching him to say "Mexican" instead of the contemptuous "Mex" used by Cox in addressing Edge.

There is still another difference with the traditional Western hero: Edge lacks the customary chivalrous attitude of the Westerner towards women, and is capable of saying to Polly Webster, the proprietress of Lakeview's only hotel, "get your mind back down

---

[8] George G. Gilman, *The Killing Claim*, New York: Pinnacle Books, 1982, p. 4. All further page references are to this edition.

between your legs and stop trying to read mine, lady" (p. 165), a remark gaining in intelligence though losing nothing of its crudity, if we realize that it is addressed to a nymphomaniac, but which could of course never have passed the teeth of the mythic Western hero.

Edge, then, is not a nice man, nor is he a gentleman, but a mean customer, though not without a caustic sense of humour, and a professional killer. When Cox, unable to live with his humiliating punishment, later tries to pull a gun on Edge, the latter, "a man of lightning reflexes, who possesses an inner monitor that warns him of danger at hand", kills the stage guard without the slightest hesitation.

When the story opens, Edge has just pocketed the bounty money he earned for bringing in a dead outlaw wanted in Denver and tracked and killed by him. About to ride into Lakeview, he is delayed by an old, half-crazed miner, Galton, who lies in his cabin, a few miles outside the town, alone and dying. Badly wounded while working his mine, he had managed to crawl back to his cabin, where without any help he had to amputate his gangrenous leg, which he then fed to his starving dog, a huge Shepherd. The animal, even though tied with a rope to the cabin, gives Edge and his horse a bad time when he tries to enter the cabin in response to Galton's call for help.

We are spared no gory detail in the description Gilman gives of Galton's revolting vicissitudes and his subsequent smelly death. Before the old miner passes away he extracts a number of promises from Edge, which the bounty hunter is at first reluctant to meet, but which, once he has made them, he faithfully keeps and executes. In this he — surprisingly — does not differ from what one expects the traditional mythic hero to do: Edge buries Galton where he said he would like to be buried, takes care of the German Shepherd, and accepts in exchange for these favours the claim on the mine, promising the dying man to restore the caved-in section and to take possession of the riches which, as Galton assures him, the mine hides.

After Galton's burial, Edge works on the claim, without, however, finding any gold but this hardly bothers him: the peaceful beauty of this part of Montana, together with the peculiar friendship that develops between him and the German Shepherd, makes his stay a pleasant and restful one, giving him a sense of contentment never experienced before. But he soon learns that he still rides "on the violence trail" (p. 41), and that even after people have died, they are still capable of playing nasty tricks on their fellow men. Running out of stores after five days, he decides to replenish them in Lakeview, but when he is about to leave the clearing, he is stopped at gunpoint by one of Galton's sons, Ralph, and the latter's wife Janet, pretty-faced though fat and the most determined of the two. What has brought them to the cabin is old Galton's letter, telling Ralph to come and see his father before he passes away and to share the mine's proceeds with his brother Lee whom he, Galton, had also alerted and forgiven for neglecting an old father.

The reason for the hostility Ralph and Janet show Edge soon becomes apparent: they believe that he is a "claim-jumper", and it takes a little show of force on the part of Edge to persuade the two greenhorns, whose knowledge of how to use guns proves minimal, that what they themselves have jumped to are the wrong conclusions: he is no claim-jumper but the rightful owner of the claim which, however, he is now quite willing to restore to the sons of the diseased, even though their father disinherited them and left the mine to him, Edge, a stranger.

What stands out so far is the role of the German Shepherd. It is the dog that makes Edge decide to stay on after Galton's burial; it is the dog's intelligent conduct that turns the odds in favour of the bounty hunter when he is held at gunpoint by Ralph and Janet. Later in Lakeview, it is the dog's presence, spooking the horses of the stage coach, that causes the fight between Edge and young Cox that ends in

Cox's death. It is again the dog that is instrumental in bringing about the final confrontation between Edge and the three outlaws who have followed him to Lakeview with the intention of killing him to avenge the death of Al Falcon, the man Edge delivered to the lawmen in Denver. It is the dog attacking one of the men during this confrontation that enables Edge to kill the three of them. And it is finally the death of the German Shepherd, reluctantly shot by Edge because he realizes that it had developed too great a taste for human flesh, that brings Edge back to Galton's place where he wants to bury the dog beside the grave of its first master. It is here that we meet again all the characters in the novel, gathered in and around the cabin: Ralph and Janet Galton, Galton's other son, Lee, who has hired a number of locals, among whom the Hall kids and Max Webster, the giant but dumb-witted brother of Polly Webster, all frantically searching for Galton's hidden treasure. Polly herself, afraid that something might happen to her brother, arrives with Edge, and is still shaking from her witnessing the shoot-out between Edge and the three outlaws. Later, after Edge has finished digging the grave for the dog, a posse led by sheriff Herman, the lawman in Lakeview who was none too happy about Edge's presence in the town, shows up. They have gathered the dead bodies of the outlaws killed by Edge, and have arrived just in time to watch the cabin explode, knocking them from their horses and killing the people inside, Galton's sons, Janet, Max Webster, the Hall kids. The townspeople among the survivors of the blast now realize what old Galton had been up to with the nearly fifty sticks of dynamite he had bought over the past few years. He had planned it all ahead, probably wired a box inside the cabin, bequeathing to his sons death and destruction instead of the gold he never possessed.

Trying to find an explanation for the deaths and the destruction she had witnessed, Polly Webster bitterly exclaims: "Greed and hatred is what's led to all the killin' and grief that's happened. Been the same since the world began, my opinion" (p. 181). From this judgement, however, one person can be excepted: Edge, the professional killer, the story's chief character. If he can be accused of anything, it is, as he himself reflects at one moment, the fact that "he had allowed others to dictate what he should do". And that was not his way at all; this, as he tells the German Shepherd, "ain't our style at all". And, "I figure we ought to do something about it before we start in to sit up and beg whenever anybody snaps their finger" (p. 95).

Here of course is the archetypal Westerner speaking, the rugged individualist, self-reliant, fearlessly independent, the man who wants to be in control of his own fate, who is no man's slave, but a man, too, who is deeply aware of the necessity to have certain standards, for if we don't have them, "we get", as Edge observes, "to be worse than animals" (p. 114).

The standards Edge himself chooses to live by are simple, clear, and not really different from those we have come to associate with the traditional Western hero as introduced by James Fenimore Cooper. Edge holds that, first, you can't draw a gun against somebody with impunity, which, decoded from Western parlance, means that nobody should get away with threats or intimidation, a prerequisite for civilized living; second, you don't shoot people for expressing an opinion, which decoded again, emphasizes the necessity of being tolerant, a guarantee for the continuation of civilized living; third, you always pay your way, because if you do that, you can't be blackmailed and consequently can't be corrupted, and this keeps the quality of civilized living up to standard.

These then are the standards upheld by Edge, the man who on account of his profession and mixed origin is doubly mistrusted by society, here represented by the Websters, mentally warped, the Galtons, all greed and hatred, the sheriff and the other law-abiding citizens, who mean well but are too unimaginative to distinguish between a man like Edge and the outlaws who were after him. The situation has again an archetypal quality, if we recall the relationship between Natty Bumppo, Cooper's Leatherstocking figure, and the citizens of Templeton in *The Pioneers*, the novels in which the frontier code clashes for the first time in Western writing with townspeople ethics. And even stronger than in *The Pioneers* one feels that also in Gilman's story the author's sympathies are with the outcast rather than with the townspeople.

To sum up: despite a tendency in this novel to depict violence with an unsettling emphasis on the gory detail, it remains recognizable, just as the violence depicted in the pre-war Western. It contains no mystery that cannot be accounted for in either psychological or social terms. Also the values underlying this post-war popular Western are not really different from those that give its pre-war predecessor the optimistic and life-affirming outlook on mankind. In *The Killing Claim* Edge may spend his share of the milk of humanity on the German Shepherd, but then there is precious little else on which he can spend it. Ralph and his rapacious wife Janet treat him with cold hostility, showing complete indifference to what he did for old Galton. Galton himself not only cheats his sons but also Edge, the man who gives him a decent burial and who takes care of his dog. Polly Webster shows some human interest in the stranger, but when Edge refuses to accept her favours, she tells her brother Max that he tried to rape her, and only the timely appearance of sheriff Herman prevents another round of bloody gunplay. The only creature in the novel willing to exchange trust and sympathy with Edge is in fact the German Shepherd, but in case some one might accuse Gilman or his creation, Edge, of sentimentality, the dog is shot, by Edge himself, because he realizes that the animal has become too dangerous to people. But when for much the same reason Polly tells him to shoot the dog, Edge nearly shoots her. In fact, shooting Polly instead of the dog would have been a more adequate reflexion of his real feelings, but he can check the impulse, because he has sufficient moral sense to know that it "would have been a bad thing to do, a hard action to live with" (p. 162).

There is really no saner man, morally speaking, than this professional killer, as also the end of the story proves when like Natty Bumppo at the end of *The Pioneers*, Edge heads for the mountains, alone, turning his back on the settlements, on civilization — here Lakeview — where life does not allow a man to make simple and straight moral decisions or choices.

In view of the tremendous popularity of novels like the Edge stories, one may conclude that if the popular Western acts as a window, then, rather than reflecting the sickness of its readers, it continues to mirror a spirit, the American spirit, which can still be said to be in a fairly healthy state, despite the increased emphasis on gory violence and a decreased concern with the niceties of speech and manners.

What seems to contradict the continuing popularity of the Western as exemplified by the success of writers like Gilman or, even more telling, a Louis L'Amour, of whose novels more than 200 million copies have appeared by now, is the diminishing interest in the Western movie — at least in Europe. The reason is to all appearances that a large part of the popularity enjoyed by the Western movie has been annexed by the science fiction film. How this could happen becomes apparent, once we have taken a closer look at the average science fiction production. What is striking is that the makers of this type of movie continue to be working within the frame of reference supplied by the Western when conceiving plot, character, and action. The locale may have changed radically, but the division into white hats and black hats has remained, even though the headdresses as such have become unrecognizably different. Also the lurking savages, the Red Indians, are still there, though now under the name of aliens. The hero may have exchanged his trusted Colt for a modern laser weapon, but he is still quicker on the draw than his formidable adversaries. He is in fact the kind of man in whom we easily recognize our Western hero, strong and fearless in holding his own in a hostile environment, a man who acts from a high sense of personal worth and a set of rigidly held beliefs. He is the kind of man who does not suffer from what Allan Bloom in his *The Closing of the American Mind*[9] calls "value relativism", a phenomenon which he holds responsible for most of the ills that at present plague American society, Western society in general. It is a condition that has emerged because people no longer believe, according to Bloom, in "a natural hierarchy of the soul's varied and conflicting inclinations". America's national hero, the mythic Westerner, is not troubled by this kind of disbelief. He knows — Edge exemplifies this — that placed before the choice to shoot either the dog you love, or the woman you dislike, you will shoot the dog, and not the woman, because, if you did otherwise, it would be "a hard action to live with".

The Mythic Westerner, then, still acknowledges "the natural hierarchy of the soul's varied and conflicting inclinations", and still acts accordingly, something people no longer seem to be able to do nowadays. Bloom has an explanation for this as well. Values, he thinks, can come into existence in two ways: as "products of reason", or as "products of folk minds". Today values are primarily recognized as products of reason. Underlying this recognition is the belief that values can be produced at will, at short notice, so to say, which means that there is nothing to stop people from creating their own identity and their own lifestyle, whereby it is of course taken for granted that these identities and lifestyles are all of equal value: the one is no better or worse than the other.

---

[9] Allan Bloom, *The Closing of the American Mind: How Higher Education Has Failed Democracy and Impoverished the Souls of Today's Students*, New York: Simon & Schuster, 1988. See in particular the chapter in which Bloom deals with the influence of nineteenth-century German philosophy on contemporary American culture, an excerpt of which appeared in *Dialogue*, no. 80, 2/88, pp. 16-26, entitled "Nietzsche in America". The quotations are taken from this excerpt.

What the second belief, the belief that values are the products of folk minds, expresses is that since minds are related to history, or culture, values are as well. They are therefore the products of a slow, instinctual growth, which implies that people's identity and subsequently their lifestyle cannot be shaped at will but must be conceived as given, something gradually to be discovered.

If doubt or disbelief arises about the truth or validity of these several values, the effect may be twofold: to those who live and act from the notion that values are the products of reason, the result will be nihilism, a state of soul which, according to Bloom, reveals itself not so much in the lack of firm beliefs as in a chaos of the instincts or passions. It is a state that prevails in the world of today. To those who act and live from the notion that values are the products of folk minds, the consequences will be far less serious. To overcome doubt or disbelief these people will simply work or fight a little harder. It is an attitude which to those in possession of "folk minds" is not hard to understand or to adopt. It may explain why the popular mind is still partial to reading Westerns, and why as long as there are those with folk minds there will be a market for the popular Western.

Chapter 9

THE NEW WESTERN:

Larry McMurtry, *Lonesome Dove*; *Anything for Billy*

1

There is, as the preceding chapter concluded, still a market for the Western. This market appears to be even more willing when it sells novels in which elements of the serious Western are interwoven with those of the popular Western. Proof of this is no doubt the publication of Larry McMurtry's monumental *Lonesome Dove* (1985), a Western in which the mythic West and the historical West are so skilfully blended that the result, an absorbing tale of close to nine hundred pages, has given the Western not only a new lease on life but a renewed popularity as well.

McMurtry had written about the West before, but in *Horseman, Pass By*, his first novel, and in *Leaving Cheyenne* (1963), as well as in *The Last Picture Show* (1966), and most recently in *Texasville* (1987), he depicts the present-day West, the scene of modern urban life in poky Texan towns, not the Old West, the scene of adventure and romance on the great plains.

Still, to those readers who up to the publication of *Lonesome Dove* had entertained a lively interest in McMurtry's literary achievements, it could hardly have come as a surprise that one day he would turn to the time of the Old West and write a full-blooded Western, replete with cowboys and Indians, sheriffs and outlaws, gunfighters and hangings. For beneath the gritty realism of his novels on small-town life in the modern West, one always felt the longing for a more daring and exciting mode of existence, the unspoken desire to accomplish deeds more in accordance with what to the popular imagination life in the Old West was believed to have been about.

In *Lonesome Dove*, McMurtry appears to have given in to the need to fulfil these longings and desires, for there is in this novel no lack of epic deeds commensurate with a legendary West, and the one that unquestionably takes the centre is the epochal, three-thousand-mile cattle drive from the Rio Grande in Texas to the highlands of Montana, a venture that had never been undertaken before. The time: the 1880s, the last decade of the more colourful episode in American history, the period of roughly 1850 to 1890, when the last Indians, the Plains Indians, were subdued, the old frontier life drew to a close as a result of the appearance of the telegraph and the railroads, and when for a brief spell the Western stage was set solely for ranchers, cowboys and stampedes, scouts, soldiers and Indians, sheriffs, gamblers and outlaws, droughts, blizzards and flooded rivers. In brief, all the traditional ingredients of the Western story, whether of the serious or of the popular brand, the stuff of which the legends were made, creating the illusion that everything in the Old West — mountain and river, man and beast, love and hatred, good and evil — was bigger and greater than anywhere else in the world.

Also McMurtry contributes in *Lonesome Dove* his share to keeping this illusion alive. He, too, exploits the mythic elements contained in the history of the American frontier experience, and the only thing that distinguishes him from his fellow writers of the popular Western in this respect is that he does it much better than they do. In achieving this he seems to place himself in the company of the serious writers of Westerns, but what sets him apart from them as well is that although *Lonesome Dove* retains all the excitement of the adventure story, and although some of the characters rise above themselves and act "heroically", the "truth of [the] action" in this novel is neither clear, nor simple, but complex and ridden with anomalies, as may become apparent from the following analysis.[1]

Augustus (Gus) McCrae, W.T. Call, and Jake Spoon, all former Texas Rangers, are what one expects members of this legendary band of law-enforcers to be: tough and courageous men who for long years fought successfully Mexican bandits and marauding Comanches.

Gus McCrae, loquacious and humane, emerges as the most attractive of the three; Call, practical but aloof and tormented by an almost Puritan sense of sin and retribution, as the most intriguing, while Jake Spoon, dashing and a ladies' man, turns out to be the weakest morally. What all three share is a general restlessness, an inability to settle and to make a family and a home. Through them, the three main characters of the novel, McMurtry has in fact reconstructed the mythic Westerner, a character of epic dimensions, commensurate with the historical import of the Western movement and the overwhelming grandeur of the landscape in which it took place. At the same time, however, a process of demythologizing is going on, revealing itself most clearly in the manner in which McMurtry has the life lines of the three men end. Jake, for example, dies a horse thief and a murderer, because he is too indulgent, too weak to stick to a moral decision he knows he should have followed. When near the Brazos he leaves both the herd and Lorena, the pretty whore whom he had promised to take to San Francisco, he thoughtlessly agrees to ride with a bunch of shady

---

[1] The quoted words are William O. Turner's, who defined the Western as an adventure story, the truth of which is "the truth of action and the possibility of a man rising above himself and acting heroically". See Part Two, Ch. 1, note 10.

characters, the Suggs brothers, common horse thieves and crazy killers, as he soon finds out. But even then he lacks the will to break with them in time, thus making himself an accomplice to a number of senseless thefts and murders he neither approved of nor wanted to participate in. All Jake asked for in life was a clean saloon to gamble in, a pretty whore to sleep with, and a little whiskey to drink. What he got in the end was a rope to hang from, and the men who provided the rope were his old *compañeros* Gus and Call. When the latter had finally tracked down the murderers of Wilbarger, the rancher who used to read Milton and to whom the horses belonged, stolen by the Suggs-brothers gang, they did what the Code of the West demanded them to do: they hanged the culprits, excepting no one.

Jake's ignominious death hardly corresponds with his fame as an ex-Texas Ranger, but Jake is only all right as long as he is among the right people. He suffers from poor judgement when he is not. Imitativeness is his strongest point, which as long as he imitates men like Gus McCrae or Call can transform him into a legendary Texas Ranger, but which in the company of lesser men can make of him a weak-willed accessory to dubious, even despicable acts.

Jake, though, dies bravely; he does not beg for his life. In the company of his old friends he is again the legendary Texas Ranger he once was, with a total disregard of death as he used to have in the past, even though, as Call concludes when he tries to account for the reckless courage of his two friends, Jake emulated Gus McCrae, who *was* a cool customer, the coolest Call had ever known.

But Gus McCrae, too, dies in a sense out of character. On a scouting trip in Montana with Pea Eye, one of Call's oldest and most faithful "retainers", he, the experienced Texas Ranger, a hardened and skilful fighter, rides into a party of Indians while incautiously looping up over a little rise. They, McCrae and Pea Eye, manage to get away, but not unscathed. With the two arrows sticking out of his leg Gus survives the Indians' hot pursuit and subsequent attack, but he reaches Miles City too late to save his gangrened leg, and following its amputation, he even loses his life.

The irony underlying his death is many-layered. He is shot by Indians, to whose plight he had always felt sympathetic, even if he had killed many in his rangering days. His encounter with these Indians is entirely accidental, as Call finds out later: they were a hunting party, not a war party. McCrae is hit by an arrow, while guns are blazing, and he, who seemed indestructable, dies, his body poisoned and putrifying, with only one leg left.

Although life to Augustus McCrae is mainly fun, he, oddly enough, has also been cast in the mould of the romantic-heroic Westerner; he hides the secret of a failure, the knowledge of an opportunity which, if only he had seized it, might have made of him a different man. This missed opportunity is Clara, the only woman McCrae had ever really loved. But Clara, though also in love with him, had married the dull but solid horsetrader Bob Allen, whom she had even followed to Nebraska because, as she had explained to a perplexed Gus, she would always know what Bob Allen did, but never what Gus McCrae was up to. Besides, two race horses would never get along, both wanting to be in the lead. Adding to Gus's perplexity was the promise she then extracted from him, which was that he must come to her again after a period of ten years, not to resume his courtship but to be a friend to her children. Since McMurtry has also made him a man who is generous, cheerful, humorous, and, although not without some vanity, totally devoid of any form of pettiness, one understands why Clara should have come up with such a peculiar wish.

It is also McCrae, not Jake, who at once starts the pursuit of Blue Duck, the Badman from Bodie in this novel, after the man has abducted Lorena, and it is Gus who slowly nurses the girl back to sanity after her horrifying experiences with the gang of renegade Kiowas and two white degenerates to whom the vicious Comanchero had sold her.

The pursuit itself belongs to the tradition of the captivity tale, becoming in the skilful hands of McMurtry a remarkable feat of action-writing, reaching surrealistic heights in the description of McCrae's meeting with Aus Frank, ex-mountainman, ex trapper, ex-storeowner, and ex-bankrobber in Waco, but now hauling buffalo bones in a wheelbarrow from the plain into the valley of the Canadian, where he piles them up into enormous pyramids; pyramids of bones of the thousands of buffalos massacred by white hunters, as one more addition to the seven wonders of the world, fittingly erected by a madman.

The final confrontation between McCrae and the gang in which the ex-Texas Ranger storms on horseback their camp in the darkness of the night, killing single-handed in a ferocious attack all six of them, is again vintage pop Western. However, McMurtry's description of Blue Duck, who escaped again as he had left camp before the attack took place, owes more to Doctorow than to Zane Grey. The evil that the Comanchero embodies is profoundly disturbing. Deeply irrational, although predictable since it is based on systematized and impersonalized forms of cruelty, it belongs to what can call into being European deathcamps rather that what one has come to associate with Red-Indian cruelty, which, even though it was "rational", remained unpredictable, as it was guided by individual or random circumstances.

Like McCrae's, Call's life also hides a secret, and just as in McCrae's case it involves a woman. There is the death of Maggie which he could have prevented if only he had not been too proud to admit that he, the famous Texas Ranger, had fallen in love with a prostitute, even though the reason why Maggie was a whore was that she had always found it hard to turn down any kind of love, hardest of all Call's, whom she loved hopelessly and desperately. But a whore was a whore, according to Call, and ashamed of his weakness to keep seeing her he had finally broken off the relationship. Maggie, unable to face up to his rebuttal, stayed drunk for a whole year, and then died not long afterwards. Her death had begun to haunt Call for years just as Jake's death started haunting him now, undermining all that he was, and making him wonder whether he was really qualified for what he knew he could do best: leading men.

It is only in his work, whether fighting bandits or Comanches as a Texas Ranger, or taking a huge herd through wild and nearly impassable country as a trail boss, that Call knows no hesitation, knows what to do and how to do it. It is the secret of leadership, as Gus in discussing this matter with him maintained, for most men doubt their own abilities, and will consequently follow those who have no such doubts and know what they are capable of doing. Call himself has in fact no sympathy for this kind of doubt, just as he has no sympathy for any kind of human weakness; he simply cannot imagine what it is like to be scared, an inability Gus attributes to the one thing Call seems to lack: imagination, a lack that may account for his great qualities as a man of action, but for which he pays dearly when he has to deal with his fellow men on the plane of feeling and emotions, even more so because he is quite capable of having deep feelings. But he cannot express or discuss them. His way of coping with an emotional situation is to spend the night alone, away from the campfire, or, as in the case of Deets's unexpected death — Deets, his black scout and Call's most trusted and loyal man from his rangering days — , to spend a whole day carving something into the board he had knocked loose from the side of the wagon. When he had finished, the improvised gravestone for Deets contained the following inscription, carved in capitals deeply into the rough board:

Josh Deets

Served with me for 30 years. Fought in 21 engagements with the Commanche and Kiowa. Cherful in all Weathers, Never shirked a task. Splendid Behaviour.[2]

The blow of McCrae's death, near the end of the novel, hits even harder, turning Call from a man with a mission into a man who has lost his sense of purpose. Even the work, the only truly important thing in his life, no longer matters, and having lost the old sense of feeling responsible for the well-being of his men as well, he even stops giving orders. The herd nevertheless reaches Montana in tact, but from this feat too Call derives no sense of fulfilment.

He delegates more and more of the work to Dish Boggert, his top hand, and to young Newt in particular, in whose skill in and appetite for ranching he detects much that reminds him of himself, even in the boy's very bearing. But he cannot bring himself to acknowledging him openly as his son, a sore point between him and McCrae who believed Maggie when she told him that the father of Newt, her son, was Call. When in spring after their first winter in Montana, Call takes leave of the men in order to fulfil a promise he had made to the dying Gus, a promise that will force him to enact on a grand scale the extraordinary journey described in Faulkner's *As I Lay Dying*, he can only admit and acknowledge his fatherhood symbolically by giving New his best horse, his favourite rifle, and the pocketwatch he had inherited from *his* father. But he cannot tell Newt, who waits with despair in his heart, that he is the boy's father. He can never tell Newt, because the boy stands before him as evidence of what he feels as his greatest failure: not to have been what he had always preached his men to be, which was to be honest to oneself.

Call, in fact, is an explosive mixture of Cooper's Leatherstocking figure, Natty Bumppo, the frontiersman , and Hawthorne's Dimmesdale, the puritan minister and leader who also lost his soul because he could not confess his love for a woman.

---

[2] Larry McMurtry, *Lonesome Dove*, 1985; London: Pan Books, 1986, p. 723. All further page references are to the Pan Books edition.

The pioneer and the minister, the two prototypes that stand at the birth of American literature, never forming an entirely happy, but often a highly dangerous combination. It may account for the murderous fury unleashed in Call when in Ogalalla he sees his tophand knocked down and Newt being vigorously quirted by Dixon, a big army scout. It is Gus who saves the army scout from being killed by dragging his partner away from the man, whose head Call in blind rage had started to bang against the anvil before the blacksmith's. Asked whether he had ever seen Call doing this before, Gus tells Dish Boggertt, awed by the fury with which his boss had punished Dixon, that, yes, he had, once before, to a Mexican bandit who had cut up three white people, but that was not the real reason. The real reason was that the Mexican had "scorned Call", and "It don't do to scorn W. T. Call" (p. 66).

Neither does it do to scorn Augustus McCrae for that matter. This becomes apparent when the drive's progress takes the Hat Creek outfit past San Antonio, a town not unknown to Gus and Call from their rangering days, but considerably changed since then. This they find out on arrival and after they have fulfilled the task of buying a new wagon, the main purpose of their visit.

Deciding to have a drink, they enter a saloon where some twenty years ago they had been hailed as heroes, but where now they are met with cold indifference, as odd "old-timers", "dern cowboys", who ought to "broom themselves off" before they walked in. The young bartender who utters these insolent remarks is also provocatively slow in serving the drinks they have ordered, and Gus, not a man to be tolerant of this kind of treatment, summarily grabs the man's head and smashes it into the bar, breaking skin and nose, blood gushing. He then has the dazed bartender take a good look at a picture propped up by the mirror, showing Gus, Call, and Jake as Texas Rangers, a photograph taken after they had successfully driven Kicking Wolf back to the Canadian. Gus next demonstrates that he still knows how to use his big Colt by shattering with one wonderful shot the glass he had slung into the air. When the proprietor, also a young man, and not the man who had been one of McCrae's cronies in the old days, loudly protests, threatening to have the sheriff arrest them, the "old-timers" have another moment of triumph, balm to their bruised egos. The sheriff that walks in is Tobe Walker, a man they know. He had also been in their Ranger troop, and a great admirer of the three famous Texas Rangers, and therefore a man unlikely to arrest them. The young man in his black suit, however, remains unimpressed. The happy reunion of the old comrades-in-arms that follows only increases his anger, and he exits in a huff.

The scene is of course one of the most effective staples in the realm of the writing of popular Westerns, and McMurtry, although dangerously balancing between functional violence and trendy sadism, makes the most of it.

The episode ends with an observation characteristic of McCrae, placing him too in the line of frontiersmen of the Natty Bumppo type. If we last another twenty years, he tells Call, when they leave the town, we'll be the Indians. And, he continues: "The way this place is settling up it'll be nothing but churches and dry-goods stores before you know it. Next thing you know they'll have to round up us old rowdies and stick us on a reservation to keep us from scaring the ladies" (pp. 326-27).

Call, level-headed as usual and never given to playful flights of fantasy, rejects this as unlikely, just as he rejects Gus's conclusion that they had spent their best years fighting on the wrong side, as utter nonsense. Of course they had not fought on the wrong side, but what he did find a miracle was that Gus had stayed on the right side for so long, on the right side of the law, that is, by seeing to it that the south-west frontier region became a safe place to live in.

But this miracle — Gus McCrae as a standard bearer of civilization — was of course not such a great miracle as Call thought it was. As long as there were still frontier regions that were *not* safe, there was no reason for people like Augustus McCrae to find the thrill of danger by defying the law. Upholding the law still involved plenty of action, enough to keep Gus from getting bored. But the irony that by doing this he helps realizing the situation which will inevitably lead to boredom is not lost on him. As he tells Call on another occasion, by killing all the bandits and Indians they killed "what made this country interesting to begin with" (p. 320).

In the last analysis it is the fear of boredom that is Gus' greatest enemy. To escape it, he had run away from home when he was thirteen, vowing that he would rather go outlaw than be a doctor or a lawyer, the two choices available in Tennessee to a boy of well-to-do parents. To defeat it, he had joined the Texas Rangers, just as he was now taking part in this cattle drive, even though he was not a cattleman and had declared the whole undertaking an irresponsible folly, which of course was also exactly what had secretly attracted him to it. And as he tells Newt when, after months of crossing dangerous rivers, of surviving stampedes, blizzards, deserts, the encounters with outlaws, and the loss of some of their best men, they have finally reached Montana, he would not have missed anything of it. It is, as he adds, exactly what he was meant for, and Woodrow Call too (p. 744).

Call's own finale in the novel is also out of keeping with his legendary stature, and profoundly ironic. Towards the end of his extraordinary solo-trip back to Texas, he is wounded in his side on the Pecos by some stray Indians whom he does not even get a proper look at, loses the buggy in which he carries McCrae's body, and covers the last five hundred miles to his destination dragging his friend's remains along on an improvised travois. But he completes the task he promised Gus to carry out: bury his body on the South Guadalupe, at the idyllic spot where Gus had spent his happiest hours with Clara.

It is, however, not simply nostalgia that had incited McCrae to make this romantic request. The real reason is grimmer. Not only is what he asked his friend and partner to do challenging enough for Call to try and accomplish it, but, more important, it would, as Gus told him, keep Call busy for another year now that the country was "about settled". Just as, in fact, the cattle drive had kept both of them busy for another year, which is what had really been behind the notion of the whole venture in the first place, Call being no more a cattleman than Augustus McCrae. Call's behaviour after he has finished the burial only confirms this. Worn out and with a festering wound, he is suddenly at a loss what to do next, or where to go. He ends up in Lonesome Dove, the town from which they had started, feeling as burnt out as the Dry Bean, which was no longer there, the only thing that had changed as he notices, because the saloon had been set fire to by Wanz, the owner, who had burnt with it. It is Dillard, the barber, who provides Call with this information, and who in answer to the latter's question in whose room Wanz had sat for a month before he burnt himself, explains: "The woman. They say he missed that whore".

To be apprised of the kind of death Wanz chose is no doubt unusual in a Western. Much more unusual, however, is the fact that the story's plot is no longer primarily seen in terms of conflicting forces — order versus lawlessness, the standard plot of the Western — , but in those of dispelling the debilitating boredom of a frugal and toilsome pioneer existence.

The whore, Dillard referred to, is of course Lorena. She has, however, long ceased to be a whore, but become a greatly appreciated member of Clara Allen's household. And it is on the Allen ranch near Ogallala in Nebraska that not only the protagonists of the main plot but also those of the two subplots converge.

If in the main plot, the cattle drive from Texas to Montana, McMurtry chiefly recreates the Old West as myth and legend through his particular choice of character and event, even though we may notice the process of demythologizing at the same time, in the two subplots we are confronted with a different West, a more pedestrian, unheroic West, in which people live in shacks with dirt floors, feel uncertain and confused and act most of the times awkwardly or foolishly, even go mad or commit suicide.

What distinctly characterizes the two subplots, which on the one hand deal with the vicissitudes of sheriff July Johnson and his family, and on the other with those of Johnson's deputy, Roscoe, is what scholarly research in the everyday reality of the frontier West has lately begun to disclose. Far from being the symbol of functional and moral order the frontier family lacked cohesiveness, was fragile instead, tending to fall apart easily under the various pressures, such as the headstrongness of its individual members and the dangers pertaining to frontier life, over which one had little or no control. As Lilian Schlissel writes: "The frontier family, long assumed to be simple by virtue of its place in history and the supposed simplicity of a frontier existence is neither simple nor easily accessible. Family life in the past century was, in fact, more complex, more diverse than it is today."[3]

That this complexity and diversity was in no small degree caused by the part women played on the frontier is also what distinguishes McMurtry's novel from the formula Western. In keeping with historical reality it is the women in *Lonesome Dove* that take a firm hand in determining their own destiny as well as in that of the men they encounter. Lorena has no intention of ending her life in Lonesome Dove as the town's only "sporting woman", but when she leaves, she leaves on her own terms, not by marrying Wanz, the proprietor of Dry Bean, which she could have done, but which she did not because she did not care for the man. When she begins to see through Jake, she

---

[3] Lillian Schlissel, "The Frontier Family: Dislocation and the American Experience", in *Making America: The Society and Culture of the United States*, ed. Luther S. Luedtke, Washington: Forum Series, 1987, p. 89.

puts her foot down and refuses to share his life as the mistress of a gambler. After her terrible experiences with Blue Duck and his gang of renegades, she becomes entirely dependent on Gus McCrae for her recovery, but once restored to sanity on Clara's ranch, she understands that she can look upon her life with Gus as another phase, an important phase but one that was past.

As for Clara Allen: she may have known doubts about her choice of Bob Allen over Augustus McCrae, but she has never regretted the choice she made nor the life she lived with her horsetrader, even though she had to live in a sodhouse for fifteen years, and lost her two small boys, a loss that had nearly finished her. Besides, when the Hat Creek outfit arrives at the ranch, she has been taking care of Bob for almost a year, washing and feeding him from the day he had fallen into a coma, completely paralyzed by the kick in the head he received from one of his half-tamed horses.

It is Clara who reads stories and novels and who would like to write some herself, who is educated and alternately sullen and vivacious, but who settles for unromantic, practical, energetic and reliable doers like Bob Allen and later, when Bob has died, for July Johnson; again, not for Gus McCrae. Although Clara's feelings for McCrae are roused again when they meet after seventeen years, she is not deceived: Gus McCrae has not really changed. But he becomes a favourite of her two daughters', as she foresaw.

Ironically enough, it is Johnson's wife, Elmira, uneducated, a prostitute before she met July and one who like her friend Jennie did not find her work objectionable at all, who can live with a man like Dee Boot, a restless adventurer and fun-loving gambler, but not with a man like July Johnson, solid but unimaginative. Life with Dee is more important to her than the security she thought she could get by marrying a sheriff, and more important than her twelve-year old boy Joe, whom she asks July to take with him when he sets out in pursuit of the alleged murderer of his brother, Jake Spoon; more important, too, than the baby she gives birth to on Clara's ranch, July's child in fact, whom she also abandons.

The youngsters in *Lonesome Dove* do get a pretty bad deal on the whole. Joe, starting to enjoy life in the open with July, is brutally and senselessly slaughtered by Blue Duck, and so is the girl Janey, thin, nimble and barefoot, not older than fourteen but already much used and abused. When Roscoe meets her for the first time she is about to kill the old man to whom she had been traded by a certain Bill, a gentleman about whom she refuses to talk to anyone. The deputy's unexpected arrival, however, makes her change her mind, and instead of killing old Sam she decides to run off and follow Roscoe, bungling but thoroughly decent Roscoe, to whom she takes an instant liking.

What is striking is that despite the harsh and loveless childhoods these children had — Joe, Janey, and Newt as well — they emerge as sane and likable persons, still appreciative of a kind or friendly gesture. It is true that Janey is tormented by bad dreams, but it has not affected her ability to hold her own in the daytime, nor her sense of loyalty, as the two highwaymen experience who in the darkness of the falling evening rob Roscoe of his money and clothes. They also tie up the girl, though not before she has put up a spirited fight. Not one to give up soon, she manages to escape later, after which the strangest battle ever described in a Western starts: Janey pelting the outlaws with rocks, at which she proves to be an expert, inflicting severe head- and armwounds on the two men, who, exasperated, return this odd barrage with a furious volley of pistolshots, while Roscoe, naked, and standing stock-still, expects to be killed any moment.

The men and women that took part in the Westward advance no doubt differed greatly, but there was one type in particular that was capable of turning the virgin, impassable wilderness of the North-American continent into what the whites believed was a place fit to live in for them and their children. The Allens and the Johnsons belonged to this particular type. They were none too capable, but hard-working, solid people, basically decent and not given to flights of imagination.

There was another type of man to whom the Westward movement afforded what was probably the last chance in the history of mankind of fully experiencing a sense of total freedom and the concomitant feeling of being able to express fully his human potentiality. To this type belonged the McCraes, the Spoons and the Calls, even though their presence on the frontier served additional purposes: for Gus McCrae, to flee the boredom of a settled existence; for Jake Spoon, to satisfy without too much exertion the hedonistic streak in his nature; for Woodrow Call, to fill the emptiness he faced with self-imposed tasks involving a degree of danger or back-breaking work sufficiently great to ensure a steady flow of adrenaline.

That this did not of necessity imply that the men belonging to this latter type shared the same underlying vision of the Westward movement, may become apparent from the following passage, a passage introduced by a question in which McCrae asks Call how far it would be to Montana. Call mentions an Indian who would have known — Black Beaver, who claimed that he had been all the way from the Columbia to the Rio Grande — , and he wonders how "a short-legged Indian" could have covered so much ground. McCrae, who may not know how far it is from Texas to Montana, can readily resolve this puzzle. As an Indian, he explains to Call, Black Beaver had all the time in the world since he didn't have to waste it on "establishing law and order and making it safe for bankers and Sunday-school teachers" as *they* had done. This is, he adds, why Call was ready to go to Montana, "to help establish a few more banks".

Call, of course, refutes this accusation, pointing out to McCrae that they had made the West safe not only for bankers, lawyers and salesmen, but for the settlers as well, and the passage continues as follows:

"Why, women and children and settlers are just canon fodder for lawyers and bankers," Augustus said. "They're part of the scheme. After the Indians wipe out enough of them you get your public outcry, and we go chouse the Indians out of the way. If they keep coming back then the Army takes over and chouses them worse. Finally the Army will manage to whip 'em down to where they can be squeezed onto some reservation, so the lawyers and bankers can come in and get civilization started. Every bank in Texas ought to pay us a commission for the work we done. If we hadn't done it, all the bankers would still be back in Georgia, living on poke salad and turnip greens."

"I don't know why you stuck with it, if that's the way you think," Call said. "You should have gone home and taught school."

"Hell, no," Augustus said. "I wanted a look at it before the bankers and lawyers get it."

"Well, they ain't got to Montana," Call said.

"If we go they won't be far behind," Augustus said. "The first ones that get there will hire you to go hang all the horsethieves and bring in whichever Indians have got the most fight left, and you'll do it and the place will be civilized. Then you won't know what to do with yourself, no more than you have these ten years."

"I ain't a boy," Call said. "I'll be dead before all that happens. Anyhow, I ain't going there to law. I'm going there to run cattle. Jake said it was a cattleman's paradise."

"You ain't a cattleman, Call," Augustus said. "No more than I am. If we was to get a ranch I don't know who would run it" (p. 83).

What this extract epitomizes is the complex character of the novel's vision of the Western experience. On the one hand we have the traditional view of the West: the West as an extension of the white man's mission to conquer and cultivate the wilderness, while civilizing the "savages". On the other, the highly critical view: the West as one of the last unspoiled and unpolluted regions on earth ruined by the arrival of white civilization. The former is represented by Call, though qualified by what actually motivates him: to lend life meaning by filling its fundamental emptiness; the latter is represented by McCrae, though equally qualified by the sort of person he is: in making the land safe for civilization he knows that he undermines his own *raison d'être*.

The complexity of the novel's vision is also mirrored in what sets Call and McCrae apart in their attitude towards the Indians. The following passage may demonstrate this. Augustus lies dying in Miles City, while Call sits at the bed of his friend, keeping watch. When McCrae awakes, feverish, Call asks him whether he wants him, Call, to do anything about the Indians, and the novel continues:

> "Which Indians?" Augustus asked, wondering what his friend could be talking about. Call's cheeks looked drawn, as though he hadn't eaten for days, though he was eating even as he asked the question.
>
> "Those that shot the arrows into you," Call said.
>
> "Oh, no, Woodrow," Augustus said. "We won more than our share with the natives. They didn't invite us here, you know. We got no call to be vengeful. You start that and I'll spoil your appetite" (p. 785).

Augustus is keenly aware of the great injustice done to the Indians by the whites. Call does not see it this way. But he has no particular quarrel with the Indians. If they do not bother him, he will not bother them. If they harass the settlers, as the Comanches did when he rangered along the Mexican border, he'll put a stop to that, and if that means killing, he will kill them. But he does not bear them a particular grudge, nor is he prejudiced. When Deets is killed in Wyoming by the young Indian who misunderstood the black's intention, Call does not take it out on the little tribe, consisting chiefly of women, children and young men. Realizing that they stole the horses to ward off impending starvation, he leaves them four of the animals.

Deets's death, incidentally, is one of the many poignant ironies *Lonesome Dove* abounds in, but it also carries a significance of a different order. When the Hat Creek men have finally overtaken the Indians, they catch them greedily eating one of the stolen horses. On seeing the armed whites, they flee, forgetting in their flight one small child, barely old enough to walk and blind as it appears. Deets picks the child up and the next thing that happens is that one of the young Indians rushes towards him, charging him with an old lance. Deets, trusting that the Indian understands that he only wants to return the child to its mother, makes no attempt at defending himself, until he realizes that the young brave is not going to stop, but then it is too late. Deets dies with a lance deep into his side and up into his chest, and there was again something in Call's life that he would never forgive himself for: concluding that the Indians were too starved to do anything, he had stood waiting with a rifle in his hands, shooting the boy when it was already too late to save Deets.

But Augustus has a different explanation of Deets's incredible death, an absurdity in more than one respect. For one thing, Deets was too professional a fighter to let himself be surprised in this manner. Deets, according to Augustus, knew that his death was coming, and he did nothing, accepted it, was ready for it. Why? Augustus does not answer this question, but the answer that forces itself on the questioner is one that would also apply to the ex-Texas Ranger himself, albeit with less serious implications for him than for a black like Deets.

What the arrival of the Hat Creek outfit in Montana signified was that the last unspoiled region of the West was about to be settled.

It would bring in the law, the church, and the school, thus putting intolerable restraints and limitations on the way in which men like Augustus and Deets had been accustomed to express their sense of individual freedom. With the disappearance of the frontier, a unique period in the history of not only the American people but of mankind in general had come to an end, the uniqueness of which found a most eloquent expression in a passage written by none other than Theodore Roosevelt, the one-time President of the United States known for his love of the Far West:

> The great free ranches, with their barbarous, picturesque, and curiously fascinating surroundings, mark a primitive stage of existence as surely as do the great tracts of primeval forests, and like the latter must pass away before the onward march of our people; and we who have felt the charm of the life, and have exulted in its abounding vigor and its bold, restless freedom, will not only regret its passing for our own sakes only, but must also feel real sorrow that those who come after us are not to see, as we have seen, what is perhaps the pleasantest, healthiest, and most exciting phase of American existence.[4]

To men like McCrae, Deets, and Call as well, whatever life could still have in store for them would pall against the significance of this phase. Everything, including death, would be better than to experience the sense of loss that was inevitably to occur, the loss of authenticity, the loss of full control over one's movements, following the encroachment of city-life and the closure of the range.

It is, in the final analysis, the nostalgic evocation of this phase in America's history that lends McMurtry's monumental novel its peculiar,

---

[4] Bayrd Still, ed. *The West: Contemporary Records of America's Expansion Across the Continent, 1607-1890*, New York: Capricorn Books, 1961, p. 229. This volume contains extracts from articles written by Theodore Roosevelt on the cattleman's frontier, articles originally published in "The Century Magazine" of 1888. The quotation is from one of these extracts.

fascinating power. There was a time and a place, it stubbornly seems to insist, in which it was possible for a man to live without having to submit to faceless bureaucracies, systems, or circumstances over which he had no control whatsoever. That time is only a few generations ago; that place is still there, though most of it has become unrecognizable. What happened precisely then and there, is impossible to retrace. A small part of it has been turned into legend; a great part of it has resulted in today's reality, which no one would welcome with great excitement, if one has to go by McMurtry's most recent book *Texasville*, the novel that gives such a chilling picture of today's West.

Lonesome Dove no doubt exploits the legends, and it makes for exciting reading. It also gives us a glimpse of what the legends conceal, and this too provides absorbing reading. The novel actually combines the best of the popular and the serious Western, but what raises the book above the genre of the Western is its combination of wistful nostalgia for something that has irreversibly passed, a phase of tremendous vitality and purpose, and the tragic sense that what in the final analysis this phase reflects is man's tireless effort to fill the void of existence with meaning, a meaning that became problematic again the moment the geographical void he entered was filled.

2

Three years after the publication of *Lonesome Dove* (1985), *Anything for Billy*, Larry McMurtry's second novel about the Old West appeared. The writing of *Lonesome Dove* had evidently whetted his appetite for the West of yore. However, *Anything for Billy*, McMurtry's version of the legendary exploits of Billy the Kid, does not take its principal lead from Owen Wister, the father of the modern Western romance and adventure story, but rather from Mark Twain, the Godfather, so to speak, of the Old West as farce and fraud writ large. It is Mark Twain who impresses his stamp on McMurtry's approach to the youngster who

240
240

killed twenty-one people before he ended his short Odyssey through the American West when he himself was shot to death at the age of twenty-two. It is Twain's presence that pervades the novel, even those parts that derive from two other influences: Richard Brautigan, one of our present-day absurdists, whose *The Hawkline Monster* (1974) seems responsible for the "Gothic" elements in McMurtry's story, and E. L. Doctorow, the expert in mingling history and fiction without creating the impression that either is sold short.

Just as in *Roughing It*, *Anything for Billy* has a narrator who like the one in Twain's book travels West in order to find the kind of excitement the rest of America seems to lack. McMurtry, however, introduces a number of delightful variants, proving that what we have is vintage McMurtry, not Twain. Not only is the company in which his narrator travels different, the inconveniences with which he has to cope on his journey from Galveston to El Paso are different as well. What is not different is the degree of hilarious exaggeration McMurtry, like Twain, expands on a mid-nineteenth-century coach ride.

Being a "Philadelphian gentleman", Ben Sippi, the narrator of *Anything for Billy*, gives up his rear seat for a front seat, an act of courtesy for which he pays dearly. Not only is he kept wedged between "a fat harness salesman" and "a weasel of a land speculator with elbows like razors" for ten long days, he also has to brace himself hour after hour "to keep from pitching forward into the lap of whoever sat across from you". The person who sits across from Sippi and with whom he has to lock knees for a thousand miles is Mrs Bargesly, the lady to whom Sippi so graciously ceded his place, a lady who during her many naps "farted like thunder", while her "four brats" developed motion sickness of such intensity that they never stopped vomiting and retching for the full ten days and nights it took them to reach El Paso.[5]

---

[5] Larry McMurtry, *Anything for Billy*, New York: Simon and Schuster 1989, pp. 58-59. All further page references are to this edition.

Besides this inconvenience, there was the infernal wind that kept blowing the travellers' headgear out of the windows, a loss that amounted to fifteen hundred hats a year, as a quick calculation showed Sippi, making it clear to him why so many Indians and outlaws wore hats made in Brooklyn: "If they grew dissatisfied with a particular hat, all they had to do was ride over to the stage road and pick a new one off a sagebrush or a prickly pear" (p. 62).

Instead of a young cub reporter, McMurtry's narrator is a writer of dime-novels, a middle-aged gentleman, married, and living with a wife and nine daughters in a big house in Philadelphia. He is in fact one of the most popular dime-novelists in the land. What he shares with Twain's narrator though, is a certain "innocence", the kind of innocence that enables young Clemens to give us his unclouded views on the American West, and Ben Sippi to leave home, wife and children and go West himself in order to actually experience what up to now he had only imagined in his writings, "his gaudy dreams" as he himself calls his dime stories.

However, robbing trains proves easier to write than to stage, which, as he soon learns, simply "wasn't in [his] breeding": engineers just laughed and waved their caps at him when he tried to stop their train by shooting in the air. (He should of course have shot at the engineers, but if he had done this he might have injured them.) Still, though he does not make a reputation as a train robber, he acquires one as the man who rode with Billy the Kid, the youngster who one day literally stepped out of a cloud into Ben Sippi's life, pistol in each hand, and metaphorically out of his legend by looking as scared as the dime-novelist himself when he found himself suddenly face to face with the notorious killer.

It is no doubt this scared look, so at odds with the Kid's fearful reputation, and a winning laugh, so unexpected on his young ugly face, which made Ben Sippi decide to ride with Billy and his rough companions, an experience that in the end enabled him to add a note of sad regret and nostalgic incomprehension to the legendary story of Billy's brief life of senseless violence. At the same time it provided McMurtry with an opportunity to deal once again with the eternal problem of *Dichtung* and *Wahrheit*.

The explanation which the novel gives of Billy's predilection for violence has a classic ring. Much abused when he was thirteen by a man called Joe Loxton, a bully, who employed the boy to clean the tables in his saloon, Billy, as he grew older, started to resort increasingly to violence himself. Like Jake in *Lonesome Dove*, Billy, too, acquired his reputation as a ruthless killer quite accidentally, though in his case it was not a lucky shot that won him fame, but a butcher knife that he happened to use while carving meat and which in a fight, started by Loxton, accidentally stuck in the latter's belly when the two hit the ground.

Even though the boy's past may go a long way in accounting for his penchant for violence, there remains enough about Billy Bone, as he is called in the novel, to keep Ben Sippi and the reader puzzled. When Sippi meets him for the first time on the clouded mountaintop, Billy had killed only one man: Joe Loxton, and his death was an accident. However, Sippi had been led to believe that the Kid had already been responsible for the deaths of at least ten white men and scores of Indians and Mexicans as well. None of this was true, as Sippi later learns from the very subject of these wild allegations. And the dime-novelist even suspects that some of the senseless killings he watches Billy do, such as the shooting of the two innocent horsetraders, the banker and the cattleman in Lincoln, the ten-year old Apache boy, and Smokie Brown, Billy's friendly jailer, could very well have been instigated by the Kid's obsessive belief that he had to live up to this reputation, a reputation from which he derived his sense of identity but which he felt he still had not earned.

The disquieting thing is, as Sippi notices, that all these senseless killings did not seem to affect Billy at all. They did not excite him, did not give him a kick, nor was there any sign that he felt any remorse. Was he perhaps psychotic? Sippi's observation that Billy "was just a puppet to his instincts, jerked this way and that by strings whose pull he couldn't predict" (p. 168) seems to affirm this suspicion. But what then was it that mustered so much loyalty from sane people like Joe Lovelady, a man who gave up a responsible job as foreman of the biggest ranch in the land just to ride with Billy and who to Ben Sippi became the dime-novelist's "model in matters of Western etiquette and deportment"; or Sister Blandina, the nun, who prevented the mob from lynching the Kid; or Katie Garza, Isinglass's spirited Mexican daughter, who helped Billy escape from prison; or Ben Sippi himself, the writer-gentleman from Philadelphia? Why were these people prepared to lay their lives on the line for an illiterate, ugly and ungainly kid, who could not hold a decent job for any length of time, who could neither shoot straight nor ride a horse well, and whose only redeeming grace was a winning laugh when he cracked his little silly jokes? Perhaps because Billy was also a kid that could say "there's no place in this world for me", in a tone "that would break your heart" (p. 147)? A kid, moreover, whose health was delicate, who was a prey to sick headaches and sudden spells of weakness, whose rough childhood had not toughened, but weakened him instead (p. 162), and who struck Sippi as "just a little Western waif, with such a lonely look stuck on his ugly young face that you'd want to do anything for him" (p. 183). When he, the great killer, slept, he looked like a twelve-year old kid. When there was a thunderstorm, the lightning terrified him so much that he hid under his saddle. He unconditionally believed the dire prophesies of La Tulipe, the old Creole woman in Greasy Corners, and was mortally afraid of what he called the "Death Dog", which, if seen, would mean that the person who saw it would die. Any mention of death for that matter turned Billy white, unless "it was death he was preparing to cause" (p. 114). In that case it was called "fun", and Billy never lost a moment's sleep over it, since he was not bothered by a bad conscience, nor ever seemed to care for his fellow human beings. When he hears from Sippi, however, how Mrs Bargesley, the Mrs Bargesley of the stagecoach ride, used "to fart like thunder", he is shocked: though "raised scrappy" in the raw mining saloons of Colorado, he was delicate about such matters. But then again, when he is told that Lovelady, his best friend, is killed by Isinglass's African negro, Mesty-Woolah, he sheds no tear, does not appear to feel any sorrow.

Billy's sense of honour, too, does not comply with the standard norm, as upheld even in the rough West: when Jody Fay enters the gully for a parley, carrying a white flag, he is shot by Billy. On the other hand, when an opportunity arises for him to escape on Sippi's mule, he refuses to take it without the latter's explicit permission.

Neither the buffalo hunters, nor the gunfighters in Greasy Corners are very fond of the Kid, whom they consider a "cold killer". The main reason why they do not hand him over to Isinglass during the Battle of Skunkwater Flats is, as Ben Sippi believes, their determination "to defy any order, no matter who it came from, or what the consequences" (p. 210). So what makes them rally behind Billy is not love but resentment, the sullen resistance to any form of authority, of degree. This, however, does not explain what attracts people like Joe Lovelady, Sister Blandina, and Ben Sippi, the narrator, to a notorious outlaw. One possible explanation — there are, as we shall see later, more — is contained in Sippi's remark when he wonders why people as diverse as nuns and ranchers should read his dime novels: "I suppose we all — even nuns — dream of a life other than the one we actually live on this indifferent earth" (p. 197). The satisfaction people derive from their own lives — however colourful or exemplary — is evidently never complete. There always remains something to be desired. When on his way from Philadelphia to Houston, Sippi is surprised to learn that the captain of the ship on which he sails is an avid reader of his Red Charlie tales, and that the first mate possesses "a well-thumbed" copy of his *Rose, the Frontier Angel*, a book which he is very reluctant to part with. Sippi's surprise increases when he hears that he is also Sister Blandina's favourite dime-novelist, while it turns into utter disbelief when he witnesses Isinglass take "a ragged and obviously much read copy" of one of his Orson Oxx stories out of his saddlebags. It is the morning after the Battle of Skunkwater Flats, in which Isinglass's Texans had killed all the gunfighters, and he himself had just shot one of his own men who had got too quarrelsome. The fictional violence of *Orson Oxx on the Pirate Isle; or, Captain Kidd's Defeat*, fabricated by a mild gentleman from Philadelphia, evidently held greater fascination to the owner of the biggest ranch in the world than the reality of the violence he himself could unleash so unthinkingly. When, incidentally, Isinglass hears that the writer of the Orson Oxx tales is his prisoner, he turns Sippi into his Sheherazade by promising him life, provided the dime-novelist keeps him awake with his tales as long as it takes the rancher to digest his supper. Knowing how to tell a tale can be an act of survival.

With Ben Sippi's arrival at Winds' Hill, Isinglass's ranch built like a castle, the novel receives a dose of postmodernist absurdism which turns the book from a Western into a Gothic horror story, a shift in genre probably meant to emphasize that the history of Billy the Kid is precisely that rather than another cowboys-and-Indians' tale. The events are consequently getting more and more gruesome, the characters increasingly more two-dimensional. Ninety-year old butlers drop suddenly dead; huge African warriors, riding the prairies on red camels, decapitate Isinglass's enemies; Billy starts slaughtering the rancher's offspring of Indian chiefs, Mexican outlaws, and innocent mutes raised in isolation by Spanish shepherds, thereto instigated by the novel's most bizarre character, Lady Cecily Snow, the imperious daughter of Isinglass's dead partner, Lord Snow.

Fortunately there is McMurtry's occasional wink at the reader, as, for example, when on his first night at the castle, Sippi receives an invitation from Cecily "to couple" with her. Isinglass's cowboys are no longer willing to oblige her in this respect, because as she explains to him, they are afraid that he, Isinglass, will kill them, so Sippy would do nicely instead. In reply to the latter's question whether Isinglass will not kill him too, she light-heartedly answers, "Of course, but he means to kill you anyway", and Sippi, understanding that nothing will be gained by restraint, accepts with eighteenth-century poise: "Ma'am, *carpe diem*, then."

There is a slight suggestion that the contest of wills between this English lady of beauty and Isinglass, the old plainsman, has allegorical significance — the worldly sophistication of England, the East, versus the primitive energy of America, the West — , but as can be expected in absurdist writing, the whole idea leads nowhere and in the absence of the required referentials soon dissolves. Cecily, made pregnant by Isinglass — he had tried before but without success — is locked up in Winds' Hill. She manages to escape, however, disappears in the snow-bound mountains, and is not seen again. It is a fate hard to reconcile with her initial presentation as a fully emancipated, totally self-sufficient modern woman of superior intellect, a scientist, whose speciality is the reproductive system of mollusks, the woman who told Sippi when he asked her why she fell for outlaws like Billy, "outlaws are not boring, that's why". They are not boring as men like ... Sippi, as she added, Ben Sippi, the dime-novelist, whom she believed to be "the most boring man" she ever met (p. 276).

The irony underlying this exchange could not be more pointed: Ben Sippi, who is successful in driving out the boredom of the real-life people who stand as models for the romantic characters in his dime novels, is thought to be a boring character by precisely those people. Sippi, on hearing Cecily's harsh judgement, is crestfallen and indignantly exclaims, "I didn't bore you at first, did I?", but Cecily's response, "Only from the moment I laid eyes on you", is even more devastating for poor Sippi. Yet, Cecily is not merely being nasty. What she says has a wider significance in that it bears directly on the mysterious relationship between reality and art. Boredom, as her remark suggests, started the moment she got to know Sippi personally, implying that before that moment he was not boring. But then she only knew him as the author of fiction which she thought was exciting. So the following paradox presents itself: a boring man, Ben Sippi, transforms the boring reality of his sedate life as a family man in tranquil Philadelphia into something that, judged by the enormous popularity of his novels, is anything but boring, and he achieves this by relying exclusively on the stereotyped view of the West as the land of adventure and romance.

What proves to be an even greater paradox, however, is that as soon as Sippi starts working from his personal experiences of the West, his writing loses all glamour and excitement. A telling example is his novel *Billy the Kid*, the book that contains Sippi's own eye-witness account of the young outlaw's last days, and which sold so poorly that it had to be written off as a failure. The reason? Too much "reality", in all probability. In *Billy the Kid* gunfighters are not portrayed as in Sippi's previous dime-novels as "a confident, satisfied lot", but as what they actually were, "mainly disappointed men" (p. 83); Apaches or bandits were not a great nuisance in the West but bugs — lice, chiggers, mosquitos, ticks, etc. — were (p. 55); the Battle of Skunkwater Flats, in which all the gunfighters were killed by Isinglass's Texans, was not a rip-roaring event, but primarily a long, dusty, day-long wait in which nothing happened, until in the evening the shooting started, but then no one could see anything, let alone determine who had shot whom; and, to give one last example, in the massacre of Greasy Corners, Billy was not shot dead in a fierce gunfight by Sheriff Tully Roebuck, as the latter claimed, but by Katie Garza, Billy's girlfriend. The killing took place before any of the men who were riding in to settle accounts with the Kid — Isinglass, Roebuck himself, Bloody Feathers, Long Dog Hawkins — had arrived.

The reason why he was killed by Katie is interesting: only one who really loved him should, the girl believed, kill Billy. But somehow the public, always ready to wallow in any form of sensationalism, refused to accept this highly romantic notion: it chose to believe Tully Roebuck's "silly memoir" instead, and in explaining that "no one wants to admit that a Mexican girl killed the greatest outlaw of the era", and that "the *Liebestod* business is hardly favored in the Old West" (p. 374), Sippi exposes the ineradicable belief in one of the West's most persistent stereotypes: the West as *macho* land.

Sippi's observation no doubt tells us as much about the public that favours Westerns as about the dime-novel writer himself. The former stands revealed as racist and anti-feminist; the latter, Sippi, as an inveterate romantic, an impression substantiated by the manner in which he chooses to remember the desperadoes who died at Skunkwater Flats:

> (...) hard though they were, I liked those gunmen who died in that wind gully. They only warred on one another, as near as I can see, and they brought some spirit to the ragged business of living, a spirit I confess I miss. Happy Jack Marco could tell a joke as brightly as any man I ever met; he had an uplifting laugh. Hill Coe rose from disgrace to die as gallantly as the hosts at the Alamo (p. 222).

To make these men interesting as fictional characters, however, more was obviously needed than a faithful portrayal of who they actually were — Ben Sippi's honest attempt in *Billy the Kid*, the novel that the public rejected. To be accepted they had to be depicted either as two-dimensional, larger-than-life heroes or villains — Sippi's previous "dime-novelistic" approach — or to be presented as the result of a skilful blending of their up-grading legendary status and their down-grading everyday ordinariness — McMurtry's own method of infusing the Billy the Kid saga with renewed interest. It is a method that consists in the application of primarily literary means, such as style, structure, and an imaginative approach to history.

It is an approach McMurtry does not allow Ben Sippi to grasp. Although disappointed by the failure of his *Billy the Kid*, Sippi remains confident that at last he "had graduated from mere tales into literary works to be proud of" (p. 378). In a frenzy of energy he writes a whole series of works in which he truthfully renders his personal experiences of the West: *Skunkwater Flats, or, The Desperate Battle, Mutes of the Mesa, The Ophelia of the Prairie*, etc., etc., but to no avail. All these books fail, and disgusted at the lack of success of his novels which, he believes, are "true to life" and full of "human depth", he decides to stop writing altogether. Sippi, as it happens, "never got over the fact that living had such a disastrous effect on [his] powers of creation", even though McMurtry makes him dimly aware of one of its causes when he has him observe that he, Sippi, was of course "never one of the great heroes of the language", heroes such as "Mr. Dickens or the poet Longfellow or W. D. Howells" (p. 380), or Larry McMurtry himself for that matter.

McMurtry's achievement of having breathed new life into such a worn-out and used-up genre as the popular Western is not merely a matter of style though, even if the style of *Anything for Billy* leaves nothing to be desired: lively and pungent, the perfect vehicle of conveying an unsentimental, caustic, grimly humorous sense of life, which nonetheless is totally devoid of cheap cynicism. It is, as I have already remarked, also a matter of structure and historical approach. It is here that McMurtry reminds us of Doctorow, especially in his ingenious blending of fiction and fact. As for the novel's structure, it is no less than a stroke of genius to make Sippi the writer of popular Westerns, ride with the hero of one of the legends of the Old West which he himself has helped to keep alive in his own writings. The experience, ironically, not only ends his career as a dime-novel writer, but also his ambition to become a serious novelist. He decides to stop writing altogether, but then something happens. Edison invents the film, and Sippi is so impressed with this new medium of popular entertainment, which, he believes, would soon make reading and writing obsolete, that he accepts an offer to become a scenario-writer for the motion-picture people.

The first film in which he has a hand is *Sweethearts of Greasy Corners*, released in 1908. The movie is based on the story of Dewey Sharp, one of the Whiskey Glass cowboys, who, as Sippi knows, had had the sense to leave Greasy Corners just before the shooting started in which Billy the Kid was killed. After the Kid's death, however, Dewey claimed that he had not left Greasy Corners at all, and had watched the shooting. Sippi, when Dewey tells him this, does not, as McMurtry puts it, "Argue too strenuously", since he has realized by now that "half the old-timers in the West had convinced themselves that they had been in Greasy Corners the day Billy Bone got killed" (p. 382). But the film is a big hit. Even Sippi himself, the man who had been there and who had written about what had really happened in Greasy Corners is deeply moved by what he knows is actually untrue, an untruth, he, like the rest of the audience, evidently wanted and needed to believe in. What the popular Western tale could no longer effect, the Western as film achieved again: Sippi cried all twenty times he saw the picture and the explanation he gives for this kind of emotionality is interesting. It was "the little actor who played Billy", who was not only good, but "too good" for the money Sippi had to pay to see the movie.

It is apparently the quality of the actor that can resuscitate what once gave the Western tale life, revitalize what had become formulaic. What "the little actor" succeeded in doing was to make Sippi relive the strong emotions of concern, compassion, fear and grief he had felt whenever he accompanied the real Billy, for the film "reminded [him] of all [his] hard goodbyes, and of [his] murdering friend, the wandering boy himself, Billy Bone, white star of the West, whose dust is now one with the billions and billions of particles that compose the ancient plain" (p. 382).

What seems clear is that both Sippi's and "the little actor'"s conception of Billy as the white star of the West differ considerably from the historical William S. Bonney, the real Billy the Kid. Or don't they?

3

Who was the historical Billy the Kid? When and where he was born no one, according to Jon Tuska,[6] knows. In 1866 he was living in Marion County, Indiana, with his mother, Catherine McCarty, and his elder brother, Joseph McCarty. He spent his early years in Silver City, New Mexico, where his mother and her new husband, William H. Antrim, had settled, and where she died in 1874. Henry's (Billy's) boyhood did not differ much from that of the average youth growing up in a mining frontier town. After his mother's death he went to live with parents of one of his schoolmates who ran a hotel, and Henry helped out by waiting on tables and washing dishes. The story of Billy killing —

---

[6] Jon Tuska, *Billy the Kid: A Handbook*, 1983; rpt Lincoln and London: University of Nebraska Press, 1986, p. 3. All further page references are to this edition, indicated in the text by T. followed by page number. There is quite a number of biographies of Billy the Kid, but, as Tuska convincingly shows in his book, most of them are not very accurate. Tuska's own biography is the result of a thorough and extensive examination of what can really be established as true about the Kid's life and what cannot, and for this reason I have followed his account in my summary of the historical Billy's life.

accidentally — his first man while carving meat, a version McMurtry has adopted, may have originated in this episode of Billy's life, but is evidently not true.

Trouble started for Henry — the real Billy — when he was arrested for stealing clothes from a couple of Chinese — to all appearances he had been the butt of a joke — and as he refused to name his accomplice, he was put in jail by the sheriff, who probably only wanted to teach young Henry a lesson. However, the boy found this out too late: he had already escaped from prison, heading for Arizona. Here he started working as a teamster for the post quartermaster at Camp Grant, and here he became known as the Kid. It is from this episode that McMurtry may have derived the notion that the Kid was harassed by a bully, for Frank P. Cahill, a blacksmith attached to Camp Grant, enjoyed bullying the boy. One day, after a card game, a fight broke out between the two, and Cahill landed on top of the boy. Desperate, the Kid pulled Cahill's gun and shot him through the stomach. The blacksmith died the following day. Billy was found guilty of murder and jailed. Until this dramatic event, reports about his character had sounded quite favourable. He had done the chores any fourteen-year-old boy did, was lively, and known not to take things that did not belong to him. When he escaped from Camp Grant and had arrived at the Knight Ranch, the place he had fled to, he returned the horse he had stolen to its rightful owner.

After three weeks at the Knight Ranch he moved on to Mesilla, and from there on to the Pecos valley in search of work. Travelling through the Guadalupe Mountains he and his companion, another youth he had befriended, were attacked by a band of renegade Apaches. Through sheer luck the Kid got away, and after a three-night walk through the foothills he reached the Jones ranch. The half-starved boy was well received by the Joneses, and it was here that the Kid introduced himself for the first time as William H. (Billy) Bonney.

When he finally arrived in Lincoln County he was hired by John H. Tunstall, who owned the Rio Feliz ranch, and who was generally known as a scrupulously honest man. A believer in the law, he refused to carry a gun. Apart from being a rancher, Tunstall was the chief financier of the Lincoln County Bank, of which the cattle baron John S. Chisum became president, and Alexander A. McSween, a lawyer, the vice-president. In the Lincoln County war which was soon to break out they could be said to represent the "honest" party, as opposed to the "dishonest" side, headed and controlled by Judge Bristol, District Attorney Rynerson, and J. J. Dolan, storeowner and beef and flour subcontractor for a number of firms that had won substantial government contracts. They, the latter, were the corrupters, even though they seemed to act within the law.

From the beginning the Kid belonged to the "honest" side, even though he and the other Tunstall men soon found themselves outlawed. The reports about Billy from those days sounded again highly favourable. "He was," as Mrs Susan McSween is said to have remarked, "universally liked" (T. 15-16). She also stated that "there was no man that the Kid liked better than Tunstall, and if the latter had not been killed by Dolan's gang, the Kid might have become a valuable citizen, since he was a remarkable boy, far above the average men of those times".

Mrs McSween's favourable impression of the Kid is corroborated by people like Henry F. Hoyt, a frontier doctor, who met Billy in Tascora, and who thought him handsome, athletic, with a ready smile, and a fearless expert at most of the Western skills (T. 60-61). This view, incidentally, seems to suggest another solution of the puzzle already referred to before, the puzzle that perfectly sane people like Joe Lovelady, Sister Blandina, Sippi himself, could take a liking to a boy who, apart from a "winning laugh", had, as McMurtry wants us to believe, no other redeeming graces. The Kid, as McMurtry has it, was not particularly handsome, but ugly; sickly rather than healthy; a bad shot, not a good shot, and a poor horseman, not an excellent one. Although McMurtry thus reversed most of the Kid's positive qualities, some memories of the historical Kid of Mrs McSween's and Dr Hoyt's description must have found its way into his portrayal of America's best-known outlaw. As for McMurtry's reasons: one can only speculate. Did he want to increase the enigma the Kid represented? Was he reluctant to suppress his scepsis vis à vis the reality of the Old West, denying the Kid any of the heroics that had turned him into a legend? Both probably.

When Tunstall in a letter to the Mesilla *Independent* exposed Sheriff Brady of Lincoln County, a member of the Bristol-Rynerson-Dolan faction, as an embezzler of taxpayers' money, he was murdered. To revenge his death and to restore order in the County, Tunstall's men formed a group, called the Regulators. They captured Tunstall's killers, Morton and Baker. Together with McCloskey, who appeared to be a spy for Dolan, they were shot, probably as they tried to break away. The Kid had no part in this shooting, although he was later reputed to have boasted he had. As a result of this shooting soon known by the name of "Dead Man's Draw", the Regulators were outlawed by Governor Axtell. The shoot-outs now followed each other in quick succession. In Lincoln, Sheriff Brady, held responsible for the death of Tunstall, was killed, the Kid was shot through the left thigh, but managed to get away with the help of Corbet, a clerk in the Tunstall store. A second shoot-out, in which the Kid was also involved, though again without really killing anyone, was at Blazer's Hill, the Mescalero Indian agency which also had an eating place. Here "Buckshot" Roberts, who was on the trail of the Regulators to earn the bounty money that Dolan had put on their heads, was shot, but the rancher Dick Brewer, the honest and loyal defender of the Tunstall and McSween's interests, as well. The Kid, who was slightly wounded, and the rest of the Regulators quickly departed. Dolan sent an account of this fight to the Santa Fe *New Mexican*, calling among other things the Kid a renegade who killed in cold blood, thus starting the legend of the Kid as a ruthless killer.

For a short period following these events it seemed as if justice would prevail in Lincoln County. McSween was exonerated of the charges brought against him, and Dolan and his henchmen Matthews and Jesse Evans were indicted for the murder of Tunstall. But the Kid and the Regulators John Middleston, Fred Waite, and Henry Brown were also indicted for the murder of Sheriff Brady. Since Dolan was supported by the Territorial officials, from Governor Axtell and U.S. District Attorney Catron to Judge Bristol and Colonel Rynerson, he was soon acquitted and free to continue his war against McSween and his followers in order to settle the question of who was in control of the Territory. He ensured himself of the assistance of the Seven Rivers gang and the notorious Dona Ana bunch for the necessary gunplay, and also succeeded in getting one of his supporters, Peppin, appointed as Sheriff of Lincoln County. The latter's first official act was to deputize a number of men from the Dolan forces.

Posses were formed to arrest the Regulators, who now served as McSween's bodyguards, and Billy the Kid was one of them. A comment made in those days by Martin Chávez, the Mexican owner of a small ranch, is interesting: "Billy was one of the kindest and best boys I ever knew. He was not bloodthirsty, he was forced into killing in defense of his own life. (...) In all his career he never killed a native citizen of New Mexico, which was one of the reasons we were all so fond of him" (T.42).

After a number of skirmishes, the main battle between the Dolan forces and McSween's men took place in Lincoln, round McSween's house, in fact. Dolan had been able to persuade Colonel Dudley of nearby Fort Stanton to assist him with his soldiers and some of his artillery, among which was a howitzer. He next managed to have McSween's house set on fire, and as McSween himself was near an emotional collapse, unable to do anything, the Kid took charge. He arranged an escape from the besieged house, but although he and two other Regulators reached safety, drawing fire to enable McSween to escape, the latter delayed his dash to freedom too long and was killed with several other men.

After his escape Billy became the leader of what was left of the Regulators. Outlawed by the Dolan forces he was left with three options: to leave the Territory; to be killed; to try to survive by his wits and by theft. John Chisum could have provided an alternative, but he refused to take McSween's place. He even refused to pay any of the Regulators, Billy included, and from then on the Kid made a living by rustling horses, cattle, in which field of activity he was not particularly concerned whether they belonged to Dolan's herds or to those of Chisum.

A change in the political climate in Lincoln persuaded the Kid to return to this town in order to find out whether he and the remaining Regulators could come to an agreement with Dolan and his accomplices. They succeeded in reaching one, but during the celebration of their peace treaty Dolan and one of his men shot Chapman, Mrs McSween's lawyer, who happened to be in Lincoln on account of his campaign against the Dolan faction. When the new Governor, General Lew Wallace (the author of *Ben Hur*), finally paid his visit to Lincoln and heard that Chapman's murderers were still not arrested, he took action and issued a list of thirty-six names of men to be apprehended for their part in the Lincoln County War. The Kid's name was also on the list, the reason being that Wallace wanted him as the main witness of the Chapman murder. Billy agreed to have an appointment with the Governor at a secret place, and Wallace promised the Kid a pardon if he let himself be arrested: this would enable him to testify to what he knew without endangering his life.

The Kid had himself arrested by Sheriff Kimball, but although the grand jury indicted the murderers of both McSween and Chapman, Judge Bristol and District Attorney Rynerson, "the Santa Fe ring", succeeded in turning all subsequent verdicts in "not-guilty". When next the Kid heard that his own case was to be heard at Mesilla, Judge Bristol's territory, he understood that Wallace would not be able to give him a pardon, and he jumped jail. In October 1879 he crossed into the Texas Panhandle and assisted by Scurlock, O'Folliard, Bowdre and a few Mexican-Americans he rustled a hundred head from Chisum, the man whom the Kid now thought mainly responsible for the bad turn things had taken for him. Chisum discovered who were behind the theft, and like Dolan, Judge Bristol, and Captain Lea, a cattleman and a friend of Chisum's, he came to the conclusion that Billy the Kid had to be eliminated.

The man who finally succeeded in achieving this was Patrick Garrett, who arrived at Fort Sumner, New Mexico, in 1878, after having done practically everything in the Western book, including rustling, without much success though. In Lincoln County he started cultivating acquaintances with leading cattlemen such as Chisum and Lea, whose support he needed in his plans to be selected sheriff of Lincoln County, one of the few projects of his that did not fail. He won the election, and there is little doubt that his promise to eliminate Billy the Kid considerably influenced the outcome. In the meantime the Kid himself could hardly be said to have prospered greatly after he had left Lincoln. He had, in fact, become a drifter, a gambler, and a petty horse thief. Although actually one of the least important among the outlaws, he had become one of the most notorious, because the Ring newspapers continued to attribute every act of lawlessness in the County to the Kid. What distinguished his illegal activities, however, was that they seemed to be undertaken primarily to expose and ridicule the hypocrisy and dishonesty of the men in power in the County, the Chisums, the Dolans, the Catrons, Bristols and Rynersons.

As part of a general call for action to get rid of the outlaws that infested the County, more posses were on the road than ever before, and one organized by the citizens of White Oaks surrounded Greathouse's trading post where the Kid and some of his fellow outlaws were staying. From this engagement probably originates McMurtry's belief that the Kid was even capable of violating the Code of the West which demanded that those who came in to parley were given a free passage back. Deputy James Carlyle, who had come in to negotiate a surrender from the Kid, was shot, but not by the Kid but by one of his own men. For what had happened? Greathouse, the owner of the trading post, had invited Carlyle to come in to parley, offering himself as a hostage. When Carlyle failed to persuade the Kid to surrender, however, he was prevented from leaving as the Kid feared that the minute Carlyle was gone, his men would start firing. The posse was then foolish enough to threaten to kill Greathouse, and when a moment later a shot was heard, Carlyle, fearing that he would be killed in turn, lost his nerve and tried to make a getaway. His men, jittery and assuming that it was the Kid who tried to escape, opened fire and killed the deputy. Realizing what they had done, they called off the siege, spreading the news that it was the Kid who had shot Carlyle.

Pat Garrett had in the meantime persuaded a posse of Texans, led by Frank Stewart, a representative of the Canadian River cattle owners and in search for rustled stock, to join his posse and to assist him in tracing the Kid. At an abandoned rockhouse at Stinking Springs the final confrontation took place. Some of the details of this fight, such as the killing of the man who was the first to appear in the dooropening, as well as the killing of the horses tied outside, one of them dropping in the doorway, remind us of the Battle of Skunkwater Flats, but McMurtry's rendering of the fight differs considerably from what actually happened. In McMurtry's version Billy escapes; in reality he surrendered, even though he had sworn that he would never be taken a prisoner. But the Texans, playing a much more civilized role here than in McMurtry's tale, had promised not to shoot him, and so the Kid, together with Rudabaugh, Wilson, and Pickett — Bowdre had been killed by Garrett — were taken to Fort Sumner and from there to Las Vegas and next to Santa Fe.

In 1881 the Kid was tried in Mesilla, a trial engineered by Judge Bristol, and he was found guilty of the murder of Sheriff Brady. He was sentenced to be hanged in Lincoln. Here an admirer of his, Sam Corbet — not a woman as in McMurtry's version —, hid a revolver in the privy behind the courthouse/jail. The Kid, notified, found it, and escaped, though he was forced to shoot his guards Bell and Olinger. Bell's death, he regretted; that of Olinger, whom he knew was a born killer, he didn't. It is true, however, that it was ultimately the Kid's love of a woman that did him in, but it did not quite happen the way McMurtry would have it. What kept the Kid near Fort Sumner after he had escaped, was Paulita Maxwell. It was she with whom he was in love, and it was her brother Pete Maxwell, the rancher for whom Billy had worked in earlier days, just as, incidentally, Pat Garrett had, but he had been fired for rustling, — it was Pete Maxwell who informed on the Kid, who told Garrett where to find him, because he wanted the relationship between his sister and Billy brought to an end. It was even at Pete Maxwell's place, in his bedroom to be exact, that the Kid was killed, accidentally to all appearances. Billy had been hiding in Francisco Lobato's camp for weeks, but he used to ride to Fort Sumner at night, probably to see Paulita Maxwell. One night, the same night that also Garrett arrived at Maxwell's house with two deputies, the Kid and Lobato decided to stop at Jesus Silva's house to have something to eat, but as the Kid wanted a beefsteak which Silva did not have, the latter told him to go to Pete Maxwell, whom he knew had killed and dressed a calf that morning. Billy, unarmed except for perhaps a knife, went over to ask Pete for some meat. Seeing two strangers outside Maxwell's bedroom, he stepped inside the room to ask Maxwell who these men were, but was then shot by Garrett who happened to have entered the room a few moments before.

T. B. Catron, one of the principal forces behind the scenes of the Lincoln County War, and J. J. Dolan, his principal field commander, emerged as the winners in what had of course basically been a fight for political and economic power in the Territory of New Mexico. Catron was elected to the U.S. Senate when New Mexico achieved statehood; Dolan ran for county treasurer and was elected to this post, as later he was to the Territorial senate. Both the Kid and Pat Garrett were simply used as tools in this contest, but there was something about the Kid that caught the popular imagination, making him grow into a legend.

What the historical account of Billy the Kid's life as summarized above has made quite clear is that McMurtry ignores most of the facts collected and checked by Jon Tuska. In McMurtry's depiction of the Kid's character there is also little that actually corresponds with the real man. The habitual cheerfulness of the historical Kid is reduced to "a winning laugh" and a penchant for little silly jokes, usually at the expense of his fellow outlaws. What McMurtry adds are the Kid's superstition, his little boy's fear of thunder and lightning and death, his sense of feeling out of place in the world, as well as the notion of the Kid as a cold, amoral killer, who showed himself so oddly unaffected by the killings he was involved in that his conduct could be suspected of being psychotic. All these additions are not supported by historical evidence. The impression is therefore strong that McMurtry in depicting the Kid relied on legend rather than historical fact. There are, as Kent

Ladd Steckmesser has examined,[7] two legendary Billy the Kids. The first is a cold-blooded murderer, a tough little thug and a thief; the second is a romantic hero, brave and likable, the victim of social injustice. It is from this first version, introduced by a vast number of dime-novels, starting with John W. Morrison's *The Life of Billy the Kid, A Juvenile Outlaw* and Edmund Fable Jr.'s *Billy the Kid, the New Mexican Outlaw*, both published in 1881, and films like "Dirty Little Billy" (Columbus, 1972, director Stan Dragoto), that McMurtry may have derived the notion of the Kid as a psychotic killer. The capacity for making loyal friends clearly belongs to the Kid of the second legend, and a third explanation of why a cold killer like Billy can find himself surrounded by loyal and concerned friends presents itself: McMurtry simply took from the legends what he liked or needed, without giving a second thought to whether or not it might affect consistency. Anybody, killer or saviour, he may have concluded, is capable of rousing exalted feelings in certain men or women.

McMurtry's view of what caused the Kid's death — the love of a woman — also seems to have its origin in the second version of the legendary Kid. The real Kid, it is true, was killed on account of a woman as well — Paulita Maxwell — , but there is no denying that the immediate cause of *his* death — his untimely search for a piece of beef — was considerably less romantic than that of the fictive Kid in *Anything for Billy*.

In dealing with Tully Roebuck, the Pat Garrett of the Billy the Kid story, McMurtry again relies on legend rather than on history. McMurtry, too, must have felt that Pat Garrett's part in the Kid's death was less heroic than Garrett's own account in his *The Authentic Life of*

---

[7] Kent Ladd Steckmesser, *The Western Hero in History and Legend*, Norman: University of Oklahoma Press, 1965, as mentioned by Tuska in his *Billy the Kid* (see pp. 198-199).

Billy the Kid [8] wants us to believe. Garrett did not know that he had shot the Kid. If it had not been Billy who entered Pete Maxwell's bedroom, Garrett would have killed an innocent man and probably be indicted for murder. When he heard that he had shot the Kid, he was so scared that he dared not enter the room again.

In McMurtry's novel, Tully Roebuck's behaviour after the Kid's death is as dubious as the real Garrett's: he claims that it was he who killed the Kid, not Katie Garza. Katie does not dispute this claim, but not because she really saw him kill the Kid, but because she promised to do what the Kid had asked her to do before he died: tell the world that Tully Roebuck (Garrett) had killed the Kid. Roebuck, as Billy put it, "got politics to think of" and his feat of having killed the Kid would give his reputation a tremendous boost. Sippi, however, is not so sure whether Billy's gesture was really as generous as it looked; he is inclined to believe that Billy asked Katie to do this because he was a bit worried about his own future reputation, which might be tarnished if it were known that he had been killed by a woman.

There is still one more character in *Anything for Billy* whose origin can be traced to the historical and legendary context of the Lincoln County war: Isinglass. It is difficult, however, to determine on whom he is modelled. John Chisum seems a likely choice, but the power he wields over his estate is only a weak reflection of Isinglass's, who possesses practically the whole of New Mexico and whose power is absolute.

What Isinglass seems to unite in his person is what "the Santa Fe ring" represented: the full weight of the county's financial and administrative and judiciary power, against which small fry like Billy the Kid and his fellow outlaws would eventually prove to be helpless. What

[8] Pat F. Garrett (pseud. Marshall Ashmun Upson), *The Authentic Life of Billy the Kid*, 1882; re-issued in 1927, New York: MacMillan, and in 1954, Norman: University of Oklahoma Press, with an Introduction of J. C. Dykes. (See for further details Tuska's *Billy the Kid*, p. 136.)

is striking, however, is that this kind of helplessness plays no role in McMurtry's story. The Kid's helplessness in *Anyting for Billy* is the helplessness of a man who is a naïf, a person, moreover, who could not, as Sippi believed, apprehend the future, neither his nor his own victims', and who was therefore destined to turn into a monster, a likable monster, but a monster all the same. That one follows with increasing fascination this in itself not very interesting monster as it wanders to its pathetic death is amazing, but only to those who no longer experience words as life intensified.

4

The Western, up to 1970, was undeniably America's most popular genre, both in fiction and in film or on television. After 1970 an equally undeniable decline set in, and in his "Reflections on the Western since 1970", included in the second edition of his *Six-gun Mystique*, John Cawelti put forward a number of reasons for this decline in popularity which the Western, Cawelti thought, was unlikely ever to regain.[9]

However, the appearance in the 1980s of Westerns like *Lonesome Dove* and *Anything for Billy*, books that have broken all popularity records, both inside and outside the country, seems to contradict this view. It is of course possible to account for this renewed popularity by looking upon these novels as as many examples of the old and trusted formula Western, only better-written, and to conclude from this that what we witness is only a temporary revival of interest in the genre. Another explanation could be that McMurtry has succeeded in breathing new life into the Western by introducing adaptations of the genre in response to the changing interests of the audience. That this is what McMurtry has actually achieved may already have become apparent from the preceding discussion of *Lonesome Dove* and *Anything*

---

[9] John G. Cawelti, *The Six-gun Mystique, Second Edition*, Bowling Green, 1984.

for Billy, but to substantiate this view it may be illuminating to examine in more detail how exactly he solved the problems Cawelti thought responsible for the decline in popularity of the Western as genre.

As one of the first possible reasons Cawelti mentions the distance between the West as myth and the West as actuality which, as he suggests, has become too great. The West has become increasingly like the rest of the country — the closing of the spatial frontier (Turner) has led to the closing of a spiritual and cultural frontier. The Old West gets associated with tourism rather than adventure.

By focussing on the one aspect of the mythic West that has acquired an increasing importance in the West as actuality, McMurtry has done something about this problem, preserved the spiritual and cultural frontier as a vital element. Instead of treating adventure and the concomitant violence as the traditional means of furthering progress, he presents them as another means of defeating the existential boredom that basically propels the activities of his main characters, the kind of boredom, the full extent of which is to be observed in today's civilization in which not only the end of ideologies but even of history itself has been announced.

Cawelti's next point is that the Western as genre can no longer be taken seriously; it has started to feed on itself through parodic and ironic versions of the type. McMurtry's solution here, that is, of restoring serious interest, is two-pronged. In the first place he considerably tones down the traditional heroics, while injecting at the same time through the subplots the writing with a large dose of gritty realism. More importantly, however, he introduces another element that equally binds myth to actuality. This is the tragic sense that even the Old West, a place and time of great vitality in the history of the land, reflects man's tireless effort to fill the void of existence with meaning, a meaning that becomes problematic again the moment the West is won.

A third reason Cawelti advances is the fact that the hero in fiction has changed, has become a more dubious kind of hero, with an ambiguous attitude towards law and order, good and evil, thus confusing the traditional expectations of dramatic and symbolic clarity associated with the Western genre. In finding an answer to this problem, McMurtry has both Gus and Call uphold the Code of the West, thus meeting halfway the traditional expectations. But at the same time he has considerably varied his heroes' motivations, as I have pointed out, and this enabled him to also meet the "modern", untraditional demands of complexity and ambiguity.

Apart from the changed nature of the hero, there is, according to Cawelti, also the changed nature of violence, sexism and racism as aspects of American culture. In the traditional Western a strong distinction is made between good violence (graceful, almost aesthetic, if done by the hero), and bad violence (ugly, if perpetrated by the villain). This distinction seems to sound hollow now. Present-day violence has acquired something vicious, and the "grace under pressure" attitude of the traditional hero seems archaic. At present violence has to be maniacal, destructive, gory, mad, random; regeneration through violence is no longer possible.

McMurtry retains this traditional distinction between good violence and bad violence — neither Gus nor Call would ever resort to violence without sufficient reason — , but there is also plenty of the vicious, maniacal, mad and gory sort, as evidenced by the Blue Duck episode and that of the Suggs brothers. Even in Gus and Call it is not entirely absent — one recalls Gus's brutal treatment of the bartender in San Antonio, and Call's vicious punishment of the Army scout in Ogallala — , but their kind of violence always serves a recognizable purpose fitting the traditional Western, a continuing antidote of sanity in a world of increasing madness.

Another difficulty in writing an effective Western nowadays is, as Cawelti notes, the contemporary concern with sexism and sexuality. The traditional Western plays down the importance of sex and women; it has, for example, not been able to accommodate the theme of homosexuality. Another example of this sexist orientation of the Western is the well-known feature of the Eastern schoolmarm and the dancehall girl in which the schoolmarm (gentility) always triumphs and the dancehall girl (representing everything that endangers gentility) always stands morally condemned. McMurtry maintains this feature but has subtly modernized it by complicating motivation and by separating the women's demand for independence from their traditional sexual roles. As for the sexuality: in *Lonesome Dove* as well as in *Anything for Billy* it is treated in such a way that it loses its bigoted air of secrecy, so characteristic of the traditional Western, but McMurtry also takes care that it never quite reaches the level of unhealthy, kinky sado-masochism, compulsory in so much of the fiction of the 1970s.

There is finally the centrality of racism to American culture. In the traditional Western the presence of blacks, Latinos, or Chinese is restricted to providing comic release, which, as Cawelti writes, is hardly in accordance with the modern awareness that these races were equally important in the development of the West than the lily-white Anglo-Saxons. Then there are of course the Indians, who were not simply the noble and violent savages of the mythic West, but who represented cultures as rich and various as those of the whites. This awareness, too, makes it difficult, Cawelti believes, to treat the Indians any longer in the traditional Western fashion.

One of the most sympathetic characters in *Lonesome Dove* is undoubtedly Deets, the black scout, a man loved and respected by Call for his loyalty and professionalism. After Deets's death something is gone in Call, and he loses all interest in his work. It is not difficult to accept that McMurtry conceived the character of Deets as a tribute to a racial group whose role in the winning of the West has systematically been ignored or overlooked. However, there is, surprisingly, less evidence in *Lonesome Dove* of a similar change in attitude towards the Indians. Indians do appear in the novel but they all play a peripheral role. The Indians that are the immediate, though not the real cause of Deets's death are a small group of pathetically poor and half-starved people. The Indians that are responsible for Gus's death also cross his path accidentally. If they have a dramatic function, it is to show up life's bitter ironies: when they were still a force to reckon with, they failed to kill Rangers like Gus and Deets; reduced to insignificance, they succeed, by accident. As for the rest, on the long drive from Texas to Montana they remain a vaguely threatening presence in the background, the part they usually play in the traditional pop Western, and this also holds good for the Kiowas, a bunch of bloodthirsty cutthroats, to whom Blue Duck sells Lorena. Blue Duck himself easily qualifies as the archetypal savage of the American wilderness, but in addition McMurtry has given him enough viciousness to even impress a modern film and television audience.

To sum up: in finding answers to the problems raised by Cawelti, McMurtry has succeeded in revitalizing the Western. By reestablishing a vital relation between the Old West and the West as actuality, he has restored the Western as an effective genre. He has achieved more. By presenting the Western as another reflection of man's tireless effort to fill the void of existence with meaning, and by showing how this meaning becomes problematic again the moment his effort seems to have been successful, he has even raised the Western beyond the narrow confines of its type. With the creation of what I would simply call the New Western, he has added to the genre a new level of significance, sufficiently intriguing to capture a large and varied present-day audience, including the more sophisticated. This appears especially from *Anything for Billy*, a Western in which McMurtry's strategy of breathing new life into the genre differs from the one he adopted in

Lonesome Dove. In this novel McMurtry achieves his aims by employing primarily literary sources and literary-technical means such as style, structure and an imaginative approach to history. The style in *Anything for Billy* — grimly humorous, unsentimental, without becoming cynical though — is the perfect expression of the novel's subject-matter. McMurtry's stroke of genius in terms of the book's structure is his bold invention of making a writer of pulp Westerns ride with the hero of one of the legends of the Old West which this writer himself, Sippi, has helped to keep alive in his own novels. It enabled McMurtry to view both the West as myth and as fact in a new light. By ingeniously manipulating legend, history and a variety of literary sources, he presents us with an interpretation of Billy the Kid's life and personality which may hardly accord with what legend or history wants us to believe, but which like *Lonesome Dove*, though with different means, has given the Western as genre a new lease on life, to be enjoyed equally by those who simply want a good read and those who are more demanding.

SELECTED BIBLIOGRAPHY

Selected Bibliography

Primary sources

Bell, Whitfield, J., Jr., ed. *The Complete Poor Richard Almanacks*. Vol. I. Barre, Mass., 1970.

Berger, Thomas. *Little Big Man*. 1960; rpt Penguin Books, 1968.

Blodgett, Harold W., and Bradley, Sculley. *The Collected Writings of Walt Whitman: Leaves of Grass*. New York, 1965.

Brand, Max. *Destry Rides Again*. 1930; rpt Pocket Books, 1944.

Brasher, Thomas L., ed. *The Collected Writings of Walt Whitman: The Early Poems and the Fiction*. New York, 1963.

Canby, Henry Seidel, ed. *The Works of Thoreau*. Cambridge edition, 1947.

Clark, Walter van Tilburg. *The Ox-bow Incident*. 1940; rpt. Vintage Books.

Cooper, James Fenimore. *The Pioneers*. 1823; New York, 1966 (7th printing).

—. *The Last of the Mohicans*. 1826; New York, 1962 (Signet Classic).

—. *The Prairie*. 1827; New York, 1964 (Airmont Classic).

—. *The Pathfinder*. 1840; New York, 1961 (Signet Classic).

—. *The Oak Openings*. New York, 1848.

—. *The American Democrat*. 1838; New York, 1969 (Penguin Books).

—. *History of the Navy of the United States of America*. New York, 1840.

Doctorow, E. L. *Welcome to Hard Times*. 1960; rpt. Bantam Books, 1975.

Gilman, George G. *The Killing Claim*. New York, 1982.

Gombrowicz, Witold. "On Bruno Schulz", *The New York Review of Books*. April 13, 1989. Vol. XXXVI, nr. 6.

Grey, Zane. *Riders of the Purple Sage*. 1912; rpt. Pocket Books, 1980.

Hawthorne, Nathaniel. *The Scarlet Letter*. The Short Stories. The Centenary Edition of the Works of Nathaniel Hawthorne. Vols I-XI. Ohio State U.P., 1974.

Hemingway, Ernest. *Death in the Afternoon*. New York, 1932. *Green Hills of Africa*. New York, 1935.

Hovde, Carl F., ed. *The Writings of Henry D. Thoreau. A week on the Concord and Merrimack Rivers*. Princeton, 1980.

McMurtry, Larry. *Lonesome Dove*. 1985; Pam Books, 1986.

—. *Anything for Billy*. New York, 1989.

Melville, Herman. *Israel Potter: His Fifty Years of Exile*. London, 1962 (Standard edition, Vol. XI).

Moldenhauer, Joseph J., ed. *The Illustrated Maine Woods*. 1864; rpt. Princeton U.P., 1974

Pynchon, Thomas. *Gravity's Rainbow*. London, 1973.

Rhodes, Eugene Manlove. *Pasó Por Aquí*. 1925; rpt University of Oklahoma Press, 1973; 3rd printing 1982.

Sands, Robert S. *Life and Correspondence of John Paul Jones*. New York, 1830.

Thoreau, Henry D. *Walden or Life in the Woods*. 1854; rpt. Doubleday Dolphin Books, 1960.

Trumbull, Henry. *Life and Remarkable Adventures of Israel R. Potter*. New York, 1962.

Twain, Mark. *Roughing It*, 1872; Penguin Books, 1981.

—. *Pudd'nhead Wilson*, 1894; Penguin Books, 1975.

Wister, Owen. *The Virginian*. 1902; rpt 1979 (Signet Classic).

Secondary sources

Anderson, Charles R., ed. *Thoreau's Vision: The Major Essays*. Engle - Wood Cliffs, N.J., 1973.

Bercovitch, Sacvan, *The American Jeremiad*. Madison, Wis., 1978.

Bercovitch, Sacvan, and Jehlen, Myra, eds. *Ideology and Classic American Literature*. New York, 1986.

Bloom, Allan. *The Closing of the American Mind: How Higher Education has Failed Democracy and Impoverished the Souls of Today's Students*. New York 1988.

Budick, Emily Miller. *Fiction and Historical Consciousness: The American Romance Tradition*. New Haven, 1989.

Cawelti, John G. *The Six-Gun Mystique*. Bowling Green, 1971. Second Edition, 1984.

—. *Adventure, Mystery and Romance*. Chicago, 1976.

Chase, Richard. *The American Novel and Its Tradition*. New York, 1957.

Clark, Robert. *History, Ideology and Myth in American Fiction, 1823-1852*. London, 1984.

—. ed. *James Fenimore Cooper: New Critical Essays*. London/Totowa, N.J., 1985.

Colacurcio, Michael J. *The Province of Piety: Moral History in Hawthorne's Early Tales*. Harvard U.P., 1984.

Cooper, James Fenimore. *History of the Navy of the United States of America*. New York, 1840.

Cunliffe, Marcus, ed. *American Literature to 1900*. London. 1973.

—. *The Literature of the United States*. Pelican, 1954.

Dekker, George. *James Fenimore Cooper: The Novelist*. London, 1973.

—. *The American Historical Romance*. Cambridge U.P., 1987.

Fable Jr., Edmund. *Billy the Kid, The New Mexican Outlaw*. Denver, 1881.

George Dekker and John P. McWilliams Jr., eds. *James Fenimore Cooper: The Critical Heritage*. London, 1973.

Dillingham, William B. *Melville's Later Novels*. Athens & London, 1986.

Dryden, Edgar. *The Form of American Romance*. Baltimore, 1988.

Emerson, R. W. *Works*. Twelve vols. New York, 1903-04.

Emerson, Everett. *The Authentic Mark Twain: A Literary Biography of Samuel L. Clemens*. Philadelphia, 1984.

Folsom, James K. *The American Western Novel*. New Haven, 1966.

Fussell, Edwin. *Frontier: American Literature and the American West*. Princeton, 1965.

Gurian, Jay. *Western American Writing: Tradition and Promise*. Deland, 1975.

Harding, Walter, and Bode, Carl. *The Correspondence of Henry David Thoreau*. New York, 1958.

Howe, Irving. *The American Newness: Culture and Politics in the Age of Emerson*. Cambridge, Mass., 1986.

Kaplan, Justin. *Walt Whitman: A Life*. 1980; Bantam Books, 1982.

Levernier, James, and Cohen, Hennig, eds. *The Indians and Their Captives*. Westport, 1977.

Levine, Robert S. *Conspiracy and Romance: Studies in Brockden Brown, Cooper, Hawthorne, and Melville*. Cambridge, Mass., 1989.

Limerick, Patricia Nelson. *The Legacy of Conquest: The Unbroken Past of the American West*. New York, 1987.

Lewis, R.W.B. *The American Adam*. Chicago, 1955.

Luedtke, Luther S., ed. *Making America: The Society and Culture of the United States*. Washington, 1987.

Lynn, Kenneth S. *Mark Twain & Southwestern Humor*. 1960; rpt Greenwood, 1972.

McGrath, Roger D. *Gunfighters, Highwaymen & Vigilantes*. Berkeley, 1984.

McWilliams Jr., John P. *Hawthorne, Melville, and the American Character: A Looking-glass Business*. Cambridge U.P., 1984.

—. *Political Justice in a Republic: James Fenimore Cooper's America*. Berkeley, 1972.

Milton, John R. *The Novel of the American West*. Lincoln and London, 1980.

Morrison, John W. *The Life of Billy the Kid, A Juvenile Outlaw.* Morrison's Sensatonal Library, 1881.

Motley, Warren. *The American Abraham: James Fenimore Cooper and The Frontier Patriarch.* Cambridge U.P., 1987.

Richardson Jr., Robert D. *Henry David Thoreau: A Life of the Mind.* Berkeley, 1986.

Rogers, Franklin R. *Mark Twain's Burlesque Patterns.* Dallas, 1960.

Sayre, Robert F. *Thoreau and the American Indians.* Princeton, 1977.

Simonson, Harold P., ed. *Frederick Jackson Turner, The Significance of the Frontier in American History.* New York, 7th printing, 1979. With an introduction [1963]

Slade, Joseph W. *Thomas Pynchon.* New York, 1974.

Smith, Henry Nash. *Mark Twain, the Development of a Writer.* Cambridge, Mass., 1962.

—. *Virgin Land: The American West as Symbol and Myth.* Harvard U.P., 4th Printing, 1975. [1970; 1950]

Sonnichsen, C. L. *From Hopalong to Hud: Thoughts on Western Fiction.* College Station. Texas, 1978.

Steckmesser, Kent Ladd. *The Western Hero in History and Legend.* Norman: University of Oklahoma Press, 1965.

Stevens, Wallace. *The Necessary Angle.* New York, 1971.

Still, Bayrd, ed. *The West: Contemporary Records of America's Expansion Across the Continent*, 1607-1890. New York, 1961.

Strout, Cushing. *The Veracious Imagination.* Wesleyan W.P., 1981.

Tocqueville, Alexis de. *Democracy in America.* New York, 1947.

Torrey, Bradford, and Allen, Francis H., eds. *The Journal of Henry Thoreau.* Boston, 1906. Vol. 4.

Tuska, Jon. *Billy the Kid: A Handbook.* 1983; rpt Lincoln & London, 1986.

Upson, Marshall Ashmun (pseud. for Pat F. Garrett). *The Authentic Life of Billy the Kid.* 1882; re-issued by Norman, 1954.

Wilson, Edmund, ed. *The Shock of Recognition*. New York, 1943.

Zweig, Paul. *Walt Whitman: The Making of the Poet*. New York, 1984.

Index

STUDIES IN AMERICAN LITERATURE